Collected Poems
1950–1993

Collected Poems
1950–1993

Vernon Scannell

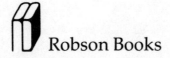
Robson Books

First published in Great Britain in 1993 by Robson Books
Ltd, Bolsover House, 5-6 Clipstone Street, London W1P
7EB

British Library Cataloguing in Publication Data
A catalogue record for this title is available from the British
Library

ISBN 0 86051 765 9

Photoset in North Wales by
Derek Doyle & Associates, Mold, Clwyd.

Printed in Great Britain by St Edmundsbury Press Ltd,
Bury St Edmunds, Suffolk.

Acknowledgements

Acknowledgements are due to the BBC, the Tate Gallery and the editors of the following journals in which a number of these poems first appeared:

Acumen, Ambit, The American Scholar, Chronicles (USA), the *Listener, The Literary Review,* the *New Statesman, Poetry Australia, Poetry Review, Quarto, Shenandoah* (USA), the *Spectator, Stand, The Times Literary Supplement, Two Plus Two, The Yale Literary Magazine.*

'Mastering the Craft' and 'The Bombing of the Café de Paris 1941' appeared in an educational book, *Mastering the Craft* (Pergamon Press, 1970). 'Talking Head' was first published in *First and Always: Poems for Great Ormond Street Hospital* (Faber & Faber 1988).

Contents

Introductory Notes

New & Collected Poems 1950–1980

For the author the publication of his *Collected Poems* is an unnerving event. He is, in effect, saying: 'This is the best of what I have thought and felt and written from the time when I first began to write verses until the present.' He is uneasily aware that the reviewers may be licking their lips, sharpening their knives and rehearsing their deflatory epigrams. Unlike the author of an isolated slim volume he cannot say: 'Here are a few exercises, an interim report, a record of some tentative steps taken towards the goal of making a complete statement as an artist and as a man. Critics, hold your fire; the best is yet to come!' The author of a Collected Poems is truly on trial for his life.

Well, here I suppose is my life, or the part of it by which I would wish to be judged. In this book I have included all of the pieces that I believe to be, irrespective of their literary quality, genuine poems, that is to say poems which have been written from a sense of compulsion, a real need to explore and articulate experiences which have been important to me. I have jettisoned a great deal, though perhaps not enough. The whole of my first published collection, *Graves and Resurrections* (1948), has been omitted as mere derivative fumbling towards a style. I have cut out those poems which on re-reading seem to be quite obviously false, banal or inept, though I am sure that there will be readers who will find much of what is included just as obviously guilty of these fatal flaws. I have not included any poems which have been written specially for younger readers or commissioned for particular occasions. I fervently, if audaciously, hope that there will be readers who will find something in these pages that will, in Doctor Johnson's words, 'enable them the better to enjoy life or the better to endure it'.

Filkins, 1980

Collected Poems 1950–1993

I have little to add to the above comments other than to express the hope that readers will find in the more recent poems no diminution in whatever merit the earlier pieces possessed and, perhaps more important, no less seriousness of purpose in the sense that Gerard Manley Hopkins used the word 'seriousness' when he explained that he did not mean ' … gravity but the being in earnest with your subject – reality'.

I have omitted little from the four collections published since 1980 with the exception of a few of the more knockabout pieces from *Soldiering On*, not because I feel any certainty that all, or any, of the inclusions possess enduring value, but because I think the reader should be left to make the final choice of what is most to her or his taste. At a time when much contemporary poetry seems to be written for specialist exegesists in the universities in order that they may practise their skills in 'deconstruction' I have, as Wordsworth said, 'wished to keep the reader in the company of flesh and blood, persuaded that by doing so I shall interest him'.

Otley, 1993

A MORTAL PITCH
1957

Something About Art

Easy at first like love:
April of the body and the white-
Gloved constables of conscience all away
On distant busy beats;
Bright shores unplundered and the boats
Nodding at the quay, Come, Come,
It's free! Easy at first
Like life itself, the act
Self-governing, not recognizing laws
Beyond fulfilment's need
Or searching for a cause beyond the warm
Compulsion of the April flesh;
Easy like love and life,
Until a dark today
Is suddenly as cold as stone,
And avaricious boatmen on the shore
Extend demanding hands,
While policemen hard as ebony
Hold heavy bruises in gloved paws.
And then like love, like life,
No longer easy as Spring kiss or breath,
His stern vocation points,
And watched on every side
By vigilant and truncheoned laws
He lifts the instrument of art,
In shadow of his conscience and his fate,
Climbs to where the terrible page
White as tomorrow waits.

Unsuccessful Poet

Pity him, even at first when it might seem
That he is not unfortunate; and praise him too.
Puff into the bladder of his self-esteem
And do not underestimate his value:
It is he who demonstrates the hardness of the work
And warns you like a notice where the dangers lurk.

Yes, even when he seems to be happy and strong
Pity him, for like curls and waistlines such happiness is
   doomed.
The first involuntary yelps that he calls song,
The moments of fragmentary vision and cosmic gloom,
The pinkish rhapsody that celebrates his first erection,
Do not condemn though they don't bear inspection.

For soon you'll see the branch of truth succumb
To the appalling dry-rot of ambition and then
Sad attempts to dress fashionably – on no income.
And after this the first chancre of self-knowledge when
Mind flinches away from the numb and wintry page
Or pen is parched before the barren acreage.

At the age of thirty or thereabouts when he says
That he is a victim of an evil age where all
Standards are debased, remember not to raise
Sceptical brows or blunt instruments; and above all
Do not judge when he goes quietly to his hovel
To put his head in the oven, or write a novel.

Two Lessons in Grammar

I

The Tenses

That which has never happened; holiday
In a glossy land of yellow and blue;
Veiled female beauty; the spicy brew
For which no surpliced barman makes you pay

In cash, disaster, morning recompense;
This you will understand is the Perfect Tense.

The Past Historic? Less easy to describe
Possessing as it does some attributes
Of the Perfect; is a mirror which refutes
Our tentative assumptions with a gibe.
The great boar-hound and girlish pages wander
Through avenues where martyrs, torn asunder,

Leave only dull brown stains and silly skulls,
And headless kings spreadeagled join the stable
Democracy of worm and vegetable.
Obsession with the Past Historic dulls
Those qualities required to understand
The Present which is really where you stand

Unhappily not knowing how to sit
In comfort and compose a farewell letter,
Knowing as well as I, or even better,
Despair's pervasive taste. This incomplete,
Uncertain lesson cannot ease your sense
Of hopelessness. You will smash the Future Tense.

II

The Sentence

Perhaps I can make it plain by analogy.
Imagine a machine, not yet assembled,
Each part being quite necessary
To the functioning whole: if the job is fumbled
And a vital piece mislaid
The machine is quite valueless,
The workers will not be paid.

It is just the same when constructing a sentence
But here we must be very careful
And lay stress on the extreme importance
Of defining our terms: nothing is as simple
As it seems at first regard.
'Sentence' might well mean to you
The amorous rope or twelve years' hard.

No, by 'sentence' we mean, quite simply, words
Put together like the parts of a machine.
Now remember we must have a verb: verbs
Are words of action like Murder, Love, or Sin.
But these might be nouns, depending
On how you use them—
Already the plot is thickening.

Except when the mood is imperative; that is to say
A command is given like Pray, Repent, or Forgive
(Dear me, these lessons get gloomier every day)
Except, as I was saying, when the mood is gloomy—
I mean imperative,
We need nouns, or else of course
Pronouns: words like Maid,
Man, Wedding or Divorce.

A sentence must make sense. Sometimes I believe
Our lives are ungrammatical. I guess that some of you
Have misplaced the direct object: the longer I live
The less certain I feel of anything I do.
But now I begin
To digress. Write down these simple sentences:–
I am sentenced: I love: I murder: I sin.

Poets Are Never Lovers

Poets are never really lovers;
If they were they would not need
To press between ambitious covers
Records of the lover's deed,
Or agonize to make the fervent
Sigh or grunt more eloquent.

Not being lovers they can see
More clearly than the fortunate
Speechless who record the glee
And glory under passionate
Eiderdowns, as gay as birds,
That love is lovelier than words.

Just as the pauper knows the power
Of the fat man's casual wad,
Or fainting in his dizzy tower
Of hunger makes of food his god,
The loveless poet alone in bed
Gauges the fortune of the fed.

Manhandling language is his job,
A task not suitable for lovers
Whose passion fattens on each sob;
And yet he does not envy others,
Unless the words turn dead as stone,
Leaving him dungeoned, and alone.

Posthumous Autobiography

Once I was a hero,
Slashing the grimy enemies who groaned
And churned their frantic fear before my calm
Fury, watched them beg for sweet reprieve
On broken knees, bawling round and loud
Beneath my blade of little ones at home.
And some I spared, mingling in my smile
Admixture of compassion and contempt.
With bandage bloody-badged upon my brow
Returned to let the English sun bring out
Brilliant blooms of medals on my breast
For favoured dainty virgins to admire.
Yes, once I was a hero but
The bombs began to fall.

Once I was a sailor
Swinging with the loll and roll at night,
Hearing the slap and wallop of the water
On creaking timbered sides; and when I slept
The fishes glided round my glassy skull.
Then when the storm enraged the grunting sea
Into a foaming epileptic fit

The ship a monstrous bronco bucked and lurched
To each enormous heave and I alone,
The only one not spewing helplessly,
Replaced the skipper on the howling bridge,
Staring the tumult out rode safely home.
Yes, once I was a sailor but
The ship put out to sea.

Once I was a lover
Walking avenues of blushes and of sighs,
Singing at night hot arias that flushed
The upper casements with a yearning light.
My bootleg kisses sent a red-head wild
Who drowned herself when I refused to smile.
Five brunettes took vows, and thirteen blondes
Wept away their beauty when I rode
Away one casual evening with a wave
Of that instructive and omniscient hand
That each had worshipped and enshrined in dream.
Yes, once I was a lover but
A woman came to bed.

Once I was a poet
Breaking the silence with an axe of bright
Articulate anger, crunching cant and lies
Between sharp lyric teeth and shrugging all
The green and silent nightingales away.
And once I was a pale religious man
My soul and conscience laundered perfectly
As white as birthday cake: rebellious psalms
Began to sing my name and when I breathed
The air about my haloed head was faint
With sweetest incense; steeples belled my name.
Yes, once I was a poet and religious,
But the terrible angels called on me.
Once I was alive.

They Did Not Expect This

They did not expect this. Being neither wise nor brave
And wearing only the beauty of youth's season
They took the first turning quite unquestioningly
And walked quickly without looking back even once.

It was of course the wrong turning. First they were nagged
By a small wind that tugged at their clothing like a dog;
Then the rain began and there was no shelter anywhere,
Only the street and the rows of houses stern as soldiers.

Though the blood chilled, the endearing word burnt the
    tongue.
There were no parks or gardens or public houses:
Midnight settled and the rain paused leaving the city
Enormous and still like a great sleeping seal.

At last they found accommodation in a cold
Furnished room where they quickly learnt to believe in
    ghosts;
They had their hope stuffed and put on the mantelpiece
But found, after a while, that they did not notice it.

While she spends many hours looking in the bottoms of
    teacups
He reads much about association football
And waits for the marvellous envelope to fall:
Their eyes are strangers and they rarely speak.
                               They did not expect this.

Waiting for Night

Here, in the clattering day where the street rings
With showers of glittering coins from the rich sun,
One walks, dazed with the bootleg warmth, emboldened
By the gay behaviour of the young. High-hung
Above the rakish roofs and kitchen gardens
The white sheets puff their chests towards the sun,

Proud as clouds of the marriage beds they honour.
And in the park's remarkable new green,
Bright and dainty as confectioner's wares
Girls wander where the lazy deckchairs lean
Striped like the humbugs of a child's desire.
Children are there, the reckless fire-eaters
Licking the solid flame from yellow torches,
Throwing the light grenades of vocal sound
For the pure joy of hearing the explosion.

But there is one who is no longer young,
For whom this annual resurrection brings
Only the sense of loss. Waiting for night
To draw soft blinds across the mirrors of
Shopwindows and the girls' indifferent eyes;
Waiting for night, his own and treacherous eyes
Kneel down before the royal sun and rest,
Pretending to a true allegiance;
Waiting for night when hate can walk upright,
And he can crush the lovers that his feet encounter
And bite their silver moon to prove it counterfeit.

The Lovers Part in Winter

It seemed appropriate that it should happen
On the day when winter consolidated
Its territorial gains; when the sky's skin
Was tight with the pain of cold and all the streams
Were paralysed, still, like a photograph.

Separately they'll hate the winter from now on,
Find its beauty not their style at all,
Hating the air in which the germ of life
Could not for an instant live. They will fear
That mass of frozen thunder, the mountain range.

The green conspirators were dead or banished,
There was no talk of bird or resurrection;
Speech lay betrayed in fragments at their feet;
The bed was cold as snow, the fire was out
And stillborn tears froze hard and cut like glass.

They had both been cruel and dishonest;
Yet pity hurt like winter when she went
Over the snow alone. And then it seemed
Her scarlet cloak, laced by the falling flakes,
Grew ermine-white except for stains of blood.

London Park in Time of Peace

On the blue breast of August bravely burns
The medallion of the polished sun,
White tourniquets of cloud conceal the wounds
Incurred in wintry battles of attrition.

The children's laughter rises like the bright
And liberated kites; adventures rock
At landing-stages waiting for the right
Adventurer to enter; lovers shock

The tight-lipped woman who, accompanied
By all she knows of love on leather leash,
Walks in the glass enclosure of despair
Towards the fragile certainty of tea.

And the iron soldier on the pompous horse
Stares upward, showing neither fear nor wonder;
The stormcloud, turgid, purple, ripe as plum,
Waits for the raping teeth of burly thunder.

The Visitation

The fire is small and hushed, the candles' speech
Is muted to a whisper while the walls
Tremble, move closer, then nervously withdraw;
Somewhere, beyond this world, a nightbird calls.

The clock counts moments in its neat black voice,
The wind complains that night is cruel to him;
Small pools of darkness brim the shallow vales
Delved in the white plain of the counterpane.

The bed seems strangely large, the intricate
Carved posts are parodied by aggravated
Semblances that mime upon the ceiling;
Only the pillowed head is unrelated.

Only the old frail skull and waxen hands
That rest upon the counterpane seem certain,
Indifferent to the terror that informs
The room's hysteria, the frightened curtain.

The noiseless gibberish of shadows grows
More feverish; bird calls from night's dark hill
Imperious; the candles weep, the fire burns low,
The clock is ticking but the hands are still.

How to Fill in a Crossword Puzzle

First adjust your spectacles and take your pen,
(A pencil will serve equally well) and pick the easiest clue:
Here you are: five letters down—'What is Man?'
Clown, Rogue, Beast, or even Saint would do.

Now let's try another going across. Here is one
Which seems more likely than the rest: 'Lethal but Sweet,'
A six-letter word, the first of which is B
If Beast were right for man—the beast with two feet.

Think hard—Lethal but Sweet. Assuming Beast is correct,
Breast might fit, the sweet but bladed breast
Of her you hugged, who bled you white and stabbed
To death your groping heart most treacherously.

If, as may well be, you have mistakenly put Beast
Adjustments are required unless you are going to let
This chequered puzzle stay unsolved. Try Rogue instead of
    Beast,
Then 'Lethal but Sweet,' could reasonably be Regret.

Of course the word Clown would fit the first clue you
    attempted
(Yes, I admit this puzzle is confusing)
Then your six-letter word going across might be
Coitus, Create, Cringe or possibly Crying.

The other word, less likely I suppose, is Saint.
Here the thing 'Lethal but Sweet' would begin with S.
Sinful it might be, Senses or simply Seduce.
The snag about these clues is the alternatives are endless.

Write in the words faintly because you may have to alter
    them,
And be warned. When the puzzle is solved, and like a
    satisfied lover
You lean back sighing and sleepy, then you will find
That the black squares hide the secrets you will never
    uncover.

Gunpowder Plot

For days these curious cardboard buds have lain
In brightly coloured boxes. Soon the night
Will come. We pray there'll be no sullen rain
To make these magic orchids flame less bright.

Now in the garden's darkness they begin
To flower; the frenzied whizz of Catherine-wheel
Puts forth its fiery petals and the thin
Rocket soars to burst upon the steel

Bulwark of a cloud. And then the guy,
Absurdly human phoenix, is again

Gulped by greedy flames: the harvest sky
Is flecked with threshed and glittering golden grain.

'Uncle! A cannon! Watch me as I light it!'
The women, helter-skelter, squealing high,
Retreat; the paper fuse is quickly lit,
A cat-like hiss and spit of fire, a sly

Falter, then the air is shocked with blast.
The cannon bangs, and in my nostrils drifts
A bitter scent that brings the lurking past
Lurching to my side. The present shifts,

Allows a ten-year memory to walk
Unhindered now; and so I'm forced to hear
The banshee howl of mortar and the talk
Of men who died; am forced to taste my fear.

I listen for a moment to the guns,
The torn earth's grunts, recalling how I prayed.
The past retreats. I hear a corpse's sons:
'Who's scared of bangers?' 'Uncle! John's afraid!'

Old Man's Song

The baby bawling, being sick,
The spotty girl with hockey-stick
Who dreams of pink blancmange and pie,
Might not be
Ideally
Happy but I know they are
Far better off than I.

I watch the warm limbs jolly by,
Feel neither grand nor fatherly:
I don't long
For those strong
Bodies but how achingly
I desire desire.

Friday night boys as bold as Bass
Release their lusts like poison gas
In punching yells or foggy songs;
That in the end
They will descend
To my cellar does not ease
This thorny hat of wrongs.

The autumn leaves romantically
Die gay and suicidally
And night is hurt by the owl's cry;
The still sleeper
Sleeps deeper
Whom no alarming clock will shock:
He's better off than I.

Cat in the night clawing silence
Howling lust that needs no licence
Makes me want to want to die;
Even though
They don't know
Dogs and bitches bogged in ditches
Are far better off than I.

Schoolroom on a Wet Afternoon

The unrelated paragraphs of morning
Are forgotten now: the severed heads of kings
Rot by the misty Thames; the roses of York
And Lancaster are pressed between the leaves
Of history; negroes sleep in Africa.
The complexities of simple interest lurk
In inkwells and the brittle sticks of chalk:
Afternoon is come and English Grammar.

Rain falls as though the sky has been bereaved,
Stutters its inarticulate grief on glass
Of every lachrymose pane. The children read

Their books or make pretence of concentration,
Each bowed head seems bent in supplication
Or resignation to the fate that waits
In the unmapped forests of the future.
Is it their doomed innocence noon weeps for?

In each diminutive breast a human heart
Pumps out the necessary blood: desires,
Pains and ecstasies surfride each singing wave
Which breaks in darkness on the mental shores.
Each child is disciplined; absorbed and still
At his small desk. Yet lift the lid and see,
Amidst frayed books and pencils, other shapes:
Vicious rope, glaring blade, the gun cocked to kill.

I Grieve for a Lost Land

I grieve for a lost land as the gulls swim
Easily on air, parodying pain
With their outrageous cries:
I grieve for a lost land as the dark stain
Of night spreads over the sad skies
And the gulls drift into silence on a chill wind.

And later, when the sea's great engines roar
Ceaselessly of death and exile, I recall
Nights starred with promises
Of a bright morning's golden madrigal
And skies blue as the nursery boys
Who blew their silver trumpets when the cows were in
    corn.

I grieve for a lost land which lies beyond
This sea which tells its hunger to the night
And shakes its rags of foam
For the idiot moon's remote delight;
I grieve for a dead child, a lost wand,
A shore to which no exile may return.

Four Dead Beats to the Bar

While day still was, four dead beats to the bar repaired,
Wearing their sultry thirsts at a Saturday angle,
Each clothed in melancholy's threadbare mantle
And the bright unenviable medals of despair.

Later they sang: blew bawdy songs from blubbery lips
Like gaudy bubbles, braved the ticking cannonade;
Toasted their toasts, composed a purple serenade
To every maid and bar, to all the whores and hips.

Then thin bells squealed that there must be no light,
No drink, nor any serenading from henceforth;
And four dead beats to a drunken rhythm waltzed
Out to be swallowed by the panting thirsty night.

The Word of Love

Perhaps it found its perfect expression
Early in life, in the fairy-tale time,
Concerning itself with a character out of fiction,
The sleeping princess or glittering snow queen,
Or focused mutely and profoundly on
A furry bear whose solitary eye was a sad button.

Certainly, as I grew tall and gruff
And the blood of the bear turned into straw
I somehow lost the habit of love.
The leggy girls, whose sharp heels tore
My flimsy dreams, with laughter crushed
The flower at the heart of my lunar lust.

Uncertain now, myopic with peering
At celluloid legends and paper lies,
The one word breaks on my disbelieving;
And yet, and yet, the dumb heart bears
The syllable like a child in its stillness
And your present absence is a mortal illness.

THE MASKS OF LOVE
1960

Romantic Suicide

He was not wicked, merely wrong,
Always wrong whatever he did,
And when he fell in love the song
He sang was pitched too high and loud
Offending those white ears he loved.
And when she went he bravely hid
His grief and walked into the water,
For that was what the poems he read
Said was the appropriate thing
To do if you had lost your lover.
He did not know the world of rhyme
Has laws outside the world of time
And what is beautiful in verse
May well outside be anything
But beautiful, indeed far worse
Than images whose conscious aim
It is to sicken and alarm.
And so he sank into the lake
And wallowed with the perch and pike
Among green wavering scenery.
Seven days were lost before they hauled
His corpse from lecherous weeds and mud,
And we who gathered there to see
That romantic suicide
Saw a fat inflated blubber,
A thing composed of greyish rubber.
His face we will not dwell upon
Though creatures in the waters had
No such pretty scruples there.
Enough to say we turned away,
And what pity might have touched
Our hearts was swamped by nausea.
All we could do was dumbly pray
That God prove less fastidious:

Extend his mercy, sweet and strong,
To one not wicked, merely wrong.

The Lynching

They rode back in trap or Ford or Cadillac.
Behind them on the tree upon the hill
Beneath the non-committal dark
Star-punctured sky their deed hung still
And black. They rode fast. One might have thought
That they were being pursued; their speed
Lunged forward with a long arm through the night
To drag the small town to their need.
And in the town the white wives in their white
Nightgowns listened to the clock
And with their wide-eyed fingers plucked
Those gowns which, fastened at the neck
And neat at feet, need not be roughed that night
To prove their husbands' manhood, or the lack.

Prostitute

All your endearments and the charms you offer,
Bulge of breast and buttock, trumpet eye,
Shall not persuade the night you do not suffer
The blade that hurts but does not purify
All your endearments and the charms you offer.

After the dark manoeuvres you may play
A few pale hours with beady words like Beauty,
While locks and curtains thwart the indigent day
And coppers are engaged on other duty:
After the dark manoeuvres you may play.

Always for you the bed meant painful labour,
But not a natal labour crowned with love;
The sheets evoke with stain and faintest odour

Nostalgia you put on like a glove;
Always for you the bed meant painful labour.

The bed, your business, factory of lust,
For other people wears a different guise
Unless the cinema abused your trust;
The dreaming virgin would not recognize
The bed, your business, factory of lust.

The vicar's pious pity is maltreated;
Your laughter like bright scissors rips it up;
Primeval sin is not to be defeated
By magic wafer or the sacred cup;
The vicar's pious pity is maltreated.

And all the endearments and the charms you offer,
The wicked stars remark them being drunk
Nightly by Time who, like a pimping lover,
Robs your white factory except for junk—
The obsolete endearments you will offer.

Remembrance Day

Apposite blood red the blobs
Of artificial poppies count
Our annual dead.
The garment of lament is worn
Threadbare and each medal hangs
Heavy its shameful head.

Bugles make their sad assault
Upon the heart and spine and throat
Ordering regret.
The names evoked are usual:
Passchendaele, Bapaume and Loos—
Our cheeks are wet.

And fumbling for the right response
We summon names more personal:
Nobby, Frank and Ted.

But wormy years have eaten their
Identities and none can mourn
These artificial dead.

And when a true emotion strikes
It strikes a crude, unsanctioned blow
Which brings a harsher chill
To hearts that know that they grow old
And must grow older yet before
That terrible Until.

Formal Problem

The poet, in his garden, holds his pen
Like a dart between two fingers and a thumb;
The target is unfortunately blurred;
He does not see as clearly as when young
Or, rather, doubt and nervousness obtrude:
He dare not risk the unreflecting fling.

How to convey the taste and texture of
This sun-drunk afternoon? How can he sieve
The essence of these greens, the grass, the trees,
The mating scents, the way the clouds behave,
And shape it to a pattern which might please
The glinting intellect and hungry Five?

And how include the aeroplane which slides
No larger than a pearl across the skies,
Its roar wrapped up in distance which conceals
A figure masked and helmeted whose strong
Finger stabs the button that resolves
The poet's problem in a flash, and bang.

Killing Flies

Compelled by their black hum
And accidental mischief, I,
Distracted from my pompous play
With words that twist and tease,
Rolled myself a paper club
And stalked my quick tormentors round
The room until they settled on
The wall, their mortuary slab.
Three I translated with one swipe
From busy bodies into dark
Smudges on my wall
Before I knew my action wrong
And guiltily let fall
The paper truncheon and went back
To where my words like insects bled
And dried upon their paper shroud,
All dead, unquestionably dead.

Two Appearances

The lean ecstatic man, the starry poet,
Expecting any day the total vision
And generously preparing to bestow it
On all of us, despite some mild derision
From that minority who doubtless find
His meditative beauty not their kind,
Walks whitely like a batsman to his crease;
While in the dirty night the ugly fellow,
His barrel belly resting on his thighs,
Calls out the temptress with a soundless bellow
And fixes her with angry bloodshot eyes,
Then forces her to bear a masterpiece.

Simon Frailman:

Ten Sonnets and an Elegiac Coda

First Sight

Simon Frailman, six feet in his dreams,
A thickening five feet eight when morning rings
And pricks him with insistent questionings:
Why did he never wear those uniforms,
The plumage and caparisons, bear arms
Or, over one heroic nipple, wings?
And now it is too late. The evening brings
A smoky sadness to the mortgaged lawns.

A moderate man with no intemperate lusts,
Content to tame the rose and civilize
The lawless strawberry, he guards the trust
Of wife and children and will never slip
The marriage leash; his quaint adulteries
Performed with lawful spouse at his thick hip.

Simon on Sunday

Printed rumours rustle through the morning.
The fragrant chamber music of the bacon
Is drowned by richer chords of roast and pudding
As Simon sprays and weeds his timid garden.
The spectres of the earlier bells compel
A melancholy that is hard to pardon
While birds in shimmering trees are simmering still
And thin stems bend beneath their fragile burden.

Evening is listless, fat with Monday morning;
Time tells its dirty secret to the heart;
The fiddles and the saxophones are moaning
As venal meat is prinked with spurious art.
A sudden chill knifes Simon to the bone:
He sees a waiting Sunday, barren as a stone.

Simon Drunk...

'It's not too late,' the glass says to his lips;
'It's not too late,' the whisper in the bowel.
The glasses wink and chink, the cigarettes
Are wagging words, but Simon draws apart.
He will be Gauguin, paint outrageous tarts,
Learn Greek, read Proust and do PT each day;
Write a witty novel or a play
And lead the leading lady well astray.

'It's not too late,' his lips say to his glass.
He feels the fireworks flowering in the dark
Beneath his sober shirt. He'll tell his boss
Just what he thinks of him and find some work
In Paris, Athens, Rome.... Then Mrs Frailman spoke:
'The Party's over, Simon. Let's go home.'

... And Simon Sober

An ashen dawn begins in Simon's mouth.
The conscious day unglues his sleep to drop
Some broken recollections in his lap
And snigger with unsympathetic mirth.
He sees himself, absurd, immodest, vain,
Swaying from maudlin right to left of wrath,
Exciting pursed contempt or nervous ruth,
His dignity, like trousers, fallen down.

The day, a soft groan, greys towards its end
Sustained by aspirin and Worcester Sauce;
A misty sexuality, a wind
Of speechless longing drifts towards his sleep
Where he, marooned upon a small remorse,
Builds resolutions he will never keep.

The Good Temptation

Frailman alone, peaceful in the sweet
Tobacco educating simple air,
Feels a spectral elbow nudge the heart

And knows what Newman knew when tempted by
Not venery but virtue, holy snare
Which draws the chosen victim to the high
Pinnacle which looks upon the wheat
Immortal and the golden everywhere.

Yet how resistible temptation of this sort.
Soon spirit aches and squints at such a glare,
And Simon turns away upon the thought
Of leaving his terrain to sojourn there
Where he may never see, or need to see,
The white and delicate legs more winkingly.

Simon Perplexed

Then Simon thinks how difficult to feel
Real love when there is no reflected pleasure,
And knows he never could sincerely kneel
To intercede for one who had his measure.

He might whip up a plausible compassion
For those whose sins are operatic, loud,
Or those whose moral dress is out of fashion,
Whose bloody heads are tinted but unbowed.

But not a simulacrum of affection
Can he display for virtue's household guard
Whose faces, even after resurrection,
Would still resemble watchful bags of lard.

And Simon swears if these are such as dwell
In Paradise, then heaven must be pure hell.

Father

Owl tinctured, blind, the wind sighs through the night,
Then mimics, with a sudden lift, a cry
Of infant fear, and Simon sits upright,
Pricked quick by this pathetic fallacy.
But none, alas, of Frailman's children now
Perturbs the evening with needs sad or shrill:

Two crude and violent boys, both low of brow,
A ten-year girl of double-barrelled will.

They do not need him now to heave them out
Of wells of furry fear or scare away
With one electric slap the grunting snout
That sniffed their beds: yet if they should display
A leaf of love his pleasure is immense
And humble from the heart's intelligence.

Simon sans Teeth

This is a stage from which there's no retreat,
Thinks Simon sadly; the lost familiars leave
A sibilance that hisses of senility;
His smile is false indeed. He cannot eat.
And Mrs Frailman and his friends deceive
Themselves, not him, when they repeatedly
Assure him that, before much longer, he
Will treat them as his own, contemptuously.

But though, for work, these teeth prove adequate
He knows and always will that they are false.
A part of him has died and, soon or late,
The rest of him must follow till that hour
When he can buy no artificial pulse
And his dead grin will gleam in some dark drawer.

Birthday Present

Forty-six years since Simon bawled his first
And unavailing no at being forced
To put on short mortality and thrust
His midget head through life's enormous noose
Which now, perceptibly, is much less loose.

He once believed his rampant greed and lust
Would leave their ageing cage or that, at least,
They'd drowse replete, resavouring the past;
And he would hang his fears and vanity
Upon a hook in dim serenity.

47

But through the jungle of his nerves the lithe
And tigerish beauties creep; now he could swear,
Until the rope of years pulls tight, he'll writhe
And hear the wanton whisperings everywhere.

Simon Gay

No causing in the sky or envelope
But joy, like oxygen, is everywhere;
And though he knows a hostile periscope
May surface soon and fix him with its glare
He rides the sparkling crest and flies his smile,
Gay in the face of preying buccaneers;
And though the clouds may shortly belch with bile
He will not shut his eyes or plug his ears.

These spells are brief and magical. He knows
Before the day is out he'll run aground
Or be capsized by envious torpedoes
Then cast up on some chill barbaric isle:
Yet Simon vows, though grievous reefs abound,
Whatever comes, the voyage is well worth while.

Elegiac Coda

And when the wingèd chariot at last
Accelerates and runs him down, what then?
No melancholy flags will sag half-mast,
The pubs will close at the usual half-past ten;
The lions in the square will be dry eyed;
No newspaper will note that he has died.

But Frailman's children, burly now or tall,
Will find with slight astonishment that he
Bequeaths, with lesser valuables, a small
And wholly disconcerting legacy:
A foliate grief that opens like a fist
To show a love they doubted could exist.

And Mrs Frailman, staring at a chair,
Whose occupant contrives by not being there

To occupy it far more poignantly
Than when his flesh flopped in it wearily,
Will know that he has cleared a way which she
Must follow after, that more easily.

The Jealous Wife

Like a private eye she searches
For clues through diaries and papers;
Examines his clothing for the guilty stains
Of crimson lipstick, wicked wine,
Or something biological.
And when no act of sensual
Crime can be at length surmised
She is most puzzled and surprised
To be assailed by disappointment
Not relief. Her steel intent
Is never to betray to him
The blonde and naked thoughts within
The purple bedroom of her mind,
But her resolve can never stand
The pressure of the need to know:
'Where?' she says and 'When?' and 'Who?'
'What time?' 'What day?' The question-marks
Like powerful iron grappling hooks
Drag him to her fantasy.
And then he cannot fail to see
Within the harem of her skull
The lovely wickednesses loll.
Thus, at night, they softly creep,
Tap at the darkened panes of sleep;
Then, white and tender, glide inside
His dream on whose delightful slope
At last her fears are justified.

Silver Wedding

The party is over and I sit among
The flotsam that its passing leaves,
The dirty glasses and fag-ends:
Outside, a black wind grieves.

Two decades and a half of marriage;
It does not really seem as long,
And yet I find I have scant knowledge
Of youth's ebullient song.

David, my son, my loved rival,
And Julia, my tapering daughter,
Now grant me one achievement only:
I turn their wine to water.

And Helen, partner of all these years,
Helen my spouse, my sack of sighs,
Reproaches me for every hurt
With injured bovine eyes.

There must have been passion once, I grant,
But neither she nor I could bear
To have its ghost come prowling from
Its dark and frowsy lair.

And we, to keep our nuptials warm,
Still wage sporadic, fireside war;
Numb with insult each yet strives
To scratch the other raw.

Twenty-five years we've now survived;
I'm not sure either why or how
As I sit with a wreath of quarrels set
On my tired and balding brow.

The Masks of Love

We did not understand that it was there,
The love we hungered for; it even seemed
Love's enemies, indifference, distaste
And cruelty, informed our father's stare
Of pained reproof, the homiletic tongue,
The sudden rage, and mother's graven face;
But we were wrong.
And when the chalk-faced master showed his teeth
And pickled us in hurtful verbiage
We labelled him Misanthropos and swore
That his vocation was revenge. But this
Was not the truth.
And later, when the easy woman gave
Free scholarship to study at the warm
College of her flesh, we called her coarse,
Promiscuous, and cunning to behave
With subsequent incontinent remorse.
We thought that we were lucky to evade
Her plot to eat us up alive, but we
Were just about as wrong as we could be.
As afterwards we were, when our sweet dove
That we had welcomed to the marriage cote
Became a beaky squawker and appeared
To loathe the bargain that her instincts bought:
And we did not permit her to reveal
The tender fingers in the iron glove
Like that whose knuckled stratagems conceal
A desperate and brooding love.

Love and Fear

This love has conjured up catastrophes:
And where my loved one walks each whispering hedge
Conceals an ambush and a levelled threat.
All dangers sidle to her trusting side;
I know contagion will be sure to covet
The breathing pastures of her tender flesh.

Disaster trumpets up reserves all over,
Calls traffic accidents beneath his flag;
Assassins pace the pavement where she idles;
Death pants with lust and trembles like a dog.
I cannot bear to have her leave my sight
To face the menace of my luck and love.

And will this fear, this bully of the heart
Grow with my love? This seems most probable,
And lovers fail because they cannot live
With that enormous beast, and cease to love.
Therefore I fear to lose this precious fear,
And cherish it, as her I hold so dear.

First Child

FOR JOHN AND JEAN BOURNE

What fed their apprehension was the fears
Of loud compulsory insomnia,
Their little liberties abruptly cancelled,
The marvel of their marriage darkening
Beneath a wagging, sanitary bunting:
All these intrusions they would have to face.
But when the niggliing interdicts and chill
Labours took up threatened residence
These seemed to be quite friendly after all.

What they had not prepared themselves to meet
Was this: the soft catastrophes, the sly
Menaces whose names are hard to spell
Creeping to her cot, the quiet killers
Loading their white guns and brooding over
That innocent and O, so fragile head.

Second Child

The world, contracted to your needs,
Receives you now, is hushed and warm
But wider than the womb.
As in a stream the sketchy weeds
Waver, your voice in silence floats
And summons instantly white flights
Of tendernesses to your room.

Soon your world will widen, noise
Grow big and blunder through the cool
Cavern where you coo-ing curl
And crow your elementary joys.
Then pain and fear will bully you
Nor may your parents rescue you
At once from that bleak school.

For them you bring gay spurts of flowers,
But also bitter herbs and grave
Auguries that they must grieve
As well as praise your ripening powers
Which open weeping gates and doors
Leading to the perilous days
And quays whence ships of exile leave.

And yet, dear egomaniac,
They would not wish you anywhere
But in the harbour of their care.
Your being there has healed a lack
And even more: love's little space
Has been extended and the harsh
Destructive seas forced back a pace.

Poem for Jane

So many catalogues have been
Compiled by poets, good and bad,
Of qualities that they would wish
To see their infant daughters wear;

Or lacking children they have clad
Others' daughters in the bright
Imagined garments of the flesh,
Prayed for jet or golden hair
Or for the inconspicuous
Homespun of the character
That no one ever whistles after.
Dear Jane, whatever I may say
I'm sure approving whistles will
Send you like an admiral on
Ships of welcome in a bay
Of tender waters where the fish
Will surface longing to be meshed
Among the treasure of your hair.
And as for other qualities
There's only one I really wish
To see you amply manifest
And that's a deep capacity
For loving; and I long for this
Not for any lucky one
Who chances under your love's sun
But because, without it, you
Would never know completely joy
As I know joy through loving you.

Jane at Play

I watch her in the garden and enjoy
Her serious enjoyment as she bends
And murmurs her grave nonsense to the toy
Circle of her animals and friends;
The doll that she quite obviously likes best
Would be to other eyes the ugliest.

For it is only later that we choose
To favour things which publish our good taste,
Whose beauty proves our talent to refuse
To dote upon the comic or defaced;
Unlike the child who needs no reference
Or cautious map to find her preference.

Yet we may be deceived by some old trick,
Robbed of our bright expensive instruments
And bundled from our path into the thick
Frondescence strangling all our arguments,
As when we see our child's plain loveliness
And blunder blind into our happiness.

Sad Story

Once upon a tomb this story closes,
A green page scrawled with a signature of roses.

She could not live with life between
Her and her love who lay unseen

And partnered only by the white
And bony gentry in the night.

Once upon a time the tale began
Of a woman who loved a death-loved man.

And so it ends upon a tomb;
A frozen bride and silent groom.

A SENSE OF DANGER
1962

The Terrible Abstractions

The naked hunter's fist, bunched round his spear,
Was tight and wet inside with sweat of fear;
He heard behind him what the hunted hear.

The silence in the undergrowth crept near;
Its mischief tickled in his nervous ear
And he became the prey, the quivering deer.

The naked hunter feared the threat he knew:
Being hunted, caught, then slaughtered like a ewe
By beasts who padded on four legs or two.

The naked hunter in the bus or queue
Under his decent wool is frightened too
But not of what his hairy forebear knew.

The terrible abstractions prowl about
The compound of his fear and chronic doubt;
He keeps fires burning boldly all night through,
But cannot keep the murderous shadows out.

Act of Violence

Flight (pursuit by only fear)
Beats on the pavement and invades the ear.
The sagging victim like a children's guy
Is dumped in the gutter. One pale cry
Flutters a moment and is blotted out.
A life has leaked away with that frail shout.
The simmering night refuses to ask why
Or who it was that had to die.

The stiff policemen will in time appear;
'In time,' I said, but let me make it clear:
In time to scent and stalk their prey,
Not save the victim for a flowering day.
This time tomorrow either mop or rain
Will certainly have wiped away the stain
That crudely signs the cold page of the street,
And I shall hide my head beneath the sheet
And mutter midnight spells to keep away
The vision of the streetlamp's bilious ray
Lighting both faces undisguised,
And recognized, and recognized.

The Ambush

Noise paled, gradual or quick, I cannot say,
And I became aware of silence everywhere;
I sucked it in when I breathed in the air.

Silence lay inside my lungs and heart
And in my brain. And with the silence came
A stillness such as paintings would disclaim.

This rural scene was not a work of art:
The fallen tree lay in real bluebells while
It played at being an actual crocodile.

The sky was real, the brambles like barbed wire
Would scratch and snag the clothing or the skin;
This Surrey wood seemed one for wandering in.

But I did not go in, though I had meant to.
I waited for a whisper, cry or screech.
The whole green parliament had stifled speech.

Irresolute I waited there until
The hostile death of noise sent me away;
I swore that I'd return on a more propitious day.

But safe in the dangerous noises of the city
I knew I'd never know what thing hid there,
What voiceless incarnation of despair

Or vigilant guerilla lying still,
With breath indrawn among the ferns and dirt,
Waiting to attack or be dealt his mortal hurt.

Hearthquake

A week has passed without a word being said:
No headlines, though that's natural, I suppose
Since there were no injured, let alone dead,
Yet I expected a paragraph or so.
But no, not even comment passed in bars,
No gossip over fences while shirts flap
And sheets boast on the line like sails on spars,
And yet it happened: I can swear to that.
I remember it as if it were last night,
My sitting smug and cosy as a cat
Until the carpet suddenly took fright
And bucked beneath my feet. Walls winced. The clock
Upon the mantelpiece began to dance;
The photograph of me aged twenty-one fell flat;
Glass cracked. The air went cold with shock.
I did not sleep at all well through that night
Nor have I since. I cannot understand
Why no one – not my nearest neighbour even –
Refers to what occurred on that strange evening
Unless, in some way difficult to see,
He is afraid to mention it. Like me.

A Sense of Danger

The city welcomed us. Its favoured sons,
Holders of office, prosperous and plump
With meat and honours, said, 'Put down your guns,
There's nothing here to fear. The industrial slump,

The Plague, the hunting-packs, the underfed,
All are gone, all caged or safely dead.

'Rest easy here. Put down your loads and stay,
And we will purify you with the kiss
Of sweet hygienic needles and display
Incredible varieties of bliss;
We'll strip your inhibitions off like trousers.
Relax. Don't brood. You'll be as safe as houses.'

But we declined, took up our guns and bags;
Turning blind backs on offers of delight
Left for the gaunt terrain and squinting crags;
With luck we'd find a water hole that night.
'As safe as houses,' they had called the town;
But we had seen great houses tumbled down.

Incendiary

That one small boy with a face like pallid cheese
And burnt-out little eyes could make a blaze
As brazen, fierce and huge, as red and gold
And zany yellow as the one that spoiled
Three thousand guineas' worth of property
And crops at Godwin's Farm on Saturday
Is frightening – as fact and metaphor:
An ordinary match intended for
The lighting of a pipe or kitchen fire
Misused may set a whole menagerie
Of flame-fanged tigers roaring hungrily.
And frightening, too, that one small boy should set
The sky on fire and choke the stars to heat
Such skinny limbs and such a little heart
Which would have been content with one warm kiss
Had there been anyone to offer this.

Death of a Jew

He wore a monocle of blood.
The crimson ribbon ran
Down one wax cheek.
His teeth had been kicked in.

Close by, on the pavement, lay
His crunched pince-nez;
The lard-fat moon ignored
His scatterbrain black grin.

The drumbeat tramping faded
Like a dying pulse;
He did not seem to hear it,
Or anything else:

But lay on the pavement grinning,
His toothless jaws wide;
And another crimson ribbon
Crawled from his side.

Ageing Schoolmaster

And now another autumn morning finds me
    With chalk dust on my sleeve and in my breath,
Preoccupied with vague, habitual speculation
    On the huge inevitability of death.

Not wholly wretched, yet knowing absolutely
    That I shall never reacquaint myself with joy,
I sniff the smell of ink and chalk and my mortality
    And think of when I rolled, a gormless boy,

And rollicked round the playground of my hours,
    And wonder when precisely tolled the bell
Which summoned me from summer liberties
    And brought me to this chill autumnal cell

From which I gaze upon the april faces
   That gleam before me, like apples ranged on shelves,
And yet I feel no pinch or prick of envy
   Nor would I have them know their sentenced selves.

With careful effort I can separate the faces,
   The dull, the clever, the various shapes and sizes,
But in the autumn shades I find I only
   Brood upon death, who carries off all the prizes.

The Telephone Number

Searching for a lost address I find,
Among dead papers in a dusty drawer,
A diary which has lain there quite ten years,
And soon forget what I am looking for,
Intrigued by cryptic entries in a hand
Resembling mine but noticeably more
Vigorous than my present quavering scrawl.
Appointments – kept or not, I don't remember –
With people now grown narrow, fat or bald;
A list of books that somehow I have never
Found the time to read, nor ever shall,
Remind me that my world is growing cold.
And then I find a scribbled code and number,
The urgent words: 'Must not forget to call.'
But now, of course, I have no recollection
Of telephoning anyone at all.
The questions whisper: Did I dial that number
And, if I did, what kind of voice replied?
Questions that will never find an answer
Unless – the thought is serpentine – I tried
To telephone again, as years ago
I did, or meant to do. What would I find
If now I lifted this mechanic slave
Black to my ear and spun the dial – so…?
Inhuman, impolite, the double burp
Erupts, insulting hope. The long dark sleeve
Of silence stretches out. No stranger's voice
Slips in, suspicious, cold; no manic speech

Telling what I do not wish to know
Nor throaty message creamed with sensual greed –
Nothing of these. And, when again I try,
Relief is painful when there's no reply.

Felo de Se

Alone, he came to his decision,
The sore tears stiffening his cheeks
As headlamps flicked the ceiling with white dusters
And darkness roared downhill with nervous brakes.
Below, the murmuring and laughter,
The baritone, tobacco-smelling jokes;
And then his misery and anger
Suddenly became articulate:
'I wish that I was dead. Oh, they'll be sorry then.
I hate them and I'll kill myself tomorrow.
I want to die. I hate them, hate them. Hate.'

And kill himself in fact he did,
But not next day as he'd decided.
The deed itself, for thirty years deferred,
Occurred one wintry night when he was loaded.
Belching with scotch and misery
He turned the gas tap on and placed his head
Gently, like a pudding, in the oven.
'I want to die. I'll hurt them yet,' he said.
And once again: 'I hate them, hate them. Hate.'
The lampless darkness roared inside his head,
Then sighed into a silence in which played
The grown-up voices, still up late,
Indifferent to his rage as to his fate.

The Fair

Music and yellow steam, the fizz
Of spinning lights as roundabouts
Galloping nowhere whirl and whizz
Through fusillades of squeals and shouts;
The night sniffs rich at pungent spice,
Brandysnap and diesel oil;
The stars like scattered beads of rice
Sparsely fleck the sky's deep soil
Dulled and diminished by these trapped
Melodic meteors below
In whose feigned fever brightly lapped
The innocent excitements flow.
Pocketfuls of simple thrills
Jingle silver, purchasing
A warm and sugared fear that spills
From dizzy car and breathless swing.

So no one hears the honest shriek
From the field beyond the fair,
A single voice becoming weak,
Then dying on the ignorant air.
And not for hours will frightened love
Rise and seek her everywhere,
Then find her, like a fallen glove,
Soiled and crumpled, lying there.

Dead Dog

One day I found a lost dog in the street.
The hairs about its grin were spiked with blood,
And it lay still as stone. It must have been
A little dog, for though I only stood
Nine inches for each one of my four years
I picked it up and took it home. My mother
Squealed, and later father spaded out
A bed and tucked my mongrel down in mud.

I can't remember any feeling but
A moderate pity, cool not swollen-eyed;
Almost a godlike feeling now it seems.
My lump of dog was ordinary as bread.
I have no recollection of the school
Where I was taught my terror of the dead.

Autobiographical Note

Beeston, the place, near Nottingham:
We lived there for three years or so.
Each Saturday at two-o'clock
We queued up for the matinée,
All the kids for streets around
With snotty noses, giant caps,
Cut down coats and heavy boots,
The natural enemies of cops
And schoolteachers. Profane and hoarse
We scrambled, yelled and fought until
The Picture Palace opened up
And we, like Hamelin children, forced
Our bony way into the hall.
That much is easy to recall;
Also the reek of chewing-gum,
Gob-stoppers and liquorice,
But of the flickering myths themselves
Not much remains. The hero was
A milky wide-brimmed hat, a shape
Astride the arched white stallion;
The villain's horse and hat were black.
Disbelief did not exist
And laundered virtue always won
With quicker gun and harder fist,
And all of us applauded it.
Yet I remember moments when
In solitude I'd find myself
Brooding on the sooty man,
The bristling villain, who could move
Imagination in a way
The well-shaved hero never could,

And even warm the nervous heart
With something oddly close to love.

The Great War

Whenever war is spoken of
I find
The war that was called Great invades the mind:
The grey militia marches over land
A darker mood of grey
Where fractured tree-trunks stand
And shells, exploding, open sudden fans
Of smoke and earth.
Blind murders scythe
The deathscape where the iron brambles writhe;
The sky at night
Is honoured with rosettes of fire,
Flares that define the corpses on the wire
As terror ticks on wrists at zero hour.
These things I see,
But they are only part
Of what it is that slyly probes the heart:
Less vivid images and words excite
The sensuous memory
And, even as I write,
Fear and a kind of love collaborate
To call each simple conscript up
For quick inspection:
Trenches' parapets
Paunchy with sandbags; bandoliers, tin-hats,
Candles in dug-outs,
Duckboards, mud and rats.
Then, like patrols, tunes creep into the mind:
A long long trail, The Rose of No-Man's Land,
Home Fires and *Tipperary*;
And through the misty keening of a band
Of Scottish pipes the proper names are heard
Like fateful commentary of distant guns:
Passchendaele, Bapaume, and Loos, and Mons.
And now,

Whenever the November sky
Quivers with a bugle's hoarse, sweet cry,
The reason darkens; in its evening gleam
Crosses and flares, tormented wire, grey earth
Splattered with crimson flowers,
And I remember,
Not the war I fought in
But the one called Great
Which ended in a sepia November
Four years before my birth.

The Men Who Wear My Clothes

Sleepless I lay last night and watched the slow
    Procession of the men who wear my clothes:
First, the grey man with bloodshot eyes and sly
    Gestures miming what he loves and loathes.

Next came the cheery knocker-back of pints,
    The beery joker, never far from tears,
Whose loud and public vanity acquaints
    The careful watcher with his private fears.

And then I saw the neat mouthed gentle man
    Defer politely, listen to the lies,
Smile at the tedious tale and gaze upon
    The little mirrors in the speaker's eyes.

The men who wear my clothes walked past my bed
    And all of them looked tired and rather old;
I felt a chip of ice melt in my blood.
    Naked I lay last night, and very cold.

Juan in Middle Age

The appetite which leads him to her bed
Is not unlike the lust of boys for cake
Except he knows that after he has fed
He'll suffer more than simple belly-ache.

He'll groan to think what others have to pay
As price for his obsessive need to know
That he's a champion still, though slightly grey,
And both his skill and gameness clearly show.

And after this quick non-decision bout,
As he in his dark corner gasping lies,
He'll hear derision like a distant shout
While kisses press like pennies on his eyes.

Incident in a Saloon Bar

Not because he was in any way remarkable
In dress, physique, or conjunction of facial parts
Did the rest of the customers feel such embarrassment
And curious fear in their superstitious hearts.

That all of them, to some degree, were so afflicted
Was evident from the way their lips grew tight,
And from the intensity with which they did not stare at
    him,
Though each could have stated his colouring and height.

Not because he was conspicuously intoxicated
Or publishing uncouth sounds or venereal signs
Did his presence so patently offend those stiff gentlemen
Who, guardsmen of propriety, presented him their spines.

Not because he was so quiet and unremarkable
That they suspected that he might be spying
Did they feel this hostility towards the lonely fellow
But simply because he was, quite quietly, crying.

Wedding

The white flower of his love grew in the shade
Of cypress and was nourished by forlorn
And haunting arias of birds afraid
Of that bright dark, the clarion murderous dawn.

The moon, diseased and beautiful, approved his choice
Of meadow saffron, wolf's-bane and the icy blade
He gave to her he loved. At last her voice
Whispered the consent for which he prayed.

But she insisted on a long engagement,
And well before the wedding day drew near
He found out what the darkening cage of age meant;
His sugared love changed into acid fear.

The date could not be cancelled, but instead
Of coloured paper snow the salt rain fell
And he, pale groom, lay blind in her deep bed,
Ears stopped against the tolling of the bell.

Elegy

The world burst (*plap!*) like a black balloon
In a black room:
Black silence, a black moon.
This occurred on a summer afternoon
In the year 1959 on July the 3rd.

The enormous nostrils of everywhere
Were pinched tight, hard;
Blind to reek, stench and sweet rumour,
To laborious sweat,
And deaf to the aria of the rose.

Music knifed in a flash
Daggered at that *plap*!

Ridiculous. And ridiculous too
That all the wild wide women then were sealed,
Stopped, blocked and chilled
When my old friend, the boozer Bellamy, expired
As, I suppose, in that same tick of time
And equally absurdly
Five hundred thousand other worlds misfired,
Speaking statistically.

Dejection

Not worthy of the fine words, this sensation –
Despair, deep-eyed may mouth its rich iambics,
Betrayal's tears move softly and in tune –
To dignify this with the name of torment
Would only puff it up, a toy balloon,
And make its owner clownish and a liar.

No dark night of the soul, but afternoon,
Quite dark it's true, and grizzled with chill rain;
The whole terrain a wintry cabbage patch;
Some stale confetti trodden in the mud.
I seek the words and images that match
The dun, the moribund, the colour of this mood,
And now intone these lines at sombre pitch,
Accompanied by one distressed bassoon.

Howling for Love

Howling for love in his unfriendly bed
At length he slept, grew muscles in his dream,
And thrashed the hairy villain with his father's face,
And kissed the woman on her tubs of cream.

The soft explosion of the sunrise flung
Him gasping in the whistling world; derisions peeped
And sniggered on the windowsill;
Through sticky lashes wincing daylight seeped.

The clanging challenge of the day began.
The shawl of sun was warm as auburn breath;
The tinkling walk of women told him love;
Dumb music churned his blood to crimson wealth.

Evening was moondrenched when he met his love;
Her breasts were smooth as peeled eggs, and she lay
Her white, unplundered beauty at his wish
And prayed that he would hold the dawn at bay.

But even as he sank into her cry
He knew betrayal curled on her dark head,
And moaned that he had never wanted this,
Howling for love in his unfriendly bed.

Cows in Red Pasture

Last summer in a Kentish field
I saw the plush green darkened by
A whim of light and darkened too
By whiteness of the sheep which stood
Diminished by the distance so
They looked like gravestones on the green,
So still and small and white they seemed.
As this warm memory blurs and fades,
The emptiness bequeathed instructs
Me, curiously, to resurrect
An older memory of a field
Which I would rather far forget:
A foreign field, a field of France,
In which there lay two cows, one white
With maps of black stamped on its hide,
The other just the colour of
The caramel that I once loved.
Both were still; the toffee one
Lay on its back, its stiff legs stuck
Up from the swollen belly like
A huge discarded set of bagpipes.

The piebald cow lay on its side
Looking like any summer beast
Until one saw it had no head.

The grass on which they lay was red.

A Day on the River

It moved so slowly, friendly as a dog
Whose teeth would never bite;
It licked the hand with cool and gentle tongue
And seemed to share its parasites' delight
Who moved upon its back or moored among
The hairy shallows overhung
With natural parasols of leaves
And bubbling birdsong.
Ukuleles twanged and ladies sang
In punts and houseboats vivid as our own
Bold paintings of the Ark;
This was summer's self to any child:
The plop and suck of water and the old
Sweet rankness in the air beguiled
With deft archaic spells the dim
Deliberations of the land,
Dear river, comforting
More than the trailing hand.

The afternoon of sandwiches and flasks
Drifted away.
The breeze across the shivering water grew
Perceptibly in strength. The sun began to bleed.

'Time to go home,' the punctured uncles said,
And back on land
We trembled at the river's faint, low growl
And as birds probed the mutilated sky
We knew that, with the night,
The river's teeth grew sharp
And they could bite.

The Wicked Words

The wicked words corrupt. The young are gorged
On printed sex and violence till they tear
The pages up, still grunting with the urge
To rip a softer substance. Everywhere
The literate werewolves roam in drooling quest
Of nice white meat. Dread walks on pointed toes.
The wicked words corrupt, should be suppressed.
The young men tick like bombs in darkened bars,
Swallow the scalding music, pupils glow
Like fuses, dangerous. Yes, I suppose
They are quite capable of violent acts,
Translating into deed the feverish prose.
The odd thing is I've never seen them read,
Not wicked words nor any words at all,
As I've seen wrinkled gents and wispy dames
Munching up the print with serious greed,
The print recording deeds of lust and terror,
Incest, murder, rape and God knows what,
Intrepid readers who would squeak with horror
To see a mouse or dog or pussy bleed
And vomit at the sight of human snot.

A Sordid Story

All the dark watchers trembled when they saw
The lovers who, as they lay down together
In desperate conjunction, also raped
Convention and made decent dewlaps shudder.

Above the town, on Beacon Hill, the rain
Homed in her hair as sweetly as on leaves,
And when he sank inside her welcoming,
'Home!' he exulted, there beneath drenched trees.

But in the town the files were being opened;
A ginger man who smelled of nicotine,
Who'd never heard of Paolo or Francesca,
Was filling in the date and place and time.

Her body made all similes of need
Die in the throat; itself was metaphor,
For, though it was substantial as good bread,
Its language was alive as no words are.

And neither tried to turn the flesh to words;
They dared not challenge time with hollow nouns
Or truss the moment with syllabic cords
However neat: no page would print their groans.

No, not their groans but fact and circumstance,
Blurred pictures of the pair, a trull and clown:
A sordid story in smudged type it danced,
Blown through the midnight gutters of the town.

My Father's Face

Each morning, when I shave, I see his face,
Or something like a sketch of it gone wrong;
The artist caught, it seems, more than a trace
Of that uneasy boldness and the strong
Fear behind the stare which tried to shout
How tough its owner was, inviting doubt.

And though this face is altogether
Loosely put together, and indeed
A lot less handsome, weaker in the jaw
And softer in the mouth, I feel no need
To have it reassembled, made a better
Copy of the face of its begetter.

I do not mind because my mouth is not
That lipless hyphen, military, stern;
He had the face that faces blade and shot
In schoolboys' tales, and even schoolboys learn
To laugh at it. But they've not heard it speak
Those bayonet words that guard the cruel and weak.

For weakness was his one consistency;
And when I scrape the soapy fluff away

I see that he bequeathed this gift to me
Along with various debts I cannot pay.
But he gave, too, this mirror-misting breath
Whose mercy dims the looking-glass of death;

For which kind accident I thank him now
And, though I cannot love him, feel a sort
Of salty tenderness, remembering how
The prude and lecher in him moiled and fought
Their roughhouse in the dark ring of his pride
And killed each other when his body died.

This morning, as I shave, I find I can
Forgive the blows, the meanness and the lust,
The ricochetting arsenal of a man
Who groaned groin-deep in hope's ironic dust;
But these eyes in the glass regard the living
Features with distaste, quite unforgiving.

An Old Lament Renewed

The soil is savoury with their bones' lost marrow;
    Down among dark roots their polished knuckles lie,
And no one could tell one peeled head from another;
    Earth packs each crater that once gleamed with eye.

Colonel and batman, emperor and assassin,
    Democratized by silence and corruption,
Defy identification with identical grin:
    The joke is long, will brook no interruption.

At night the imagination walks like a ghoul
    Among the stone lozenges and counterpanes of turf
Tumescent under cypresses; the long, rueful call
    Of the owl soars high and then wheels back to earth.

And brooding over the enormous dormitory
    The mind grows shrill at those nothings in lead rooms
Who were beautiful once or dull and ordinary,
    But loved, all loved, all called to sheltering arms.

Many I grieve with a grave, deep love
   Who are deep in the grave, whose faces I never saw:
Poets who died of alcohol, bullets, or birthdays
   Doss in the damp house, forbidden now to snore.

And in a French orchard lies whatever is left
   Of my friend, Gordon Rennie, whose courage would
   toughen
The muscle of resolution; he laughed
   At death's serious face, but once too often.

On summer evenings when the religious sun stains
   The gloom in the bar and the glasses surrender demurely
I think of Donovan whose surrender was unconditional,
   That great thirst swallowed entirely.

And often some small thing will summon the memory
   Of my small son, Benjamin. A smile is his sweet ghost.
But behind, in the dark, the white twigs of his bones
   Form a pattern of guilt and waste.

I am in mourning for the dull, the heroic and the mad;
   In the haunted nursery the child lies dead.
I mourn the hangman and his bulging complement;
   I mourn the cadaver in the egg.

The one-eyed rider aims, shoots death into the womb;
   Blood on the sheet of snow, the maiden dead.
The dagger has a double blade and meaning,
   So has the double bed.

Imagination swaggers in the sensual sun
   But night will find it at the usual mossy gate;
The whisper from the mouldering darkness comes:
   'I am the one you love and fear and hate.'

I know my grieving is made thick by terror;
   The bones of those I loved aren't fleshed by sorrow.
I mourn the deaths I've died and go on dying;
   I fear the long, implacable tomorrow.

WALKING WOUNDED
1965

Autumn

It is the football season once more
And the back pages of the Sunday papers
Again show the blurred anguish of goalkeepers.

In Maida Vale, Golders Green and Hampstead
Lamps ripen early in the surprising dusk;
They are furred like stale rinds with a fuzz of mist.

The pavements of Kensington are greasy;
The wind smells of burnt porridge in Bayswater,
And the leaves are mushed to silence in the gutter.

The big hotel like an anchored liner
Rides near the park; lit windows hammer the sky.
Like the slow swish of surf the tyres of taxis sigh.

On Ealing Broadway the cinema glows
Warm behind glass while mellow the church clock chimes
As the waiting girls stir in their delicate chains.

Their eyes are polished by the wind,
But the gleam is dumb, empty of joy or anger.
Though the lovers are long in coming the girls still linger.

We are nearing the end of the year.
Under the sombre sleeve the blood ticks faster
And in the dark ear of Autumn quick voices whisper.

It is a time of year that's to my taste,
Full of spiced rumours, sharp and velutinous flavours,
Dim with the mist that softens the cruel surfaces,
Makes mirrors vague. It is the mist that I most favour.

Talking of Death

My friend was dead. A simple sentence ended
With one black stop, like this: My friend was dead.
I had no notion that I had depended
So much on fires he lit, on that good bread
He always had to offer if I came
Hungry and cold to his inviting room.
Absurdly, I believed that he was lame
Until I started limping from his tomb.
My sorrow was the swollen, prickly kind,
Not handsome mourning smartly cut and pressed:
An actual grief, I swear. Therefore to find
Myself engaged upon a shameful quest
For anyone who'd known him, but who thought
That he was still alive, was something strange,
Something disquieting; for what I sought
Was power and presence beyond my usual range.
For once, my audience listened, welcomed me,
Avid for every syllable that spoke
Of woven fear and grieving. Nervously
They eyed my black, ambassadorial cloak.
Their faces greyed; my friend's death died, and they
Saw theirs walk in alive. I felt quite well –
Being Death's man – until they went away,
And I was left with no one else to tell.

Act of Love

This is not the man that women choose,
This honest fellow, stuffed to the lips with groans,
Whose passion cannot even speak plain prose
But grunts and mumbles in the muddiest tones.
His antics are disgusting or absurd,
His lust obtrusive, craning from its nest
At awkward times its blind reptilian head;
His jealousy and candour are a pest.

Now here is the boy that women will lie down for,
The snappy actor, skilled in the lover's part,
A lyric fibber and subvocal tenor
Whose pleasure in the play conceals his art;
Who, even as he enters her warm yes,
Hears fluttering hands and programmes in the vast
Auditorium beyond her voice
Applauding just one member of the cast.

Telephoning Her

The dial spins back, clicks still. Just half an inch
Of silence, then the abrupt eruption blurts
Its two quick jets of noise into his ear.
Again the double spurt; again. Three, four.
She does not answer. Give her just two more.
Yet still he holds the instrument to his ear,
But no longer is imagination bare.
Inside his head the room assumes its shape:
The dishevelled bed, a stocking on the floor.
The tortured clown grimaces in his frame;
The room seems empty, but how can he be sure?
And with uncertainty the light grows dim,
But not before he sees a movement there,
Quick twitching of the coverings on the bed,
Or thinks he might have noticed something stir.
Darkness grows thick as tar. Then he can hear –
Though not in the liquorice-black thing that he holds –
Her voice, thick with the body's joy and mind's despair,
Moaning a foreign word, a stranger's name.
Derisively the darkness jerks again,
Spits twice into his violated ear.

It's Sure to End in Tears

'It's sure to end in tears.
These rough games always do.
Come downstairs! Where's that book
That Auntie Georgie gave you?
Get your crayons, make a picture.
Stay apart. Don't touch.
You know as well as I what happens
When your games start getting rough.
Now don't get so excited dears
Or everything will end in tears.'

And she was right. Things always did:
Wild giggle in mid-air would flip
A sudden somersault and turn
To yell of pain. The dizzy branch
Of fun would crack; a shrill swoop down,
Black flash of bump, and pain began;
Or, more insidious than pain,
Excitement's swing came lurching low
To darkened ground where nothing grew
And all the air was sick and stale.
The best games always ended so,
With pain or boredom, screams and jeers;
Were always sure to end in tears.

So let us, Love, be circumspect,
For we are wiser than we were;
We are not children and must act
With pressed decorum, keeping far
Apart on couches, stay downstairs,
Read serious books, play nothing rough;
And if, at times, caught unawares,
We think of those hot games and laugh,
Perhaps, in folly, wish once more
To swing branch high, roll on the floor,
We'll summon that calm voice which said,
'It's sure to end in tears' and go
Sober to our separate beds
Where, should we weep, no one will know.

Voyeur

Find the hidden face. A prize is offered.
The scene is green and summer. On the grass
The dresses spread, exhausted butterflies,
And smooth brown legs make soft confessions to
Rough trousers. Excited air
Is hushed with kissing.
Now search for the solitary, the uncoupled one:
Not in the leafy tentacles of trees,
He is no climber,
But close to earth, well-hidden, squat.
You see him now? Yes, there! His snarling grin
Bearded with leaves, his body bushed,
Invisible. See how his eyes are fat with glee
And horror. They fizz with unfulfilment's booze.
His tongue makes sure his lips are still in place
With quick red pats.
You've found him now, and you can take your prize,
Though, as you see, we do not offer cash:
Just recognition and its loaded cosh.

Walking Wounded

A mammoth morning moved grey flanks and groaned.
In the rusty hedges pale rags of mist hung;
The gruel of mud and leaves in the mauled lane
Smelled sweet, like blood. Birds had died or flown,
Their green and silent attics sprouting now
With branches of leafed steel, hiding round eyes
And ripe grenades ready to drop and burst.
In the ditch at the cross-roads the fallen rider lay
Hugging his dead machine and did not stir
At crunch of mortar, tantrum of a Bren
Answering a Spandau's manic jabber.
Then into sight the ambulances came,
Stumbling and churning past the broken farm,
The amputated sign-post and smashed trees,
Slow wagonloads of bandaged cries, square trucks

That rolled on ominous wheels, vehicles
Made mythopoeic by their mortal freight
And crimson crosses on the dirty white.
This grave procession passed, though, for a while,
The grinding of their engines could be heard,
A dark noise on the pallor of the morning,
Dark as dried blood; and then it faded, died.
The road was empty, but it seemed to wait –
Like a stage which knows the cast is in the wings –
Wait for a different traffic to appear.
The mist still hung in snags from dripping thorns;
Absent-minded guns still sighed and thumped.
And then they came, the walking wounded,
Straggling the road like convicts loosely chained,
Dragging at ankles exhaustion and despair.
Their heads were weighted down by last night's lead,
And eyes still drank the dark. They trailed the night
Along the morning road. Some limped on sticks;
Others wore rough dressings, splints and slings;
A few had turbanned heads, the dirty cloth
Brown-badged with blood. A humble brotherhood,
Not one was suffering from a lethal hurt,
They were not magnified by noble wounds,
There was no splendour in that company.
And yet, remembering after eighteen years,
In the heart's throat a sour sadness stirs;
Imagination pauses and returns
To see them walking still, but multiplied
In thousands now. And when heroic corpses
Turn slowly in their decorated sleep
And every ambulance has disappeared
The walking wounded still trudge down that lane,
And when recalled they must bear arms again.

A Case of Murder

They should not have left him there alone,
Alone that is except for the cat.
He was only nine, not old enough
To be left alone in a basement flat,

Alone, that is, except for the cat.
A dog would have been a different thing,
A big gruff dog with slashing jaws,
But a cat with round eyes mad as gold,
Plump as a cushion with tucked-in paws –
Better have left him with a fair-sized rat!
But what they did was leave him with a cat.
He hated that cat; he watched it sit,
A buzzing machine of soft black stuff,
He sat and watched and he hated it,
Snug in its fur, hot blood in a muff,
And its mad gold stare and the way it sat
Crooning dark warmth: he loathed all that.
So he took Daddy's stick and he hit the cat.
Then quick as a sudden crack in glass
It hissed, black flash, to a hiding place
In the dust and dark beneath the couch,
And he followed the grin on his new-made face,
A wide-eyed, frightened snarl of a grin,
And he took the stick and he thrust it in,
Hard and quick in the furry dark.
The black fur squealed and he felt his skin
Prickle with sparks of dry delight.
Then the cat again came into sight,
Shot for the door that wasn't quite shut,
But the boy, quick too, slammed fast the door:
The cat, half-through, was cracked like a nut
And the soft black thud was dumped on the floor.
Then the boy was suddenly terrified
And he bit his knuckles and cried and cried;
But he had to do something with the dead thing there.
His eyes squeezed beads of salty prayer
But the wound of fear gaped wide and raw;
He dared not touch the thing with his hands
So he fetched a spade and shovelled it
And dumped the load of heavy fur
In the spidery cupboard under the stair
Where it's been for years, and though it died
It's grown in that cupboard and its hot low purr
Grows slowly louder year by year:
There'll not be a corner for the boy to hide
When the cupboard swells and all sides split
And the huge black cat pads out of it.

Hide and Seek

Call out. Call loud: 'I'm ready! Come and find me!'
The sacks in the toolshed smell like the seaside.
They'll never find you in this salty dark,
But be careful that your feet aren't sticking out.
Wiser not to risk another shout.
The floor is cold. They'll probably be searching
The bushes near the swing. Whatever happens
You mustn't sneeze when they come prowling in.
And here they are, whispering at the door;
You've never heard them sound so hushed before.
Don't breathe. Don't move. Stay dumb. Hide in your
    blindness.
They're moving closer, someone stumbles, mutters;
Their words and laughter scuffle, and they're gone.
But don't come out just yet; they'll try the lane
And then the greenhouse and back here again.
They must be thinking that you're very clever,
Getting more puzzled as they search all over.
It seems a long time since they went away.
Your legs are stiff, the cold bites through your coat;
The dark damp smell of sand moves in your throat.
It's time to let them know that you're the winner.
Push off the sacks. Uncurl and stretch. That's better!
Out of the shed and call to them: 'I've won!
Here I am! Come and own up I've caught you!'
The darkening garden watches. Nothing stirs.
The bushes hold their breath; the sun is gone.
Yes, here you are. But where are they who sought you?

Unacademic Graffiti

The coin slips down with a metallic gulp;
The door submits, steps back, slams shut again.
Buttocks are bared; the seat is slightly warm,
Distasteful relic of a former reign.
The cell is small and mainly functional,
Yet something more: this privacy is rare,
Perhaps unique, self-conscious, quintessential.
This, and of course the business why we're here,
May be the reason why the mental bowels
Move to expel dark cargo of their own.
There, on the door and on the gaolish walls
Are aspirations that we can't disown:
The chronic thirst for immortality,
Someone's name carved by a penknife blade,
Not ours of course though it might easily be
Were we not quite so prudent or afraid;
And we, too, might have drawn those zeppelin cocks,
Ballooning balls and ladies on their backs
With wide flung legs revealing beetling twats
Had we not often felt the punch guilt packs.
And we feel solitude encouraging
Confessions that no penitent would make;
The words upon the walls are whispering
Our loneliness and lust, despair and hate.
We notice, unsurprised and unappalled,
That someone's done an abstract with his shit.
It's time to go. Heave off. The chain is pulled.
Gurgle and gush. Outside the lamps are lit
But in the padlocked park the night is thick;
Down baffled alleys desperations sob;
In blinded upper rooms the air is sick,
And everywhere the human engines throb.

Report on Drinking Habits

I

He is always well-shaven; often
His jowl is powdered like something
Carefully prepared for the oven.
He is plump but not corpulent.
It is talk he wants rather than drinking,
Though nowhere else than in a saloon
Could he find the conversation
He needs, metallic as a spittoon,
Masculine as beef and mustard.
He always buys a round before leaving
But never stays for more than half an hour
And two or three drinks, and no one
Has ever observed him hungover.
His eyes' brightness advertises
Good meals and unadventurous sleeping.

II

This one is a different case: he starts
Fast, towsing his glass like a dog
With bone, welcomes it when the drink hurts
Exploding in dark diaphragm.
The presiding clock watches his knees sag.
He is not much interested in talk
And the most he will ever eat
Is a sandwich, or sausage on stick;
He is sometimes accompanied
By a mournful woman who does not speak.
Three hours produce a visible change:
His eyes smear and his face grows fat,
A dredged cadaver's except for the tinge
Of diseased sunset through the sweat.
Closing time strikes like a fatal attack.

III

But for this other one drink is not
A murderous necessity,
A vice or pleasant social habit;
For him it is a vocation.
Virtue is no more than capacity.
He will talk because, by speaking, he
Can show that he is capable.
If you meet him in the lavatory
He will remark on the weather,
But his words are never memorable.
Like a professional athlete he
Paces himself and finishes
Strongly. Nobody will ever see
Him collapse or even falter.
At the last bell he quietly vanishes.

IV

Watch the next customer; observe him
Grabbing with eyes and mouth and fist.
He likes to talk, also, as the rim
Of gripped glass trembles to get in,
Promises to be better than the last.
Gay joker early in the evening,
Later a mournful bulldozer
Incorrigibly revealing
Public parts he believes are secret;
From the opening bell a certain loser.
In the morning it will be never
Again, never to be realized.
Observe this fellow in the mirror:
The daft mask mocks all promises,
Sticks fast and hurts, and must be recognized.

Mourning

We sat in the kitchen and listened to the rain
That spluttered on the pane like something frying.
The silence simmered but we did not season it;
We had mislaid effective flavouring.
Each of us knew the other's heart was tight,
Swollen and taut, like something overripe;
But neither spilled a drop of salty water.
I do not know how long we stayed like that,
An hour, at least, for the room was growing dark
When one of us rose and switched on the light.
Chairs groaned and sighed, and then at last she spoke:
We had to decide what to eat that night.

Revenant

There is a smell of negligence;
Dust pads the evening shadows;
The room has become small.
I remember the bird-shaped stain
Brown on the yellow wall.

This room was once familiar,
In which I move, a stranger;
The window holds a view
Faded like a print;
Even the smell is new,

New, yet also ancient,
And the dusty stuff I finger,
The books I must have read,
One cuff-link, postcards, letters,
Seem things left by the dead.

The room attends my going;
Watchfully it waits
To occupy itself.

My feet move down the stairs,
Noiselessly, with stealth.

Since Donovan Died

Death has been named so many times before,
Its avatar determined by blind needs:
Pale rider, lover, angel, king, slammed door;
Scientific fact or worm that feeds
Under numb earth plumping with pale blood;
As if our naming could propitiate,
Redeem the voices from dumb cells of mud.
I will not flatter Death, conceal my hate,
But name it, yes. Since Donovan died I've felt
Anger like a cinder in my gut,
So dirty was the trick that he was dealt,
Such innocent trust was chosen for a butt.
So I name Death, not proud, of regal stock,
But pale, malevolent; a cruel boy
Who pulls the thin black arms out of the clock,
Burns calendars alive with sniggering joy.

Frankly Speaking: An Interview

'Listeners will be interested to hear
This programme where our greatest man of letters
And possibly the greatest man in any
Sphere of intellectual endeavour
Speaks frankly from the wisdom gathered over
A long and varied life. This mellow store
I'm sure will edify and entertain
Without imposing on us too much strain.
We're speaking from the great man's lovely home
And seated in his splendid book-lined room....'

Eight million listeners act their patient role:
They listen. The sharp young voice begins to probe
With confidence, and then the old one comes,
Dusty and frail. One almost smells the mould
Of yellow pages, but no illumination
Brightens bed-sitter, drawing-room and kitchen.
The notions are banal, the phrasing dull;
The stout words with their double chins wheeze out:
The Absolute, the True, the Beautiful.
Then as time wastes, the mouth begins to utter
Dry syllables that flutter like hurt moths.

Determined not to fail, the interviewer
Affects a brisker tone, a little too
Like a policeman's for this interview:
'Now you, sir, as a most exceptional man
Who's pondered long and deep on what goes on
Upon this earth and in the human heart,
Perhaps you'll tell us now what you believe
About the life to come beyond the grave.'

A silence seems to chill the air and threaten
The listener in his armchair or warm kitchen;
And then the great man speaks, quite clearly now:
'Get out! Get out of here you prying fool!
Let in the white men in their soft black boots
Who come with measuring instruments to prove
I'm no exception to their iron rule.'

This Summer

See the stout man with the bald head
Pink as plastic in the polishing sun
Pause on the threshold emerging from the bank,
Petrified by dazzle.

Heat crumbles the afternoon to dust;
Windscreen and chrome flash desperate messages;
A girl in yellow walks past Woolworths,
Her legs oiled with lust.

And who lingeringly chiselled them,
Those indolent limbs lacquered in oil and gold?
Who but him, and of his making
The lush eatable hair.

The crazed man with the hot bald head,
He made them, stunned with lust and summer
On the steps of the Westminster Bank,
Overdrawn and hopelessly happy.

Six Year Darling

The poets are to blame, or partly so:
Wordsworth's pretty pigmy, plump with joy,
And Henry Vaughan's white celestial thoughts
Mislead as much as Millais' chubby boy
Or daddy-blessing Christopher at prayer.
These fantasies are still quite popular.
Pick up any children's book and you will see
That all the illustrations are as false
As muscle-builders' ads: angelic girls
And sturdy little chaps with candid eyes –
Not to please the children, understand;
You'll find few kids who're kidded by the act,
Though later most of them will take the bribe
And speak of infancy as paradise.
Will this boy, here, be legatee of lies?
Perhaps he will, and maybe just as well
If one day he is going to breed his own.
But now he knows that things are otherwise:
Not paradise, no glimpse of God's bright face,
But time of simple goods like warmth and sweets,
Excitement, too; but often pain and fear,
And worse than either, boredom, long and grey,
A dusty road to nowhere, hard to walk,
Going on and on, desolate and bare,
Until it breaks upon the hidden dark.

I'm Covered Now

'What would happen to your lady wife
And little ones – you've four I think you said –
Little ones I mean, not wives, ha-ha –
What would happen to them if ...' And here
He cleared his throat of any reticence.
' ... if something happened to you? We've got to face
These things, must be realistic, don't you think?
Now, we have various schemes to give you cover
And, taking in account your age and means,
This policy would seem to be the one ...'

The words uncoiled, effortless but urgent,
Assured, yet coming just a bit too fast,
A little breathless, despite the ease of manner,
An athlete drawing near the tape's last gasp
Yet trying hard to seem still vigorous there.
But no, this metaphor has too much muscle;
His was an indoor art and every phrase
Was handled with a trained seducer's care.
I took the words to heart, or, if not heart,
Some region underneath intelligence,
The area where the hot romantic aria
And certain kinds of poetry are received.
And this Giovanni of the fast buck knew
My humming brain was pleasurably numb;
My limbs were weakening; he would soon achieve
The now explicit ends for which he'd come.
At last I nodded, glazed, and said I'd sign,
But he showed little proper satisfaction.
He sighed and sounded almost disappointed,
And I remembered hearing someone say
No Juan really likes an easy lay.
But I'll say this: he covered up quite quickly
And seemed almost as ardent as before
When he pressed my hand and said that he was happy
And hoped that I was, too.
                              And then the door
Was closed behind him as our deal was closed.
If something happened I was covered now.
Odd that I felt so chilly, so exposed.

A Note for Biographers

Those early chapters are the ones to watch:
It is too cosily assumed that all
That happens to the eminent will clutch
The reader's buttonhole. Where infants crawl
Is much the same for every baby born,
And later, when the subject walks erect
In private park or back street of a town
The difference is much less than you'd expect.
The little master in expensive tweed
And scabby little mister in huge cap
Suck in same air, are laughed at, bored, afraid:
Their joys and terrors more than overlap,
They are identical. When Christopher
Crouched by father's side to sight that deer
The nightmare that he'd long been tensing for
Banged loud, awake, and father saw his fear.
The boy felt terrible, but no more so
Than little Eddie when Mum said she knew
About the Sunday penny meant to go
Dark in the soft religious bag, not to
The shop which sold sweet paper bags of guilt.
When Christopher was given his Hornby Train
His joy was bright as rails; but Eddie felt
As much delight to wear Dad's watch and chain
Although the watch's pulse had given up
And neither fly-blue arm would move again.
All children's lives are very much alike,
So my advice is keep that early stuff
Down to a page or two. Don't try to make
Nostalgia pay: we've all had quite enough.
What captivates and sells, and always will,
Is what we are: vain, snarled up, and sleazy.
No one is really interesting until
To love him has become no longer easy.

Moral Problem

Impartial dark conceals the true relation
And hides his screwed grimace, the eyeless grin;
His wife receives his violent visitation,
With muffled cries of welcome lets him in.
His vehement dream reshapes her body to
The sweet task that he really wants to do.

His brother exiled to a foreign city,
Months from his heart's address, his candid bed,
Writes to his love a letter long and witty
But leaves frustration's vocables unsaid;
But lust and longing urge him like a knife
To buy a whore and dream he's with his wife.

And who commits adultery? I question:
The one whose need evokes the girl next door
And makes his wife a page in his hot fiction,
Or he who loves his wife inside a whore?
The question whimpers, asking to be fed;
Better all round to wring its neck instead.

Millionaire

His public face is not entirely human,
Though whether more or less is hard to say;
A flourish of his gold-nibbed wand will bring
Obsequious flunkeys, each with loaded tray,
All the world's sweetmeats to his peevish tongue.
The ennui of possessions, shrivelled appetite
Have moulded him a mask, austere, remote,
But not the luminous and moony skull
Of the voluntary holy anchorite.

Contemptuous of all sensual bargains offered,
Yet frightened of the chill, ascetic cell,
His dreamed apotheosis of the human
Derided by the silk and gold and skill
Of master craftsmen with the tape and shears

All helpless to conceal that crumpled skin
Dry and heavy over lizard eyes,
Does he suspect, through sweet bluff of cigars,
A faint stink of the reptile house creeps in?

A world ago, one wonders, did he dream,
Hungry in ghetto or industrial slum,
Of nodding beauties, steaks and grand hotels,
Or did the ache for power provide the fuel
That drove the panting engine of ambition,
Fired by a vision, anarchic, beautiful, cruel?
Or fear perhaps? A zany dream of freedom?
Even if he knew he would not tell,

Though at cold lonely moments he might curse
The fortune that has come to own himself
And locked him in its huge expensive purse.
But now his folded face shows no emotion.
The chauffeur parcels up his legs in plaid,
Salutes and soothes the limousine from the kerb,
Smooth as a liner on a lake of oil,
Reticent as a hearse.

The Great Old Men

Imagination will not see them as
Toddlers nor as adolescent boys,
These monumental gentlemen who gaze
Serenely from smooth paper that employs
Our weekly interest and rewards it well
With far catastrophes and framed displays
Of foreign pain and sewers one can't smell.

The great old men have silver hair, and who
Could see it otherwise? Who see it sprout
In shocking red or bootbrush black; believe
Those graven visages could pimple out
In pustules, little swellings that betray
The dark tumescences whose heavings leave
Night smears upon the body of the day?

Their lives are formed like perfect paragraphs
Or sweet equations, rational and calm;
They marry garden ladies or remain
Celibate but tranquil as a psalm,
To die with dignity in careful rooms,
And after death continue to explain
Our dark predicament from tomes and tombs.

I raise plumed admiration; I bow low
To see each grave contemplative, each brave
And venerable explorer of the mind
At last borne slowly to a solemn grave;
But grief is formal: sombre clothes disguise
The heart's composure; though I draw the blind
No salt glass splinters in the heart's cold eyes.

My heart's own heart is gripped, the eyes are smashed
By other lives and deaths; the obdurate boys
Who would not leave the playground till the bell
Tolled black, who would not sacrifice their toys,
Their tales, their rhymes, their wild games by the sea
For any grown-up prize; whose early knell
Rolled under waves, clanged from the gallows tree.

Not old and wise, not silvered and serene,
But flogged by sensual storms and appetites
That no white meat nor violent wine could ease,
Trampled at noon by hooves from thrashing nights,
They put rope chokers on, capsized in gin
Or dived heart first in fanged and slavering seas.
With love I take their orphaned poems in.

Love in Any City

It could have been any city – London, Rome,
Paris, New York, Chicago – any home
For simmering crowds and parks and monoliths
Pocked with a hundred peeping squares, where myths
Proliferate against the darkening sky
In brilliant beads of light or, in the sly
And sweetened shadows, joggle on a screen;

A place where the poor and sick are rarely seen
But covered up like sores, where the air is rich,
Spiced and spiked to aggravate the itch
Of need for what one can't or dare not say.
She seemed the City's child in every way:
No wimpled pretty, stroking her sad lyre,
Impatient for her silver-plated squire,
She couldn't show that soft pre-raphaelite
Hair that syrups smoothly over white
Marmoreal shoulders, neither were her eyes
Those wistful jellies of astounding size;
And yet, though many might not notice it,
Her gaze reflected sympathy and wit
In such a way that it could claim a kind
Of magic that obscurely undermined
His selfish palisades. And though both used
A taut elliptic idiom which refused
A melting welcome to the lyric or
Enraptured paean, by which they set small store,
When streets were hushed, swept bare by the night's
    smooth broom,
A meadow breeze swayed cool in the grateful room
In which, like branches on related trees,
They stirred towards each other, touched and clung,
Awed by the haunting music that was sung.

When We Were Married

She took the book from the shelf
And turned the pages slowly.
'I loved this book,' she said,
'When we were married.

'That song that teases silence
Was a favourite of mine;
It did not grow tedious
While we were married.

'I ate some food tonight
But did not relish it.

It was a dish that I enjoyed
When we were married.

'When we were married,' she said,
And her lashes were glistening,
'I felt at home in this house, that bed.'
But the man was not listening.

Taken in Adultery

Shadowed by shades and spied upon by glass
Their search for privacy conducts them here,
With an irony that neither notices,
To a public house; the wrong time of the year
For outdoor games; where, over gin and tonic,
Best bitter and potato crisps, they talk
Without much zest, almost laconic,
Flipping an occasional remark.
Would you guess that they were lovers, this dull pair?
The answer, I suppose, is yes, you would.
Despite her spectacles and faded hair
And his worn look of being someone's Dad
You know that they are having an affair
And neither finds it doing them much good.
Presumably, in one another's eyes,
They must look different from what we see,
Desirable in some way, otherwise
They'd hardly choose to come here, furtively,
And mutter their bleak needs above the mess
Of fag-ends, crumpled cellophane and crumbs,
Their love-feast's litter. Though they might profess
To find great joy together, all that comes
Across to us is tiredness, melancholy.
When they are silent each seems listening;
There must be many voices in the air:
Reproaches, accusations, suffering
That no amount of passion keeps elsewhere.
Imperatives that brought them to this room,
Stiff from the car's back seat, lose urgency;
They start to wonder who's betraying whom,

How it will end, and how did it begin –
The woman taken in adultery
And the man who feels he, too, was taken in.

The Old Books

They were beautiful, the old books, beautiful I tell you.
You've no idea, you young ones with all those machines;
There's no point in telling you; you wouldn't understand.
You wouldn't know what the word beautiful means.
I remember Mr Archibald – the old man, not his son –
He said to me right out: 'You've got a beautiful hand,
Your books are a pleasure to look at, real works of art.'
You youngsters with your ball-points wouldn't
    understand.
You should have seen them, my day book, and sales ledger:
The unused lines were always cancelled in red ink.
You wouldn't find better kept books in the City;
But it's no good talking: I know what you all think:
'He's old. He's had it. He's living in the past,
The poor old sod.' Well, I don't want your pity.
My forty-seventh Christmas with the firm. Too much to
    drink.
You're staring at me, pitying. I can tell by your looks.
You'll never know what it was like, what you've missed.
You'll never know. My God, they were beautiful, the old
    books.

Tightrope Walker

High on the thrilling strand he dances
Laved in white light. The smudged chalk faces
Blur below. His movements scorn
And fluently insult the law
That lumps us, munching, on our seats,
Avoiding the question that slyly tweaks:
How much do we want to see him fall?

It's no use saying we don't at all.
We all know that we hate his breed.
Prancing the nimble thread he's freed
From what we are and gravity.
And yet we know quite well that he
Started just as we began,
That he, like us, is just a man.
(We don't fall off our seats until
We've drunk too much or are feeling ill.)
But he has trained the common skill,
Trained and practised; now tonight
It flogs our credence as high and white
In the spotlight's talcum he pirouettes,
Lonely, scorning safety nets,
The highly extraordinary man.
But soon, quite softly, boredom starts
Its muffled drilling at our hearts;
A frisson of coughs and shuffles moves
Over the crowd like a wind through leaves.
Our eyes slide down the air and walk
Idly round the tent as talk
Hums on denial's monotone.
It's just as well the act ends soon
Or we would leave, though not stampede,
Leave furtively in twos and threes,
Absence flooding the canvas house
Where he, alone, all unaware
Would go on dancing on the almost air
Till fatigue or error dragged him down,
An ordinary man on ordinary ground.

Peerless Jim Driscoll

I saw Jim Driscoll fight in nineteen ten.
That takes you back a bit. You don't see men
Like Driscoll any more. The breed's died out.
There's no one fit to lace his boots about.
All right son. Have your laugh. You know it all.
You think these mugs today that cuff and maul
Their way through ten or fifteen threes can fight:

They hardly know their left hand from their right.
But Jim, he knew: he never slapped or swung,
His left hand flickered like a cobra's tongue
And when he followed with the old one-two
Black lightning of those fists would dazzle you.
By Jesus he could hit. I've never seen
A sweeter puncher: every blow as clean
As silver. *Peerless Jim* the papers named him,
And yet he never swaggered, never bragged.
I saw him once when he got properly tagged –
A sucker punch from nowhere on the chin –
And he was hurt; but all he did was grin
And nod as if to say, 'I asked for that.'
No one was ever more worth looking at;
Up there beneath the ache of arc-lamps he
Was just like what we'd love our sons to be
Or like those gods you've heard about at school…
Well, yes, I'm old; and maybe I'm a fool.
I only saw him once outside the ring
And I admit I found it disappointing.
He looked just – I don't know – just ordinary,
And smaller, too, than what I thought he'd be:
An ordinary man in fact, like you or me.

Time for a Quick One

Noon holds the city back;
Its suburbs are five miles away
Where the baker's cry is greyer than the sky
And drapes itself about the television masts.

Here, alcohol explodes
In secret salvoes, glasses chime.
The stew of noise boils over, spills outside,
Calls hungry volunteers to join the garrison.

A veteran lights a fag.
His face is pigmented with rage,
Flayed raw by booze; both eyes have gone to bed.
A new recruit salutes and takes his life in hand.

Malingerers and old sweats,
Stout corporals and cute subalterns
Shout for reinforcements and more rations.
The smoke cuts harsh at eyes and din thumps louder
  drums.

Outside, the suburbs start
Their noiseless, disciplined advance.
The city waits with finger firm on trigger.
The fort is now surrounded. Soon closing-time will strike.

After the Fireworks

Back into the light and warmth,
Boots clogged with mud, toes
Welded to wedges of cold flesh,
The children warm their hands on mugs
While, on remembered lawns, the flash
Of fireworks dazzles night;
Sparklers spray and rockets swish,
Soar high and break in falling showers
Of glitter; the bonfire gallivants,
Its lavish flames shimmy, prance,
And lick the straddling guy.
We wait for those great leaves of heat
And broken necklaces of light
To dim and die.
And then the children go to bed.
Tomorrow they will search grey ground
For debris of tonight: the sad
And saturated cardboard stems,
The fallen rocket sticks, the charred
Hubs of catherine-wheels;
Then, having gathered all they've found,
They'll leave them scattered carelessly
For us to clear away.
But now the children are asleep,
And you and I sit silently
And hear, from far off in the night,
The last brave rocket burst and fade.

We taste the darkness in the light,
Reflect that fireworks are not cheap
And ask ourselves uneasily
If, even now, we've fully paid.

My Three Hoboes

In the bullion bar of a bright hotel
I gave three tramps a splendid feed.
Though I was poor I fed them well,
Knowing the acreage of their greed.
All around, the double-chinned,
The thin and plump of various ages,
Lacquered with privilege, golden-skinned
Because they paid the sun good wages,
Laughed and drank and did not see
The scruffy hoboes I'd brought there;
In fact they did not notice me,
But we watched them with our reptile stare,
We watched the blond boys and their trulls
Whose taut instructive favours draped
Hard uniform of bones and skulls;
We eyed the stout papas and gaped
At slender daughters' pulchritude,
But not a glance came back our way
As I provided yet more food
For my rough guests.
                              I always pay
When my familiar vagrants come
To these palatial joints with me –
Lust and loathing and the other bum,
Envy, strongest of the three.

Dirty Story

The laughter at the bar rumbles rich,
Masculine as steak. More drink is served.
Tankards clang and tumblers ring;
Dull memories are cuffed and searched,
Together heads are bent, intent, and words
From someone wind the spring of mirth again:
Heard the one about the blonde with worms?
Listen. She was sitting on a gate…
And so a verbal art is carried on,
Simple as tales of bunnies, elves and moles,
With vicars, golfers, spinsters and cute dolls,
Rabbis and rissoles, condoms and commodes.
Each fable, rhymed, or plain vernacular job,
Insists upon the funniness of lust,
Betrayal, shame, the belly-shaking joke
Of pain and innocence and wounded love.
Again the laughter thickens, swirls like smoke:
'Oh, very good!' they gasp: 'Oh Gawd! oh my!'
They laugh till they begin, almost, to cry.

Ruminant

The leather belly shades the buttercups.
Her horns are the yellow of old piano keys.
Hopelessly the tail flicks at the humming heat;
Flies crawl to the pools of her eyes.
She slowly turns her head and watches me
As I approach: her gaze is a silent moo.
I stop and we swap stares. I smoke. She chews.

How do I view her then? As pastoral furniture,
Solid in the green and fluid summer?
A brooding factory of milk and sausages,
Or something to be chopped to bits and sold
In wounded paper parcels? No, as none of these.
My view is otherwise and infantile,
But it survives my own sour sneers.

It is the anthropomorphic fallacy
Which puts brown speculation in those eyes.
But I am taken in: that gentleness endears,
As do the massive patience and submission
Huge among buttercups and flies.
But, in the end, it is those plushy eyes,
The slow and meditative jaws, that hold
Me to this most untenable of views:
Almost, it seems, she might be contemplating
Composing a long poem about Ted Hughes.

My Pen Has Ink Enough

My pen has ink enough; I'm going to start
A piece of verse, but suddenly my heart
And something in my head jerks in reverse.

I can't go on – I did, with switch in tense,
And here's the bleak, accusing evidence;
I don't know why, or even what I seek.

This thought jabbed hard: how insolent to make
These blurred attempts when Shakespeare, Donne and
    Blake
Have done what they have done. And yet it tempts,

This longing to make wicks of words, light lamps
However frail and dim. And, hell, why not?
I've had six children yet more casually got.

EPITHETS OF WAR
1965

Epithets of War

I

August 1914

The bronze sun blew a long and shimmering call
Over the waves of Brighton and Southend,
Over slapped and patted pyramids of sand,
Paper Union Jacks and cockle stalls;
A pierrot aimed his banjo at the gulls;
Small spades dug trenches to let the channel in
As nimble donkeys followed their huge heads
And charged. In the navy sky the loud white birds
Lolled on no wind, then, swinging breathless, skimmed
The somersaulting waves; a military band
Thumped and brayed, brass pump of sentiment;
And far from the beach, inland, lace curtains stirred.
A girl played Chopin while her sister pored
Over her careful sewing; faint green scent
Of grass was sharpened by a gleam of mint,
And, farther off, in London, horses pulled
Their rumbling drays and vans along the Strand
Or trundled down High Holborn and beyond
The Stadium Club, where, in the wounded world
Of five years later, Georges Carpentier felled
Bulldog Joe Beckett in a single round.
And all is history; its pages smell
Faintly of camphor and dead pimpernel
Coffined in leaves, and something of the sand
And salt of holiday. But dead. The end
Of something never to be lived again.

II

The Guns

A few were preserved years after they had died,
Kept in hushed museums as stuffed animals are;
One, a trench mortar, rested amiably inside
The recreation ground of a midland spa.
The kids took no more notice of it than
The parched fountain or the grass on which they ran.

They were too young to have heard the gun's enormous
    tongue,
Though the blind voice still broke their parents' sleep:
Black sacks of spilled thunder avalanched among
The pastures of dreamed peace; again pacific sheep
Were slaughtered in hot laughter's howl and boom;
Wraiths of dead cordite smelled sweet in the waking room.

Dawn tamed the darkness in the skull, put thunder down.
Rain slanted hair-thin through the haggard sky;
Again gun-carriages rumbled through the broken town;
Capes gleamed, dark metal, as the infantry marched by.
The guns were silent, but their speakings echoed still:
Anger of names – Cambrai, Bethune, Arras, Kemmel Hill.

Night will surge back, sure as a counter-attack;
Lewis-guns and Vickers will chatter in their fever;
Again the big guns will slam and slash and hack
At silence till it folds about their heads forever;
Then even the names will fade, mere sounds, unbroken
    code,
Marks on the page: Passchendaele, Verdun, The Menin
    Road.

III

Casualties

They were printed daily in the newspapers.
A woman in Nottingham went mad reading them;

114

She drowned herself in the Trent.
Her name was not included in the casualty lists.

She was mother of two million sons.
At night a frail voice would quaver,
Cry from its bed of mud:
'Stretcher-bearers! Stretcher-bearers!' She could not go.

She could not bear it. Her mind broke.
Barbed-wire scrawled illiterate history
Over the black dough of Belgian fields,
Was punctuated by anatomies.

In Trafalgar Square an English lady
Distributed white feathers among civilians.
Children with sad moustaches and putteed calves
Prepared to be translated.

The crazed mother heard them at night
Crying as hot stars exploded
And the earth's belly shook and rumbled
With giant eructations.

The ambulances lurched through the mire in the brain;
Uniformed surgeons in crimson aprons
Laboured at irreparable bodies;
Dawn bristled on their skullish jaws.

And two million of an innocent generation,
Orphaned by a doomed, demented mother,
Unlearned an axiom: they discovered
Only the lucky few meet death once only.

IV

War Songs

A lesson that their children knew by heart
Where it lay stonily in that September.
Conscripted man, anonymous in hot
Brown or blue, intoned his rank and number.
The discs, strung from his neck, no amulet

Against the ache of loss, were worn in darkness
Under grave blankets in the narrow cot
After the bugle's skirmish with night's silence.
In trembling cities civil sleep was probed
By the wild sirens' blind and wounded howling;
White searchlights hosed the sky; black planets throbbed;
At night all buildings put on total mourning.
And, when dawn yawned, the washed skies were afloat
With silver saveloys whose idle motion
And conference with puffed clouds appeared to mock
Bereaving night and morning's lamentation.
And then, down country lanes, the crop-haired sons
And nephews of the skeletons of Flanders
Made seance of their march, as, on their tongues,
The old ghosts sang again of Tipperary,
Packing kit-bags, getting back to Blighty,
But soon, bewildered, sank back to their graves
When others songs were bawled – a jaunty music
With false, bragging words: The Siegfried Line
Transformed with comic washing hanging from it,
Sergeants and Corporals were blessed, the barrel rolled;
But behind the grinning words and steady tramping
The Sergeant of the dark was taking names
And marking time to that lugubrious singing.
We're saying goodbye to them all: and, far away
From gunpit, barrack square and trench, the mother
Sewed the dark garments for tomorrow's mourning.

V

Eidolon Parade

A grey wind prowls across the lake of stone,
The flag flicks like a summer horse's tail,
The brass voice of the bugle climbs and clings
High before it crumbles, falls and fades.
CSM Hardy, back from Salerno Beach,
Glitters with sea salt, winkles nest in his eyes,
But his voice grinds loud as ever as he calls
The Nominal Roll: Corporal Mick McGuire
Has returned from Alamein, each orifice
Is clogged with sand; but tonight he will appear

Once more at the Church Hall, battle-dress pressed
And patent leather highlights on his feet;
And when the lights are dimmed, the last waltz makes
Its passionate interrogation: *Who's*
Taking You Home Tonight? who but McGuire,
Although his terrible kiss will taste of sand
Gritting on shocked teeth, and his cold cheek
Will seem to her a stony reprimand.
And, while the Corporal tangoes, Private Bain,
A bunch of quarrels hanging from each wrist,
Will sluice his guts with twenty black-and-tans;
But he stands still now, sober, at attention
With that small company paraded there
Waiting for inspection: Dodger Rae,
Equipment scruffy and an idle bootlace,
Is put on an eternal two-five-two;
Spike Liston, gaunt as a Belsen boy or saint,
Still rages for more grub; Bull Evans broods
On all the thighs he'll never lie between
Or lie about, his pack and pouches stuffed
With fantasies and condoms; Les King, who crooned
Like Bing, is back from Mareth where he lay,
The tunes mislaid, gargling with his blood.
His songs are out of date. And there are others
Whose faces, though familiar, fade and blur.
The bugle publishes another cry.
Two more commands explode; butts and boots
Crash and ring; another echoing shout
And, by the left, they start to march away.
The steady tramping dims into a mist.
The stone ground stretches in its vacancy;
One final flick of flag, the mist comes down,
And silence stuns with its enormous weight,
And there is nothing left to do but sleep.

Scottsburg USA

'He's a bootlegger,' said the young ladies, moving
somewhere between his cocktails and his flowers.
'One time he killed a man...'

THE GREAT GATSBY

'There was music through the summer nights'.
Zelda was young, an unusual flower,
She swayed in the wind from gold trumpets.
Saxophones sighed for her.
Her sex was a dark nest, warm in the fork
Of white and welcoming branches.
At dawn the barbered lawns
Sparkled with specially imported dew.
The ocean rehearsed its morning performance.
Scott polished the jewel of his gift.
It would last long, longer than he would last.
He would keep it through the slow fall
When the shed leaves deadened the footsteps
Of the pale bailiffs, when the young flower
Grew brittle, crumbling in its expensive vase.
The band packed its instruments and left.
The last guests departed for more hospitable views.
The grass greyed and grew long on the lawns.
Scott walked the streets of winter alone
Where the stores offered only alcohol and accusations.
In sleep his booze-battered, rueful countenance
Looked bitterly wise yet remarkably innocent.
The stone gleamed in a drawer in his desk
Like a small strong lamp in a coffin.
The blinds were drawn.
The long jag was over.

View from a Wheelchair

Every day is visiting day;
There are no temporal restrictions.
You cannot tell them to go away;
They fuss, or are negligent, or bored.
The world is an open ward
Populated by nurses, orderlies,
And simpering visitors with flowers.
I resent with equal rancour
Both indifference and pity.
Children insult me with their agility.
I am an old baby with a blue chin,

At night my teeth snarl in a tumbler.
As evening darkens in my ward
There are voices from beyond,
Clear cries of the unmutilated,
Murmur of sensual conspiracy,
Salutations, prodigal laughter:
The blind effrontery of health.
I will strangle my ears; I will call
And demand to be put to bed.
But I do not pray for a miracle –
You must not deceive yourself there –
And you must not assume my condition
Is not of my own choosing. I am not sure.
I am less unfortunate, maybe,
Than your insolent pity believes:
The muscles in my wheels do not get tired;
Like a horse I can sleep standing.
And there is something sacred about me,
Something that can haunt, and make you tremble.
I am sick of the fear, the pity, the revulsion.
I want them to put me to bed.
Their gratitude for my not being them
Is a nauseous, poisonous toffee.
It is dark and cold. They must put me to bed.
They do not know that I walk in my sleep.

Uncle Edward's Affliction

Uncle Edward was colour-blind;
We grew accustomed to the fact.
When he asked someone to hand him
The green book from the window-seat
And we observed its bright red cover
Either apathy or tact
Stifled comment. We passed it over.
Much later, I began to wonder
What curious world he wandered in,
Down streets where pea-green pillar-boxes
Grinned at a fire-engine as green;
How Uncle Edward's sky at dawn

And sunset flooded marshy green.
Did he ken John Peel with his coat so green
And Robin Hood in Lincoln red?
On country walks avoid being stung
By nettles hot as a witch's tongue?
What meals he savoured with his eyes:
Green strawberries and fresh red peas,
Green beef and greener burgundy.
All unscientific, so it seems:
His world was not at all like that,
So those who claim to know have said.
Yet, I believe, in war-smashed France
He must have crawled from neutral mud
To lie in pastures, dark and red
And seen, appalled, on every blade
The rain of innocent green blood.

Any Complaints?

Lawrence – not the bearded one – the one
Who dressed up as a wog and crashed his bike
Doing a ton, if those old jobs could make it then,
Lawrence said something about courage: Courage is like
A bank account; you keep on writing cheques
Until the day comes when there's nothing there,
No more to draw. You're broke. What next?
They tie you to a gunwheel in the lashing air
Or blind you with a bandage and lead you out
As target for small arms.   If you are very rich,
Got plenty in that bank, you'll probably get hit
But by the other lot; wind up in a different ditch
But just as dead. With extraordinary luck
You might survive and get back home quite safe.
But what if all your days you've been dead broke,
Never owned a cheque-book in your life,
Nothing in the bank at all?   You go to jail
Or try to bluff it out, let others pay your way.
It's not an easy game, and if you fail,

Are shown up as a fraud, no matter what you say
You'll get the gunwheel or the firing-squad.
It isn't fair? All right, but don't tell me.
The Company Commander is the man to see
Or, better still, complain direct to God.

A Kind of Hero

At school he was revered yet lonely.
No other boy, however much
He might dream of it,
Dared to be his friend.
He walked, gaunt and piratical,
All bones and grin,
Towards his inescapable end.

Revered, but not by authority,
He poured ink into the new hat
Of the French Master,
Painted the blackboard white,
Swore at the huge Principal,
Refused to bend
And invited him to a free fight.

In memory he is beautiful,
But only his desperate gold
Hair might have been so.
Vaguely we understood,
And were grateful, that he performed
Our lawless deeds:
Punished, he allowed us to be good.

The end: he was killed at Alamein.
He wore handcuffs on the troopship
Going out: his webbing
All scrubbed as white as rice;
And we, or others like us,
Were promoted
By his last, derisive sacrifice.

View from a Deckchair

I rest in the canvas lap and let fall my book.
The breeze, browsing, flips a few pages,
Leaves it, then comes back for a second look.
My eyelids close, like mouths, on the images.

The sky is green with the smell of crunched grass
Whose dark, shed juice seasons the simmering air;
Eyelids slide open, eyes see a butterfly pass,
Pause, wings frittering, treading the air's water.

Summer mothers me; here I feel secure;
My neighbours are not likely to break down the fences;
The only guns they carry are for making war
On garden pests. Their televisions have valid licences.

Vapour-trails, squeezed out on the bland blue,
Perturb only slightly; the bee's buzz does not sting.
Even when a motorbike rasps in the avenue
The heart bucks only a little, and I stay sitting,

Or, rather, reclining in my garden chair,
And can stay here for at least another hour
Before the benevolent and grass-flavoured air
Loses its warmth, and the chill tastes sour.

Cigarette

It tap-danced on the shining silver case,
Jumped to his mouth, wagged jaunty from teasing lip,
Its whiteness darkening the uncle face;
Thin snake's blue ghost rose curling from the tip.
Emblem of manhood and emancipation,
But something more: it burned yet was renewed
Pure as before; scent stirred sweet perturbation
In the thrilled blood, first inkling of the feud,
Still unresolved, between desire and fear.
My first cigarette was smoked in the boiler shed

Behind the Sunday School in my tenth year.
Veil-dance of smoke revolved in my dazed head,
Strong the sense of falling, though I stood;
I thought that I did wrong, and think so still.
They told us that tobacco-smoking would
Stunt our growth. They tell us now fags kill,
And I believe, though when I ruminate
I see that even smokeless inhalations
Are paces, if not quite so long and straight,
Towards the darkest of all destinations.
I take another, light it, noting how
The stained air holds no sweet reverberations
And that I have no sense of falling now.

View from a Barber's Chair

In the glacial mirror
The skull is preserved;
Dun flesh clings to it
Obstinately alive.
The basin below
Is smooth and white –
Hard flesh of shelled egg –
Taps gleam like spoons.
The head is perched
On a white mound,
Its eyes aggrieved.
Behind, in the gloom,
White deference bends,
Snips and combs;
A glimmer of scissors
Kisses, bites,
Snips locks that, falling,
Tickle the air,
Fall faster than leaves
But quiet and light
On the slope of snow.
Electric buzz

And nibble at neck;
Sweet buzz replies
Warm in the blood;
Surrender's signal,
A yielding hum,
Purred submission
Invite violation,
A numb need
For a cruel Todd,
Which dies away
When the bowing voice
Tickles the ear:
'Next gentleman, please.'
The white mound melts,
Slides down the glass
And disappears.
The stunned head hangs
Amazed a moment,
Then floats away.
The mirror gurgles
In the basin's throat.
The next gentleman
Is gowned in snow.

A Song to Celebrate

Your hair tastes of darkness.
The sea fondles the long drowned.
The shore extends a delicate limb,
The waves relish its whiteness.

Your mouth tastes of moonlight.
The city revs its dark engines;
Lamps are bright burs on the night's coat.
I would wear you like a cloak

And would be your robe for all weathers.
Your flesh tastes of sunlight.
The sea concedes defeat. The drowned
Rise white and dance naked.

Pistol

This one is not black,
Squat, packed with deeper black;
It does not squint.
The silver barrel
Thrusts clean from the chamber
And polished butt's
Mahogany curve
Whose smoothness soothes the hand.
Who would deny
Any healthy boy
Such an old-fashioned and
Beautiful toy?

A Long Sentence

begins slowly, uncertain of
its terminus, but after
the first hesitancies,
destination still hidden,
the pace increases, grows more sure
though with a confidence
that will not be for long sustained
when it becomes apparent
that movement is towards
not revelation or release
but a darkness darker far
than any known midnight,
dungeon, tunnel, desperation,
and all sentences must end
with an abrupt full-stop,
punched in like a nail, its black head
showing on the page, like this.

The Sunday People

After the dolour of bells
The place was shut,
Though at certain intervals
Noises squeezed out
Through venerable walls;
Then all was quiet
Before faint vocables
Told they were out.

The Sunday People, slow
On mournful feet,
A dark irregular queue,
Trickled from the great
Hunk of masonry
And moved through the morning light
As now, through memory,
Linen and faces white.

The smell still lingers; the smell
Of flowers and sick
Comes back when church bells call;
These, too, begin it:
The wax-faced queue who fill
This Sunday memory,
Lovers of hymn and hospital,
Roast beef and cemetery.

Moods of Rain

It can be so tedious, a bore
Telling a long dull story you have heard before
So often it is meaningless;
Yet, in another mood,
It comes swashbuckling, swishing a million foils,
Feinting at daffodils, peppering tin pails,
Pelting so fast on roof, umbrella, hood,
You hear long silk being torn;

Refurbishes old toys, and oils
Slick surfaces that gleam as if unworn.
Sometimes a cordial summer rain will fall
And string on railings delicate small bells;
Soundless as seeds on soil
Make green ghosts rise.
It can be fierce, hissing like blazing thorns,
Or side-drums hammering at night-filled eyes
Until you wake and hear a long grief boil
And, overflowing, sluice
The lost raft of the world.
Yet it can come as lenitive and calm
As comfort from the mother of us all
Sighing you into sleep
Where peace prevails and only soft rains fall.

Mercenaries

At first we were attracted by the pure
Thrill of playing childish games with all
The seriousness of children; or, unsure
Of our own strength, our stamina and will,
Enlisted, hoping to survive the test;
Others liked the reckless uniform.
But one lure winked that no one could resist,
The dream that strengthened all and kept us warm
On cold patrols and lonely nights on guard,
A fantasy of total anarchy
Made flesh at last, the marvellous reward
Of absolute permission, liberty
That babies, lunatics and millionaires,
And they alone, are able to afford:
The spoils of war, the naked town sprawled out
Inviting us to enter and enjoy.
But when – the last defenders put to rout –
We seized the city like a promised toy,
The most inviting doors were booby-trapped,
The wine was sour, they'd buried all the gold;
The dogs and children snarled and cursed and snapped,
And every woman was gun-hard and cold.

Black Dog

Across grass gnawed by dingy snow
Half-thawed, now frozen, a soiled shroud
Patched and torn on a cold torso,
The dog prowls on numb pads;
The dark hedge drinks his darker shape
And he is gone.
                The last light rots,
Crumbles to night; the cold clamps hard.
Grey rats freeze on the ditch's verge;
The lane is smeared with gritty lard.
Time to go home. Yet no desire.
The black dog waits, sprawled by the fire;
In that small house looks very large,
Owns all within, including those
Soft furnishings that ache and age.

Dreamgirl

Her name is not important. On the screen
Or front page of the polished magazine
What slaps you in the eyeballs is her tits,
Soft bombs whose threats to burst score accurate hits;
The mouth your eyes can taste, her ripened eyes
Before which all equivocation dies;
Lithe legs and gorgeous haunches spread and curve
On red divan of tight sprung vein and nerve.

You want her. Yes. But reason intervenes:
She cannot really be just what she seems.
If fantasy should muscle into fact,
Surely you'd find her actual presence lacked
The opulence her image offered you:
If not a lie, then not entirely true;
Some artifice, small sympathy; worse still,
Cold waxwork lacking passion, needs or skill.

But Brother, eye to keyhole, have you thought?

Behind the door might lie a different sort
Of creature, someone much more terrible,
Whose writhings, far from being artificial,
Would flush with blood, would sweat and burn and grip,
Whose five-thonged need would flog you like a whip.
Stay kneeling there; reality can bite.
Settle for screen and page. You've got good eyesight.

No Sense of Direction

I have always admired
Those who are sure
Which turning to take,
Who need no guide
Even in war
When thunders shake
The torn terrain,
When battalions of shrill
Stars all desert
And the derelict moon
Goes over the hill:
Eyes chained by the night
They find their way back
As if it were daylight.
Then, on peaceful walks
Over strange wooded ground,
They will find the right track,
Know which of the forks
Will lead to the inn
I would never have found;
For I lack their gift,
Possess almost no
Sense of direction.
And yet I owe
A debt to this lack,
A debt so vast
No reparation
Can ever be made,
For it led me away
From the road I sought

Which would carry me to –
I mistakenly thought –
My true destination:
It made me stray
To this lucky path
That ran like a fuse
And brought me to you
And love's bright, soundless
Detonation.

Summer in the Park

Sun leans lightly on all temples;
In the park the far trees
Melt at their shadowed knees.
Summer supplies its simples
For all but one disease:
Young dogs, young sons, young mothers,
Gold waterfall hair of daughters
Float over trim green seas.
He could munch them up and swallow them,
Yes, even the melting trees,
The staid man on the seat
Whose heart's teeth ache with love
And its impossible sweet.

Blood Letter

Frail leech that craves an open vein,
Paper vampire, blood-letter,
Go in your mild envelope
Disguised as harmless paper.

Dissemble in the postman's sack,
Mix with football coupons, views
Of beaches, blackmail, racing tips,
Poems and domestic news.

Go to her whose heart your need is,
But temper your red hunger, rest
Gently on her pulses, be
Tender at her breast.

And hope that she will welcome you
To ease her fever and make better
Such distemper as she suffers,
Letter of blood, love-letter.

Growing Pain

The boy was barely five years old.
We sent him to the little school
And left him there to learn the names
Of flowers in jam jars on the sill
And learn to do as he was told.
He seemed quite happy there until
Three weeks afterwards, at night,
The darkness whimpered in his room.
I went upstairs, switched on his light,
And found him wide awake, distraught,
Sheets mangled and his eiderdown
Untidy carpet on the floor.
I said, 'Why can't you sleep? A pain?'
He snuffled, gave a little moan,
And then he spoke a single word:
'Jessica.' The sound was blurred.
'Jessica? What do you mean?'
'A girl at school called Jessica,
She hurts – ' he touched himself between
The heart and stomach ' – she has been
Aching here and I can see her.'
Nothing I had read or heard
Instructed me in what to do.
I covered him and stroked his head.
'The pain will go, in time,' I said.

The Toys of Love

His cuddly toy of love
Was bought to keep him warm;
In bed he held it tight
And did not fear the storm
Which flogged the howling night
Until it bled to dawn.

His woolly toy of love
No longer soft and white
Grew bristly, cold and thin,
Consoled no more at night;
Its mouth chewed on a grin,
Showed teeth and they could bite.

His silver gift of love
He used with joy and skill
And wore it on his thigh,
Was thrilled by it until
He found it was no toy,
Was loaded, and could kill.

A Quaint Disorder

A quaint disorder, this:
I do not sleep too well
For fear the dark hours build
A solitary cell;
My intellect expels
Its former policies,
Disburdened can explore
Remoter galaxies.
My heart snarls at the way
The minutes pitter past
Towards the last abyss.
I tremble at the vast
Arsenals that Chance
Commands, could call upon

To lay mines in your path.
The moonlight that once shone
Benignly frightens me,
As does deceitful air;
Time's frequent felonies
Are crueller than they were.
Food no longer tempts
The withered appetite;
I hunger only for
That longed-for, good tonight
When you, desired physician,
Will come with healing art
And magical prescription
To purge my febrile heart
Of all its grave distempers
And burn my fever-chart.
A quaint disorder, this,
Which stabs with hope and doubt,
And one – with all its pains –
I would not be without.

A Game of Shove-Ha'penny

In a pub in Hampstead on a Spring evening
A couple were playing shove-ha'penny. They wore
The uniform of the district and of youth:
Sweater, jeans and unwrinkled skin.
Her bottom and breasts were roundly confident
And her hair was dark with a gleam of copper
Within. The man was dark and thin.

He bent over the table playing that game
With bitter concentration. She took her turn
But her play was more perfunctory. She wept.
She shoved the discs across the board
And, all the time, the tears blurted from her eyes
And moved down her face like little snails; they left
A pale brown spoor where they had crept.

For a long time they did not speak. Then he turned,
Looked at her directly; his eyes jabbed hate.
He cursed her, but she did not respond except
To deliver another tear.
His stare was without pity, informing her
That pain is not like beauty: only its host
Is moved by it when love is not there.

The Rivals

All, all of them wanted her.
I watched them, ready to frustrate
Whatever strategy they used,
Doubly armed with fear and hate:
Prince Mincing and Lord Bulge were there,
Paul Profile and Lance Glitterteeth,
Sir Timothy Tarmac, hand on hilt
And golden blade half out of sheath.
I blocked her view when they came flaunting
Their wealth, fine clothes, virility,
Firm jaw, white smile of dancing master;
I showed my own agility.
But there was one whose gaunt appeal
I had not reckoned with. She fell
For him, the one I'd overlooked,
She, with her dainty sense of smell,
Fastidious ways, she fell for him,
The bony one with stinking breath
And sergeant's stripes, the clever fellow
In whose small room she lies beneath
A stiff cold quilt, without a pillow.

The Moth

'The moth has got into it.'
I heard the woman speak from another room.
What the moth had entered I did not know,

Nor why that singular creature should own
The definite article before its name.
The woman said 'The moth' as she might say
'The dog', a minor member of the family,
Yet in my mind's commodious bestiary
There was no space for such a stray.
I knew that it was time for me to go.
I crept away. I left some clothes:
A sweater, vest, two pairs of socks with holes.
Sometimes I think of the moth in its cage,
Its great khaki wings heavy with dust
And the woman feeding it, pushing through the bars
The tasteless garments to assuage
An appetite that must
Make do with such rough food as she, too, must.

Wife Killer

He killed his wife at night.
He had tried once or twice in the daylight
But she refused to die.

In darkness the deed was done,
Not crudely with a hammer-hard gun
Or strangler's black kid gloves on.

She just ceased being alive,
Not there to interfere or connive,
Linger, leave or arrive.

It seemed almost as though
Her death was quite normal and no
Clue to his part would show.

So then, with impunity,
He called up that buttocky beauty
He had so long longed to see

All covering gone: the double
Joggle of warm weighty bubbles
Was sweet delirious trouble.

And all night, all night he enjoyed her;
Such sport in her smooth dimpled water;
Then daylight came like a warder.

And he rose and went down to the larder
Where the mouse-trap again had caught a
Piece of stale gorgonzola.

His wife wore her large woollen feet.
She said that he was late
And asked what he wanted to eat,

But said nothing about the murder –
And who, after all, could have told her?
He said that he fancied a kipper.

Death in the Lounge Bar

The bar he went inside was not
A place he often visited;
He welcomed anonymity;
No one to switch inquisitive
Receivers on, no one could see,
Or wanted to, exactly what
He was, or had been, or would be;
A quiet brown place, a place to drink
And let thought simmer like good stock,
No mirrors to distract, no fat
And calculating face of clock,
A good calm place to sip and think.
If anybody noticed that
He was even there they'd see
A fairly tall and slender man,
Fair-haired, blue-eyed, and handsome in
A manner strictly masculine.
They would not know, or want to know,
More than what they saw of him,
Nor would they wish to bug the bone
Walls of skull and listen in

To whatever whisperings
Pittered quietly in that dark:
An excellent place to sip your gin.
Then – sting of interruption! voice
Pierced the private walls and shook
His thoughtful calm with delicate shock.
A waiter, with white napkin face
And shining toe-cap hair, excused
The oiled intrusion, asking if
His name was what indeed it was.
In that case he was wanted on
The telephone the customers used,
The one next to the Gents. He went.
Inside the secretive warm box
He heard his wife's voice, strangled by
Distance, darkness, coils of wire,
But unmistakably her voice,
Asking why he was so late,
Why did he humiliate
Her in every way he could,
Make her life so hard to face?
She'd telephoned most bars in town
Before she'd finally tracked him down.
He said that he'd been working late
And slipped in for a quick one on
His weary journey home. He'd come
Back at once. Right now. Toot sweet.
No, not another drop. Not one.
Back in the bar, he drank his gin
And ordered just one more, the last.
And just as well: his peace had gone;
The place no longer welcomed him.
He saw the waiter moving past,
That pale ambassador of gloom,
And called him over, asked him how
He had known which customer
To summon to the telephone.
The waiter said, 'Your wife described
You, sir. I knew you instantly.'
'And how did she describe me, then,
That I'm so easily recognized?'
'She said: grey suit, cream shirt, blue tie,
That you were fairly tall, red-faced,

Stout, middle-aged, and going bald.'
Disbelief cried once and sat
Bolt upright, then it fell back dead.
'Stout middle-aged and going bald.'
The slender ghost with golden hair
Watched him go into the cold
Dark outside, heard his slow tread
Fade towards wife, armchair, and bed.

A Simple Need

Well, no. Not now I suppose. Not now.
Not in the eyes of the law, I'm not any longer
Married. Yet still I feel she belongs to me,
In a way. Not that she ever really did,
Belong to me I mean. Right from the start I felt
That she was marking time, rehearsing, using me
As stand-in for the genuine first night.
Well, time will mark her in its own good time,
Though that's not what I want. I'm not vindictive.
I'd hate to see her sucked dry by the years.
She always seemed so ripe. I used to think
She's like a plum, a big plum with the smooth
Bloom on summer skin, a plum of plums,
The way they halve! Ridiculous, I know.
But listen, let me tell you something. Listen.
I never caught her out. I never once.
I'd come back two days early from a trip,
Wait till the lights were out. I'd leave the car
A block away and creep up pussyfoot.
I never caught them at it. Never once.
The joke is she got rid of me. Cruelty she said.
I can't go near. Not now. They'd jail me if I did.
But one of these fine nights I'll go,
I've got to go. Just to see them at it once,
That's all. Just see the two of them.
It's only fair.
Drink up. We've time for just one more.
That's all I want: Just see them at it once.

The Mourners

The boy was dead, his body lay
In the smart box.
The vicar said that death and life
Compose a paradox.

Maybe. I watched the father, who
Had not seen
His son for eighteen months or more,
Face raised like a tragic queen;

Tears candidly confessed his grief,
Marched from his eyelids,
Medalled his cheeks. Some time now since
He left his wife and kids.

No histrionics from the wife,
No jewellery of tears;
She would leave for home, a cold house,
Light lamps against her fears,

Build fires against the evening chill,
And yet not cry;
Feed the living children; pray
That none of these would die.

Fear of the Dark

Along the unlit lane on a night
When the stars are blind, the moon masked,
Footsteps follow. I knew a man
Of six foot three who, on dark nights,
Held two lit cigarettes between his lips
Hoping by this bright stratagem
To fox footpads, mislead murderers.
I used to laugh at him, but not now.
I clench teeth and fists and walk fast.
When I reach the house I switch on lights.

The darkness seems defeated, yet
Open the door, the light does not flow far
Beyond the threshold; it stops dead
A few feet from the step, I hear
The darkness growing; it is enormous,
It is in this room in thin disguise.
I am afraid of it, and with good reason.

THE WINTER MAN
1973

Comeback

The wind is in a whipping mood tonight.
Whatever changes, these old noises don't.
My Grandad must have heard it much the same
And lain in bed and known that sleep had gone
To find a quieter place.

                                When I was twelve,
And that's a good half century ago,
I used to lie awake, not that the wind
Could scare sleep from my bed, but something could:
A sharp electric charge of restlessness
Would needle and excite for hours on end,
And, in imagination, I would touch
Each object of my shadow treasury –
An odd collection for a kid to love –
Not foreign stamps or hollow eggs in beds
Of cotton-wool, not model aeroplanes
Or rolling-stock, nor hoarded coins or cards,
But articles of apparatus, kit
And clothing of a special usefulness,
The paraphernalia of the fighter's craft.
It seems unlikely now that all that gear,
Which came to be the tackle and the tools
Of my life's trade, could thrill me in those days
As later only women's secrets could.
Yet that's the way it was, and even now
I catch a tiny tremor of the old
Excitement on the sagging wires of nerve
Recalling how I'd lay the objects out –
The black kid boots, white ankle-socks, the gloves
Like giant kidneys, skipping-rope and towel,
The glittering robe embroidered on the back
With my brave name; black satin trunks
With yellow stripes and wide band at the waist;

And no less sacred, no less magical,
The grim and necessary armour of
Gum-shield, jockstrap and protective cup.
Not that I really owned these things. Not then.
The only kit I had for training nights
Was my old sand-shoes, cotton football shorts
And winter vest. But one day I would wear
The finest stuff. I knew I'd make the big time,
And I did.

     Listen to that wind.
It's strange how all its anger comforts you,
Maybe because it means I'm not alone;
We share the long hours of the night, the two
Of us, the old and tireless wind and me.
Does the wind have memories to shuffle through?
If so, they can't be very cheerful ones,
Judging by that sound.

     Oh, yes, I knew
I'd get to be a champion one day,
Though that was not the most important thing.
Important, yes, but what meant more to me
Was making myself good enough to wear
The garb the great ones wore. And even more
Important was the pleasure in the game,
Though 'pleasure' seems too weak a word for that
Drench of power that filled you when you fought
And overcame with cunning, speed and skill
A tough opponent. Many times I've made
A perfect move, smooth as satin, quick as a cat,
The muscles thinking faster than a wink,
A double feint and counter, something you
Could never in a thousand lessons teach
An ordinary fighter to perform:
A miracle, a gift. Those moments make
Your life worthwhile.

     The other stuff was muck:
I mean the silver trophies, medals, praise;
And later, fighting pro, the fancy belts,
The pictures on the sports page, interviews,
The youngsters scrambling for your scribbled name,

Even the big-time purses and the girls,
The bitches who would suck the virtue from you,
Press near your fame until the glitter dimmed,
They'd smear you with their artificial honey
And leave you spoiled and shamed.

                              I think it's strange
That when you've reached the top and won the crown
And every childish fantasy is fact,
It's strange how disappointing it all seems.
Success and fame, I've had the two and found
That both were fragile as those eggshell globes
They hang on Christmas trees. I used to think
The boys who'd never made the top, the ones
Who fought for peanuts in the shabby halls
And lost more often than they won, I thought
Them pitiable. Not now. They never knew
The failure of success, and they were real
Members of our craft, good workmen, proud
To wear the badges of the trade, a breed
That, if it dies, would surely mean the end
Of what I still believe the greatest game.

                              I won my first
Big title at the Albert Hall.
I fought a good old-timer from the North,
Birkenhead I think it was. He knew
The moves, was cagey as a monkey-house,
But he was past his best and in the seventh
I felt him weaken; as his strength seeped out
I seemed to suck it in like Dracula.
I put him down three times and in the ninth
He took a fast right-cross and folded up.
I knew he wouldn't rise. I did my dance
Above his fallen body, and the crowd
Bellowed their brainless worship of my feat.
I never thought that night my turn would come,
That eight years later in the selfsame ring
My nose would squash against the dust and resin
As I lay flat; I'd hear the same applause
But for the other man, new champion,
A youngster, strong, ambitious, arrogant.
By that time I had fought in Canada,

Twice at the Garden in New York, Berlin,
Milan and Paris, Rome, the Blackfriars Ring
And Stadium Club and places I've forgot.
I'd made and spent a fortune for those days,
And now they wrote me off. Another fool
Who once had been a fighter, now a ghost,
A fading name in yellowing papers, soon
Remembered only by a very few
And even they would get the details wrong
And, after too much booze, remember fights
I'd never had.

                    The wind is dying down
But still it makes its music, now less wild
But melancholy. It seems to sense my mood.
I doubt if I shall sleep tonight at all.
To tell the truth I have a taste for that
Sad sound of wind with darkness in its throat;
I like it when it snatches rain like seeds,
Throws handfuls at the window. But tonight
Is dry. No rain. No sleep. Only the wind
And memories.

                    After that defeat
I drank too much. I played the horses, too,
And lost the little capital I'd saved.
I was not old – a little over thirty –
Young enough in years, but I had fought
Two hundred contests as a pro, was tired.
But there was nothing else to do but fight.
It was my trade, the only one I knew.
And so I made my comeback, cut out booze,
Began to train with rope and heavy bag,
Run in the misty mornings through the park
And spar in the gym at night. I got a fight
In Leeds and put my man away in three.
I went back to the Club and showed them there
I still knew more about my business than
Those youngsters with their blasting energy
But little sense of what to do with it:
They sprayed their shots all round the field of fire;
I hoarded ammunition, only pressed
The trigger when I knew my shots would tell.

Once more my name appeared in fresh black ink,
My picture on a million breakfast tables.
They matched me for the title once again.
The fight was held in summer, out of doors,
White City was the place. The night was fine
And thousands came to see the veteran
Hand out a lesson to the cheeky boy
Who called himself the Champion. I knew
I'd win the title back. I'd seen him fight:
He was young and strong, with fair ability,
But I was master of a hundred tricks
He'd never heard about. I might be old
But I was also wise.

                    The fight began
At nine o'clock at night as dark came down.
The arc-lamps gushed white brilliance on the ring.
Beyond the ropes, the crowd, a factory
Of noise and appetites, was idling now
Though very soon I knew the huge machine
Would roar to tumult, hammer out acclaim,
And I would be the target of that praise.
The comeback would succeed, though history
Was littered with the names of those who'd failed.
I would not fail.

                    The first round proved to me
That my opponent was no better than
A score of fighters I had met before
And beaten easily. I jabbed and moved,
Slipping his leads and hurting him inside.
I took my time, collected points and foiled
His two attempts to trap me on the ropes.
The round was mine.

                    The second round began
With brisker action from us both; he swung
A left and followed with an uppercut
Slung hard towards my heart. I moved away,
Stepped in and jabbed and jolted back his head;
I saw my chance and threw a big right hand.
I felt the jar to elbow as my fist
Connected with his jaw. He should have gone.

Most would. He staggered back but did not fall.
The engines of applause were roaring wild.
He faded back. I knew I had him then.
I took my time. I was too old a hand
To crowd in, throwing leather at his head.
I stalked him to the ropes and measured him:
A feint downstairs, a jab – I saw his chin
And threw again the punch to douse the lights –
I never knew what happened. Something burst
Inside my head; my skull was opened up
And starless midnight flooded into it.
I'll never know what happened on that night,
Why my right fist did not connect and end
The fight with me as Champion. They said
He beat me to the punch. Maybe. It seemed
A thunderbolt had fallen from the skies,
A biblical defeat, the fall of Pride.
One thing was sure: I had not won the bout
Nor would I ever have another chance.
I'd never be a champion again.

                         I said that I'd retire,
Hang up the gloves for good, but very soon
I went into the ring, though now I knew
That I would never make the top again.
I fought in little halls and local baths,
Making a pound or two but taking some
Beatings from boys who five years earlier
Could not have laced my shoes. Sometimes I'd dream
That I would even yet surprise them all,
Come back and dazzle them with my old skill.
I nursed the dream till not so long ago
And then I gave myself a shake and said,
'Stop acting like a kid. You're grown up now.'
I got a job as trainer at a club
In Bermondsey. It's fine. I like it there.
I taught those boys some things they'd never learn
From amateurs. I still work there. It's good.
I like to see them in the ring. I like
The smell of rubbing oils, to hear the swish
And slap of skipping-rope, the thud of fist
On bag. I like it all. I don't complain.
I'm quite a lucky man.

The windows pale.
The wind itself seems tired now. I lie
Stretched out, but not to take the final count;
I have a round or two left in me yet.
My body is my own biography:
The scars, old fractures, ribs and nose, thick ear;
That's what I am, a score of ancient wounds
And in my head a few remembered scenes
And even those I'm not too sure about –
I've heard them say my brains are scrambled now –
I'm not too sure. Not sure of anything,
Except I'm proud of what I've been – although
I would have liked another chance – sure, too,
I'll never make another comeback now
Unless the dead can make it, as some say.

Here and Human

In the warm room, cushioned by comfort,
Idle at fireside, shawled in lamplight,
I know the cold winter night, but only
As a far intimation, like a memory
Of a dead distress whose ghost has grown genial.

The disc, glossy black as a conjuror's hat,
Revolves. Music is unwound: woodwind,
Strings, a tenor voice singing in a tongue
I do not comprehend or have need to –
'The instrument of egoism mastered by art' –

For what I listen to is unequivocal:
A distillation of romantic love,
Passion outsoaring speech, I understand
And, understanding, I rejoice in my condition:
This sweet accident of being here and human.

Later, as I lie in the dark, the echoes
Recede, the blind cat of sleep purrs close
But does not curl. Beyond the window
The hill is hunched under his grey cape

Like a watchman. I cannot hear his breathing.

Silence is a starless sky on the ceiling
Till shock slashes, stillness is gashed
By a dazzle of noise chilling the air
Like lightning. It is an animal screech,
Raucous, clawing: surely the language of terror.

But I misread it, deceived. It is the sound
Of passionate love, a vixen's mating call.
It lingers hurtful, a stink in the ear,
But soon it begins to fade. I breathe deep,
Feeling the startled fur settle and smooth. Then I sleep.

The Discriminator

I can afford to discriminate
In the matter of female pulchritude,
Though I will readily admit
That, to many observers, my attitude
Must seem pernickety, even absurd.
This, of course, is not the way of it
Though I understand why the less fastidious
Call me poseur or hypocrite.
Take that girl over there – fine tits
I will concede, but her ankles are too thick.
Her eyes are pleasing, opalescent, dark
As a glass of stout held up to light,
But the mouth is so slack as to make you sick.
Her blonde companion, I must remark,
Is far too wide in the hips. She might
Be pretty enough, but in a style
So commonplace you must have seen
The same face in a hundred city streets.
I note your disbelieving smile.
Don't be deceived, young man; the time
Will come when you, too, will apply
The cool astringent judgement you observe
Me exercising now. Your eye
Will be, as mine, fastidious and cold,

And you will then display the fine
Wisdom and discernment of the old,
Enjoy the wages of experience,
Reject expediency and compromise
With the stern impartiality of age
And age's impotence.

The Defrauded Woman Speaks

The legend of my love and its defeat
Is soiled and crushed beneath indifferent feet.
Excrement and mud are smeared across
The words that cannot apprehend my loss.
I'm reckoned as pathetic or a joke,
Perhaps a bit of both. They say: 'She's broke.
He's robbed her of her savings, every cent,
A cool twelve thousand, all the lot he spent
On other, younger women.' And it's true.
I'm broke all right, and broken-hearted, too,
Though not because of all I had to spend
But just because the whole thing had to end.
I was not fooled, was always well aware
That he was lying, but I did not care.
The other women hurt, but what hurts more
Is that I'd never known such joy before
And never will again. You wonder why
I went into the box to testify
Against him. Vengeance maybe. I don't know.
One thing I'm absolutely sure of, though,
And this is it: I swear I'd gladly give
However many years I've left to live
For just another month with him; again
To hear his sweet deceitful whisper feign
A lovelier love than plain and honest fare;
To feel his hands exploring flesh and hair,
Re-educating lust until it knew
How false such categories as false and true.

Confrontation

When we finally met, the hatred
That for weeks had been savoured
Was drained of taste;
We let it fall.
We looked at each other without fear,
With shyness and curiosity,
No loathing at all.

The impulse to smash bone and tear flesh
Was gone; no aftertaste
Lingered and sickened.
One did not forgive.
Forgiveness and blame were irrelevant
As knuckle-duster, cosh, revolver,
Or slick shiv.

My need was for the affection
I felt for him, and he
I am sure wanted mine.
Courteously we waited,
Uncertain, yet each with the knowledge
That through the bonds of her body
We were related.

I felt a rare generosity,
A kinship and sympathy;
Believed, in us both,
These might uncover
New areas of magnanimity,
Dismissing such trivia as who
Was husband and who lover.

Love Nest

Perched high, it swayed when the wind was wild.
Roots were loosening in the stone.
It was not safe. Underground thunder

Rumbled, made it jerk and shudder.
He knew one day, or rather night,
The nest must fall: the place of loving
Was the place of death. He saw the picture:
Their fallen bodies on the ground,
Soldered together like a single creature,
Without a stitch or feather on,
For the world and his wife to look upon.

Picture of the Bride

Alone, among the grey crosses and stones,
The slabs of marble, slippery as brawn,
Absolute as theirs the stillness she owns;
Her whiteness darkens the shades on the lawn.

Her features are hidden under the veil
Which also conceals the gleam of her hair;
Sepulchral she seems, not humanly frail,
Whiter and taller than any tomb there.

Sleeping Beauty

It was evening when he reached the place.
Outside, the air was motionless.
He listened for the sound of sigh or snore.
Silence trickled down his face;
He touched his sword for confidence,
Then parted the dark foliage at the door.

He entered. She was beautiful.
He pressed his mouth to hers; her lips
Grew warm and parted, breathing quick yet deep;
Her waking welcome magical
Until her sharp teeth came to grips
And munched; for she was starved from that long sleep.

A Mystery at Euston

The train is still, releasing one loud sigh.
Doors swing and slam, porters importune.
The pigskin labelled luggage of the rich
Is piled on trolleys, rolled to waiting cars,
Grey citizens lug baggage to the place
Where fluttering kisses, craning welcomes wait.
A hoarse voice speaks from heaven, but not to her,
The girl whose luggage is a tartan grip
With broken zip, white face a tiny kite
Carried on the currents of the crowd.
The handsome stranger did not take her bag,
No talent-scout will ask her out to dine.
Her tights are laddered and her new shoes wince.
The Wimpy bar awaits, the single room,
The job as waitress, golden-knuckled ponce.
Whatever place she left – Glasgow, Leeds,
The village on the moors – there's no return.
Beyond the shelter of the station, rain
Veils the day and wavers at a gust,
Then settles to its absent-minded work
As if it has forgotten how to rest.

The Widow's Complaint

You left as you so often left before,
Sneaking out on tiptoe,
No slam of door,
Off to drink with enemies of mine,
And of yours –
If you could only see it –
Drunkards and bores
Whose grossest flatteries
You swilled down with the booze
That you never had the gumption to refuse.
You won't come back this time.
No need to prepare
A welcome for you – clamped silence

And belligerent stare –
No need for morning nostrums or to hide
The whisky and car-keys,
Tighten my lips and thighs
Against your pleas,
No need for those old stratagems any more.
But you might have let me know what was in store;
Your last low trick
To leave me with no clue
That you had gone for good,
My last chance lost
To tell you what I've so long wanted to,
How much I hate you and I always have,
You pig, you bastard,
Stinking rat –
Oh, love, my love,
How can I forgive you that?

Five Domestic Interiors

I

The lady of the house is on her benders;
She's scrubbed and mopped until her knees are sore.
She rests a second as her husband enters,
Then says, 'Look out! Don't walk on my clean floor.'
He looks up at the slick flies on the ceiling
And shakes his head, and goes back through the door.

II

She holds her chuckling baby to her bosom
And says, 'My honey-pie, my sugar bun,
Does Mummy love her scrumptious little darling?
You're lovely, yes, you are, my precious one!'
But when the little perisher starts bawling
She says, 'For God's sake listen to your son.'

III

Sandbagged by sleep at last the kids lie still.
The kitchen clock is nodding in warm air.
They spread the Sunday paper on the table
And each draws up a comfortable chair.
He turns the pages to the crossword puzzle,
Nonplussed they see a single large black square.

IV

The radio is playing dated music
With lilac tune and metronomic beat.
She smiles and says, 'Remember that one, darling?
The way we used to foxtrot was a treat.'
But they resist the momentary temptation
To resurrect slim dancers on glib feet.

V

In bed his tall enthusiastic member
Receives warm welcome, and a moist one too.
She whispers, 'Do you love me? More than ever?'
And, panting, he replies, 'Of course I do.'
Then as she sighs and settles close for slumber
He thinks, with mild surprise, that it is true.

Song for a Winter Birth

Under the watchful lights
    A child was born;
From a mortal house of flesh
    Painfully torn.

And we, who later assembled
    To praise or peer,
Saw merely an infant boy
    Sleeping there.

Then he awoke and stretched
    Small arms wide
And for food or comfort
    Quavering cried.

A cry and attitude
    Rehearsing in small
The deathless death still haunting
    The Place of the Skull.

Outside, in the festive air,
    We lit cigars.
The night was nailed to the sky
    With hard bright stars.

Cold Spell

Take a black length of water,
                        leave it rippling as the day dies,
By morning it will be stretched taut,
                        pale and motionless, stiff silk.
Take a solitary puddle,
                        let it be nursed under sharp stars,
At dawn it will be a small blind mirror,
                        cold and milky.
The field in a single night
                        will age, grizzle and grow brittle;
Grasses will welcome destruction,
                        crunching underfoot.
Take a deep inhalation
                        and release slowly,
In the scentless air you will see
                        drifting bundles of breath.
Take a look at the sycamore and oak trees,
                        they will shame your softness
With their black calisthenics
                        gaunt against grey sky.
At sunset the dark cottage windows
                        will flush with a vinous infusion.
The furrows of mud in the field

                                   might break a careless toe.
The cold spell works. Listen:
                    you can hear
The tap of hammers, the scrape of chisel,
                         the silver engines.
For disenchantment you must draw
                    fur and fire
Close, close to you, or better,
                         embrace a live body,
Drink broth of warm breath,
                    eat each other.

Picnic on the Lawn

Their dresses were splashed on the green
Like big petals; polished spoons shone
And tinkered with cup and saucer.
Three women sat there together.

They were young, but no longer girls.
Above them the soft green applause
Of leaves acknowledged their laughter.
Their voices moved at a saunter.

Small children were playing nearby;
A swing hung from an apple tree
And there was a sand pit for digging.
Two of the picnicking women

Were mothers. The third was not.
She had once had a husband, but
He had gone to play the lover
With a new lead in a different theatre.

One of the mothers said, 'Have you
Cherished a dream, a fantasy
You know is impossible; a childish
Longing to do something wildly

'Out of character? I'll tell you mine.

I would like to drive alone
In a powerful sports car, wearing
A headscarf and dark glasses, looking

'Sexy and mysterious and rich.'
The second mother smiled: 'I wish
I could ride through an autumn morning
On a chestnut mare, cool wind blowing

'The jet black hair I never had
Like smoke streaming from my head.
In summer, swoop on a switchback sea
Surf-riding in a black bikini.'

She then turned to the childless one:
'And you? You're free to make dreams true.
You have no need of fantasies
Like us domestic prisoners.'

A pause, and then the answer came:
'I also have a hopeless dream:
Tea on the lawn in a sunny garden,
Listening to the voices of my children.'

End of a Season

The nights are drawing in; the daylight dies
With more dispatch each evening;
Traffic draws lit beads
Across the bridge's abacus.
Below, black waters jitter in a breeze.
The air is not yet cold
But woven in its woof of various blues,
Whiffs of petrol and cremated flowers,
A cunning thread runs through,
A thin premonitory chill.
The parks are closed. Lights beckon from the bars.
The sporting news has put on heavier dress.
It is not autumn yet
Though summer will not fill
Attentive hearts again with its warm yes.

Far from the city, too, the dark surprises:
Oak and sycamore hunch
Under their loads of leaves;
Plump apples fall; the night devises
Frail webs to vein the sleek skin of the plums.
The scent of stars is cold.
The wheel-ruts stumble in the lane, are dry and hard.
Night is a nest for the unhatched cries of owls;
As deep mines clench their gold
Night locks up autumn's voices in
The vaults of silence. Hedges are still shawled
With traveller's joy; yet windows of the inn
Rehearse a winter welcome.
Though tomorrow may be fine
Soon it will yield to night's swift drawing in.

The athletes of light evenings hibernate;
Their whites are folded round
Green stains; the night
Reminds with its old merchandise –
Those summer remnants on its highest boughs –
That our late dancing days
Are doomed if not already under ground.
The playground gates are chained; the swings hang still;
The lovers have come down
From their deciduous hill;
Others may climb again, but they will not.
And yet the heart resumes its weightier burden
With small reluctance; fares
Towards Fall, and then beyond
To winter with whom none can fool or bargain.

Beside the Sea

Dark as braves, red as bricks from kilns
Or brown as loaves from ovens,
The faces of the veterans confirm
That the business of the sun had flourished
Before this diligent rain began.

And sun will hammer out its gold again,
Though when it does the gloom
Inside the heart and head will not disperse
Entirely: beneath the shimmering
Exuberance dark threads will creep,

Will drag against the flow, cold undertow,
While various boats put out
For trips across the bay, and on the beach
Little fists are fastened round
Olympic cones of frozen fire.

Sand will be slapped and deck-chairs fatten, groan,
As naked boys conceal
Their willies under prudently hung towels
And shops will flush with smooth pink rock
Seductive under cellophane.

But, as the sun presides and we applaud,
Dejection will persist,
A mist from off the sea, invisible,
Whose clinging weight will lie upon
The spirits like damp clouts.

Deny it as we might while daylight cries
With gulls and objurgations,
With noon's delight and shine,
At night we know, hearing its far, caged roar,
The greed and true vocation of the sea.

Incident at West Bay

He drove on to the quay.
His children, Mark and Jane,
Shrilled their needs:
A ride in a boat for Mark,
Ice-cream and the sands for Jane.

Gulls banked and glided over
The nudging dinghies; waves
Mildly admonished
The walls with small slaps.
It was the first day of the holidays.

'Wait there,' he said, 'I'll bring
Ice-cream.' Out of the car
He felt the breeze
Easing the vehemence of the sun.
He said, 'I won't be long.'

He walked a few steps before
He was hit by a shout; he spun
Quickly round
To see his car begin
To move to the edge of the quay.

It was blind; it could not see.
It did not hesitate
But toppled in.
The sea was shocked, threw up
Astonished lace-cuffed waves.

He ran, he followed, plunged,
And in the shifting green gloom
He saw the car's
Tipped shape; he clutched handle, lugged.
His lungs bulged, punishing.

Through glass he saw their faces
Float, eyes wide as hunger,
Staring mouths,
Their lost and sightless hands.
In his chest the sea heaved

And pressed, swelled black and burst
Flooding his skull; it dragged
Him up to air.
They hauled him out and spread him
Oozing on the slimed stone.

They pumped the salt and darkness
From his lungs and skull;
Light scoured his eyes.
The sun said, 'Rise.' The gulls
Fell silent, then echoed his long torn yell.

Battlefields

Tonight in the pub I talked with Ernie Jones
Who served with the Somersets in Normandy,
And we remembered how our fathers told
The sad and muddy legends of their war,
And how, as youngsters, we would grin and say:
'The old man's on his favourite topic now,
He never tires of telling us the tale.'
We are the old men now, our turn has come.
The names have changed – Tobruk and Alamein,
Arnhem, the Falaise Gap and Caen Canal
Displace the Dardanelles, Gallipoli,
Vimy Ridge, the Somme – but little else.
Our children do not want to hear about
The days when we were young and, sometimes, brave,
And who can blame them? Certainly not us.
We drank a last half pint and said goodnight.
And now, at home, the family is in bed,
The kitchen table littered with crashed planes;
A tank is tilted on its side, one track
Has been blown off; behind the butter-dish
Two Gunners kneel, whose gun has disappeared;
A Grenadier with busby and red coat
Mounts guard before a half a pound of cheese.
Some infantry with bayonets fixed begin
A slow advance towards the table edge.
Conscripted from another time and place
A wild Apache waves his tomahawk.
It's all a game. Upstairs, my youngest son
Roars like a little Stuka as he dives
Through dream, banks steep, then cuts his engine out,
Levels, re-enters the armistice of sleep.

War Cemetery, Ranville

A still parade of stone tablets,
White as aspirin under the bland
Wash of an August sky, they stand
In exact battalions, their shoulders square.

I move slowly along the lines
Like a visiting Commander
Noting each rank, name and number
And that a few are without names.

All have been efficiently drilled,
They do not blink or shift beneath
My inspection; they do not breathe
Or sway in the hot summer air.

The warmth is sick with too much scent
And thick as ointment. Flowers hurt,
Their sweetness fed by dirt,
Breathing in the dark earth underneath.

Outside the cemetery walls
The children play; their shouts are thrown
High in the air, burst and come down
In shrapnel softer than summer rain.

The Soldier's Dream

After the late shouts, the silences
Shattered like windows, rises
The bugle's husky hymn;
After the boozers' fumbled voices,
Their studs on stone, songs and curses,
The hard blokes are dumb.

After the last fag doused, small brightness
Crushed by the heel of darkness,
Lights out: the night commands.

After groans and expectorations,
Creakings like an old ship's timbers,
Sleep condescends.

In that consoling ambience
Images with unsoldierly elegance
Advance and are recognized.
After the day's gun-metal,
The khaki itch, such softness beckons,
Intentions undisguised.

Such challenge yet complete submission,
Small arms that need no ammunition
Beyond being feminine;
And other naked limbs, much longer,
Cancel parades, the day's loud anger,
With their own disciplines.

And after the cordite's lethal sweetness,
Reek of oil on steel, such fragrance,
A delicate silent tune;
And then the white thighs' open welcome,
The belly and breasts so suave and silken,
The moist dark between.

The bearded grin of generation
Calls the idler to attention,
Rouses the martial man,
Renews him as annihilator,
Restores his role, the man of leather,
Sinew, muscle, gun.

Muzzle flash and blast, bright blaring
Of the bugle of the morning,
The dream and darkness fled;
Orderlies of light discover
The soldier struggling with the lover
On the snarled, dishonoured bed.

Stanley's Dream

The village hall was changed: someone had moved
The church pews into it. There were many people there.
It was a summer evening, fragrant from
Anthologies of flowers. He could not see
All faces clearly, though one he saw quite plain:
Thomas Ashman, the carpenter from Trent.
But Thomas had been dead for eighteen months.
Or had he? Stanley was no longer sure.
Maybe he had dreamt that Thomas died,
For there was no mistaking that grained face,
And no one could deny he was alive
Since he was beckoning with urgent hand.
Stanley waved back and went across the room.
Then Thomas showed that he should bend his head
Close to his secret whisper. Stanley bent,
Then swiftly Thomas grabbed his neck and pulled
His startled face towards his own and pressed
His cheek to his old friend's, and Stanley felt
A coldness like a winter stone. The scent
Of flowers grew intolerably sweet,
The cold bit deep. He struggled to get free
And broke away from that embrace and from
The toils of sleep, but in his waking room
He felt the coldness burning on his cheek
And phantoms of dead flowers explored his throat.

Charnel House, Rothwell Church

I remember the visit now,
See those tiers in the hall of my skull,
The little heads on shelves;
My nose remembers the smell,
Damp and chill, but not rank;
I remember the way they looked down,
Their eyes small, starless caves

In the grey and ochre and brown
Of skulls as cold as stones,
Looked down at the beautiful, neat
Composition of their stacked bones.
What a waste to gaol them away;
I would like some for my friends,
One to give to my wife
Next time I must make amends
For neglect or cruelty.
When I am away from home
It would not be any trouble,
It has no hair to comb.
And if she awoke to face it
Calm on her neighbour pillow
Where tenderly I'd place it
She'd welcome this better fellow,
The lack of fetid breath,
Know any words it could utter
Would have nothing to do with death.

Lives of the Poet

In Spring he saw the hedges splashed with blood;
Rags of flesh depended. In the moonlight
From a chestnut branch he saw suspended
A man who cocked an inattentive ear.
He heard worms salivate and paced his song
To the metronome of the hanging man,
Wore black to celebrate this time of year.

In August, from deceitful beaches, waves
Hauled drowners deeper in; he watched their arms
Wink in the obsolescent sun;
His ears discerned those other melodies
Beneath the chesty self-praise of the band,
The sound of blues. The shifting sand
And sea entombed clean bones, old summer days.

Now Autumn, vicar of all other weathers,
Performs its rites he joins the harvest chorus

At the cider-press and celebrates
In dance of words the seasons' grand alliance,
Puts on his snappiest suit on Friday nights
And stomps gay measures: no dirges now,
For Winter waits with ice and truth and silence.

Legs

Of well-fed babies activate
Digestive juices, yet I'm no cannibal.
It is my metaphysical teeth that wait
Impatiently to prove those goodies edible.
The pink or creamy bonelessness, as soft
As dough or mashed potato, does not show
A hint of how each pair of limbs will grow.
Schoolboys' are badged with scabs and starred with scars,
Their sisters', in white ankle-socks, possess
No calves as yet. They will, and when they do
Another kind of hunger will distress
Quite painfully, but pleasurably too.
Those lovely double stalks of girls give me
So much delight: the brown expensive ones,
Like fine twin creatures of rare pedigree,
Seem independent of their owners, so
Much themselves are they. Even the plain
Or downright ugly, the veined and cruelly blotched
That look like marble badly stained, I've watched
With pity and revulsion, yet something more –
A wonder at the variousness of things
Which share a name: the podgy oatmeal knees
Beneath the kilt, the muscled double weapons above boots,
Eloquence of dancers', suffering of chars',
The wiry goatish, the long and smooth as milk –
The joy when these embrace like arms and cling!
O human legs, whose strangenesses I sing,
You more than please, though pleasure you have brought
    me,
And there are often times when you transport me.

Six Reasons for Drinking

I

'It relaxes me,' he said,
Though no one seemed to hear.
He was relaxed: his head
Among fag-ends and spilt beer.
Free from all strain and care
With nonchalance he waved
Both feet in the pungent air.

II

'I drink to forget.'
But he remembers
Everything, the lot:
What hell war was,
Betrayal, lost
Causes best forgot.
The only thing he can't recall
Is how often before we've heard it all.

III

'It gives me the confidence I lack,'
He confided with a grin
Slapping down ten new pennies
For a pint and a double gin.

IV

'It makes me witty fit to burst,'
He said from his sick-bed. 'There's nothing worse
Than seeing a man tongue-tied by thirst.
Hey! Bring me a bed-pun quickly, nurse!'

V

From behind a fierce imperialistic stare
He said, 'The reason's plain. Because it's there!'

VI

'It releases your inhibitions,
Let's you be free and gay!'
The constable told him brusquely
To put it away.

Drunk in Charge

We'd had a damned good party in the mess
The night before, went on a bit too long,
I wasn't feeling quite on form next day.
The Scotch I drank for breakfast didn't help.
I'd half a mind to go and see the quack
Except it wouldn't look too good, I mean
Going sick the morning of the big attack.
I soldiered on. I took a nip or two
While Grieves, my servant, laid my doings out.
An idle beggar, Grieves, but not too bad
As long as you administer the boot
From time to time. Certainly the chap's
Devoted to me, follow me to hell
And back he would. I thought I'd feel all right
After a decent shit, a bath and shave,
A breath of air, but nothing did much good:
Guts still complained, I couldn't see too well.
I took another nip before I mounted.
I rode out well enough and told my men
I knew they wouldn't let me down today –
Stout fellows, every one of them. We trotted off.
We heard the cannon of the enemy
Begin its din. We reached the starting line.
The bugle called. This was the time to show
My quality. I lit a long cheroot,
Pulled out my sabre like a long thin fish
And shouted, 'Charge!' My damned cheroot went out.
'Hold on, my lads! Hold on!' I lit it up
And roared again through its blue fragrance, 'Charge!'
My chestnut stumbled and it nearly fell.

I spurred him on but he reared up and tried
To throw me – a lesser rider would have gone.
I almost lost my long cheroot. I tried
To make him gallop but he wouldn't run.
Either he was lame or else a coward.
My squadron overtook me, thundered past,
Those gallant troopers, surging on towards
The wall of cannonade and musketry,
Hot for a glorious death or victory,
Fine fellows, splendid soldiers every one,
And not a smoke between the lot of 'em.

Not a Bad Life

I am my own hero and I worship me.
Often I loom at night outside the women's conveniences
And mumble through the bullets of my teeth.
When I spit, the leech of phlegm
Spawns a litter of condoms in the gutter.
I am not queer. I shall sleep
In bed soundly, deaf to the day's grim music
Which cannot disturb my repose.
When day slumbers
And the tolerant night gets up
I follow my customary employment:
I am a traveller
In ladies'
Undergrowth.
The commission is generous
And the wages are not derisory,
Could be called, I think,
A pretty good screw.

Polling Day

Politics, said Bismarck, is not
An exact science. Neither is science,
At least it's not to me.
Towards each of these important matters
My attitude is less than reverential
Yet I accept that one cannot deny
The relevance of both, not now
Especially as I approach the booth,
Once more prepare myself
To make this positive, infrequent act
Of self-commitment, wishing that I could
Do more than scrawl a black anonymous mark –
The illiterate's signature
Or graphic kiss – against my favourite's name.
Incongruous, one thinks;
But is it so? In my case not entirely
Since I am voting unscientifically
For one who might be midwife to a dream
Of justice, charity and love
Or scatter obstinately truthful seeds
On these deceitful plots.
No argument or rhetoric could lend
My gesture and my hope more confidence,
So oddly apt this cross, illiterate kiss.

The Winter Man

I

Numb under the fresh fall
The stone of pavements did not feel
The blunted heel. Parked cars were furred
With ermine capes of recent snow;
Substantial silence showed both tint
And texture, bandaging the town
In lint of winter.
                              Looking down

From a window in a high warm room
A man recalled how, once before,
The slow hypnosis of the snow
Had veiled his senses in a trance,
How that pale dance composed its own
Spectral music and deceived –
When the sewing flakes had ceased –
With its white lie, a fraudulent
Paradigm of innocence.
And now, once more, the town wore white,
But he knew well the cold could kill,
That this bland lenitive possessed
No healing skill, would soon be soiled
And, like discarded dressings, show
The old wounds underneath, unhealed.
He did not trust the lying snow.

He turned away, sat by his fire,
A man of thirty-four, unsure
What stance to take, poised as he was
Precariously between the traps
Of youth and middle age; he feared
In equal parts the anguish of
Youthful passion and the absurd
Attitudes of ravenous love
Adopted by the man too old
To play the Prince with word and sword;
And yet he craved such exercise,
Yearned for the natural warmth it lent,
Half believed he could survive –
Without being too severely hurt –
Just one more non-decision bout.
He picked up his book but had not read
A page before the stillness jerked,
Pierced by a double jet of noise
Blurting through the silent room,
Official as a uniform.
The black shell raised, he said no more
Than half his name before a voice
Breathed close; he could have sworn he felt
The warmth of every whispered word.
She knew she did not have to say
Her name, less individual

Than that soft signature of sound.
He said: 'It seems so long ago,'
And thought: How long? A year, or more?
Impossible to measure such
Desolation, so much hurt.
It seemed so long ago...

II

Clock and calendar would both agree
That it was fourteen months ago when he,
Bored on a snivelling November night,
Stale as old crust, unable to read or write,
Called on some friends who would not aggravate
His subcutaneous itch, might mitigate
The threat of an enveloping despair.
When he arrived, at once he saw her there,
And all else in that room, human or
Inanimate, whatever dress it wore,
Was darkened and diminished by the claim
Her presence made, a solitary flame
Brilliant among spent ashes of the day.
Although the clock and calendar might say
That moment lifeless lay a year away
He reckoned otherwise: its essence stayed
Fixed in the heart, whatever else betrayed.
And other things remained to tantalize,
Awaken thwarted hungers and surprise
With half recaptured joys: a ride –
So trivial an occasion to provide
A charge of such excitement and regret –
A ride in leather dusk when fingers met,
Uncertain for a second, then they clung
Miming longer limbs as if they'd flung
All clothing off; those moving hands amazed
With conscious nakedness and praised
Each other's strangeness and audacity.

Other minute events he could recall,
Gestures of lust and tenderness so small
No onlooker would know they had occurred.
And yet it was not long before he heard

A harsh inflection in her voice and she
Revealed impatience that could rapidly
Become contempt for all he seemed to be,
And had his reason not been on its knees
He would have known, however he might please
Her eyes and mind and flesh on friendly days,
He never could possess her and must face
The truth that her desire was spiked with hate.
So when, as winter laid down arms to spring,
The season when, in fiction, everything
In nature welcomes lusty grooms and brides
But is, in fact, peak time for suicides,
He realized, once the first raw pain had eased,
Like a man informed he's mortally diseased,
Her words confirmed what he had always known:
In spring she turned indifferent as stone
And told him that the time had struck to go,
Her winter love had melted with the snow.

For days he dozed, bemused, and then began
The ache that trailed him like a Private Eye
To cafés, bars, surprising him with sly
Disguises in the street or public park,
Tapping his line, transmitting in the dark
Messages whose sense he could not quite
Seize before each cypher slipped from sight.
He found, again, he could not read or write.
Down avenues of summer, lovers walked;
The green tongues in the trees above them talked
A language that endorsed their bodies' speech,
Yet with the sun's connivance could not reach
Those icy fetters clamped on feeling's source.
And when sun paled with Autumn's sick remorse
And leaves swam in the morning milk of air
As smoke from garden bonfires rose like prayer,
He was unmoved; until fresh winterfall
Prepared white silence to sustain that call
Thrilling the waiting stillness of his room,
A double blade that stabbed with hope and doom.

III

He said, 'It seems so long ago,'
And waited, holding to his ear
The black shell in which low susurrus
Rose and fell, a dream of surf.
He would not go.
Yet even as intention shaped
He felt it melt, a single flake
Of snow that settles on warm stone.
Slowly he lowered the telephone,
Found his coat, switched off the lights
And went down to the white, stunned street.
The coldness glittered in his eyes.
Beneath the stroking wind the fur
Of snow was riffled, then smoothed down.
The stars were frozen chips of flint.
The flesh grew warm, his eyes were bright.
Anticipation drummed and strummed;
Uncertainty sniped at his heart,
Premonitory fear was sharp
And lingered on the tongue, although
A sweeter taste was there also,
Wafer of hope, a desperate joy.
His footprints trailed him through the snow.

THE LOVING GAME
1975

The Loving Game

A quarter of a century ago
I hung the gloves up, knew I'd had enough
Of taking it and trying to dish it out,
Foxing them or slugging toe-to-toe;
Keen youngsters made the going a bit too rough;
The time had come to have my final bout.

I didn't run to fat though, kept in shape,
And seriously took up the loving game,
Grew moony, sighed, and even tried to sing,
Looked pretty snappy in my forty-drape.
I lost more than I won, earned little fame,
Was hurt much worse than in the other ring.

Wicket Maiden

It is a game for gentle men;
Entirely wrong that man's spare rib
Should learn the mysteries of spin.

Women should not be allowed
To study subtleties of flight;
They should bowl underarm and wide.

Or, better still, not bowl at all,
Sit elegant in summer chairs,
Flatter the quiet with pale applause.

It shouldn't happen, yet it did:
She bowled a wicked heartbreak – one,
That's all. God help the next man in.

Enemy Agents

Expert in disguise and killing-blows,
Fluent in all languages required,
They wrote me ardent letters, but in code.
My vanity and ignorance combined
To make me perfect victim for their game.
I took them at face-value every time.

Repeatedly they practised their deceits
And I was fooled, but slowly I became
Alert and learnt few things are what they seem,
Few people, too; so I grew narrow-eyed
And wore suspicion's habit like a coat.
I boasted not just second but third sight.

But then the top man, whom I'd never seen,
The power above the throne as you might say,
Assigned a partner to me. I could see
At once that she was candour's self, her whole
Demeanour spoke of truth. I'll never learn.
Most ruthless of the lot, her cover blown.

Where Shall We Go?

Waiting for her in the usual bar
He finds she's late again.
Impatience frets at him,
But not the fearful, half-sweet pain he knew
So long ago.

That cherished perturbation is replaced
By styptic irritation
And, under that, a cold
Dark current of dejection moves
That this is so.

There was a time when all her failings were
Delights he marvelled at:

It seemed her clumsiness,
Forgetfulness and wild non-sequiturs
Could never grow

Wearisome, nor would he ever tire
Of doting on those small
Blemishes that proved
Her beauty as the blackbird's gloss affirms
The bridal snow.

The clock above the bar records her theft
Of time he cannot spare;
Then suddenly she's here.
He stands to welcome and accuse her with
A grey 'Hello'.

And sees, for one sly instant, in her eyes
His own aggrieved dislike
Wince back at him before
Her smile draws blinds. 'Sorry I'm late' she says.
'Where shall we go?'

Separation

They stand still as trees
In the drifting mist
Of an autumn evening,
Silent as elms
With branches becalmed,
All language drowned,
A man and a woman
Quite motionless,
Yet the space in between
Is slowly increasing.
No gesture from either,
Regret or farewell,
As the interval widens
And they wait for the night
In stillness and silence,
For the moon's blind stare
Or the seal of darkness.

An Anniversary

Endlessly the stream slides past,
Jellies each white flat stone
Which stares through its slithering window at
The sky's smeared monotone.

Two willow leaves glide smoothly on
The water's shimmering skin:
Inches apart they float along,
The distance never changing.

Once, on a branch in the sun, they danced
And often touched each other;
They will not touch each other again,
Not now, not ever.

Marriage Counsel

Your problem is not unusual,
Indeed its absence would be that
(Regard this room as a confessional,
Nothing you tell me will leak out).
So far, it seems, your principal trouble
Is your wife's indifference, her failure to hear
Whenever you speak, in bed or at table,
Her remote and unrecording stare.
These are not uncommon features of a marriage,
In fact the contrary would be true.
You suspect an urgent need for copulation
With an unknown someone, the opposite of you?
She puts black stuff round her eyes and wears
Unaccustomed underclothes,
Ambiguous, weightless as mist? She dyes
The grey bits of her hair and shows
A strange new taste for vulgar romantic songs?
None of this need suggest another man.
You say she has never had strong lungs
Yet, despite Government Health Warnings, she has begun

To smoke cigarettes – expensive, King-size.
It may be the menopause, although
Her new vocabulary might give cause
For perturbation. It could show
That she is being refashioned utterly,
Which certainly suggests a mentor, a new friend.
In this case you must try to be
A different person too. It need not be the end.
Re-woo her. Win her hand again.
And if you fail – which might well occur –
This reflection should ease the ensuing pain:
Consider – you will not really have lost her
Because, from all you say, she is other
Than the woman you married. She is remade.
In this case you have never possessed her
And cannot therefore be betrayed.
Later, the former, the familiar wife
May return. It has often happened before.
But, if she does, do not expect life
To be suddenly charged with honeyed splendour
And harmonious chords. You must not be surprised
If you find your need and passion are dead.
There are times when defeat is to be prized
Above victory.
   Good day to you. You will forget
All I have said.

When Love Has Gone

   When love has gone
This at least, or most, stays on:
   When tenderness
Fades and brittles till the press
   Of days destroys,
All arias are pulped to noise,
   Prismatic dome
Drained and stunned, cold monochrome,
   This needs remains:

To clamp each other in soft chains,
  The dragging links
Of flesh and, as the last flame sinks,
  In darkness drown
Clinging, bearing each other down.
  And yet, God knows,
You could not tell these cries from those
  That used to flow
When love, it seemed, would never go.

Captain Scuttle Ashore

I've sailed so far and heard the sea's
Drunk shanties rolling under
A moon as fat and powder white
As a spot-lit prima donna.

Black sea ran through my hempen veins;
I drank it down like porter;
My heart was calloused like my hands,
I pissed and bled salt water.

But I'd one pretty whistle in my ditty-box
And, man, the tunes it's played
In knocking-shops and snazzy flats
From Brest to Adelaide.

In shacks and pads and pent-houses
And on the sun-burnt sands,
And once in a Methodist chapel,
I laid them all, like plans.

But this soft inland breeze that sighs
Now I'm ashore for good,
Brings a warm sweet rain that pierces me
As never north sleet could.

And my old concertina heart
Is squeezed by cunning fingers;
No jig or hornpipe rollicks out
But a melody that lingers,

A melancholy air that floats
Through twilight of the blood
And curls around the nervous roots,
Yet is not wholly sad.

There's a kind of joy in the tune that leads
Me to this breathing shore
Where, warm in the briny undergrowth,
I know I'll sail no more.

I'm home at last, I'm harboured now,
Tied up till the day I die,
Held fast by ropes of glossy hair
And anchored to a thigh.

Though white ships round my blue skull glide
And storms bang far and deep,
I'll stay where the waves like lions prowl in
And, tamed, lie down to sleep.

Amities

Amities composed in gentle weather,
Flowering in temperate field or harbouring wood,
Or sealed at ease in warm and fragrant bed

Flinch cravenly when winter swings its axe,
Raise hands in negative surrender when
Threatened by adversity's muscle-man.

It is the friendships built in bitter season,
When menace prowls the street and fields; when food
Is scarce and all you're left to share is need,

These are conjunctions nothing can unmake;
They will survive until all climates merge,
Proof against clock and calendar's furtive rage.

Spot-check at Fifty

I sit on a hard bench in the park;
The spendthrift sun throws down its gold.
The wind is strong but not too cold.
Daffodils shimmy, jerk and peck.

Two dogs like paper bags are blown
Fast and tumbling across the green;
Far off laborious lorries groan.
I am not lonely, though alone.

I feel quite well. A spot-check on
The body-work and chassis finds
There's not much wrong. No one minds
At fifty going the speed one can.

No gouty twinge in toe, all limbs
Obedient to such mild demands
I make. A hunger-pang reminds
I can indulge most gastric whims.

Ears savour sounds. My eyes can still
Relish this sky and that girl's legs;
My hound of love sits up and begs
For titbits time has failed to stale.

Fifty scored and still I'm in.
I raise my cap to dumb applause,
But as I wave I see, appalled,
The new fast bowler's wicked grin.

Self-inflicted Wounds

Soldiers who decided that
dishonour was a wiser
choice than death, or worse, and spat
into the face of Kaiser
Bill and the Fatherland or

King George's Union Jack
and took up their rifles for
the purpose of getting back
to Blighty by sniping at
their own big toes or trigger-
fingers were called things like 'rat'
but preferred scorn to rigor-
mortis and considered gaol,
for however long, a soft
touch after trench and shell-hole,
but it is only the daft
who think that self-inflicted
injuries hurt less than those
sustained by folk addicted
to being punched on the nose
or greeting mutilation
welcomingly for the sake
of glory and the nation.
The wounds and scars that ache
the worst, and go on aching,
are from blows delivered by
oneself; there's no mistaking
that sly pain, and, if you cry,
you cannot expect a breath
of sympathy; you will find
no healing of any kind
till he comes who began it
all, and cures all, Doctor Death.

The Wrong of Spring

Oh, this risen beauty, treacherous and cold,
Concealing in yellow sleeves its glittering knives
Intended for the tender parts of coves
Who are too old
To dance on green a lithe white measure now,
It is unbearable – well, almost so.

And we grey inconsolables remain
Immured in winter's club; each holds his card
Of membership for which he's overpaid,

187

And through the window
See daffodils and girls, recalling how
We too walked golden there so long ago.

We dare not venture out; the knives are sharp;
The wind, the flowers, those limbs so delicate,
Yes, even they can pierce the faltering heart;
And we are prudent men
Not warmed by dreams of our lost Aprils, nor
By how we longed to be club-members then.

Our Father

'I was surprised,' my old friend said one night
As we sat there with our drinks and talked
Companionably of things
Linked by threads as thin as our grey hairs,
'I was surprised to find, when I was quite
Grown up – ready to try my wings –
Not that I hated Dad,
But there were many lads who claimed that they loved
    theirs.

'My father really thought that he was God
And sat upon his own right hand –
So that it couldn't see
What tricks the left was up to: sinister
Was just the word for what that member did.
He seriously claimed to be
Pure beyond reproach:
Pure hell the punishments he would administer.

'A sadist, liar and a fornicator
And, worst of all, strict temperance man,
The perfect hypocrite.
Not once do I recall a single word
Of kindness or affection from dear pater:
He was, in short, a total shit.
I never saw him smile
Far less laugh out; oh yes, he was a walking turd.

'Perhaps you think that I exaggerate,
Oedipal loathing has upset
My power to see the man?
Not so: I saw him on his dying bed.
I feel for him more pity now than hate;
I wish him peace. He lay in sweat
And silence for nine days,
Then spoke. "I'm sorry!" were the last words that he said.'

Wish You Were Here

The sun's brass shout is muffled by a wad
Of woolly cloud; this wind has wandered from
An earlier mood, say March.
Its energy has no good humour in it.
It floats a shiftier beach a foot above
The firm original,
Insinuates grit in sandwiches and eyes.

In spite of drifting sand, a muted sun,
We all, in our own ways, apply ourselves
To this, our annual task
Of relaxation or more active pleasure.
A yellow plastic ball bobs out to sea;
Young men with muscles prance
Or pose and touch their bulges pensively.

They do not touch my heart, as children do
Whose serious play is wholly lacking that
Self-consciousness that robs
The body's speech of plausibility.
The children ply their spades with diligence
Or dare the slavering waves.
Unknowingly they mould a memory.

The old are unselfconscious too. The wives
Lie back in deck-chairs, eyes tight-shut against
The wicked wind-blown sand.
Their husbands, bald and bracered, sleep until
The pubs renew their welcome, opening

Their doors like loving arms.
Incontinent and feline, seagulls yaup.

And I, who feel I'm neither young nor old
But obsolete, lie on my bed of beach
And feel the sabulous wind
Spreading its thin coarse sheeting over me.
Ambition, hope, desire are cold. I'll stay
For sand to cover me,
Forgotten culture, not worth digging for.

A Circle of Animals and Children

The first animals spoke in the darkness;
Comforting. They uttered very simple words.
Their fur was familiar and their names
Easy to say. They had small eyes that never blinked.

I loved them, if love is being grateful
For their presence in my bed. This could be so.
They never disobeyed and seldom hid –
Teddy, Bunny and Jumbo with hide of velvet.

Next came the animals who could not speak:
The hamster, rabbits and cocker-spaniel
That looked like a black compassionate judge
Who would sentence no one. I loved him and liked most
   dogs.

Until my first child was born. This changed things.
All my delighted tenderness, fear and joy
Were concentrated through a burning-glass
Of gratitude and awe. I had no love to spare.

I watched my son, saw him learning to love,
The first and fumbling rehearsal conducted
Among my old, almost forgotten pets
With chronically astonished eyes. He spoke with them.

And later, predictably, I saw him
Banish the animals who had shared his bed
And take to his heart a brisk terrier,
Giving the little yapper love for a season.

Until his first child was born. This changed things.
He left, with wife and baby, for New Zealand.
Later, my other children went away.
I was alone with time for animals again.

They are company through the winter evenings
By the fireside. They walk with me in summer.
I spoil them, solicit their tolerance,
My mongrel – black dog – and the animal of death.

Our Pale Daughters

When our pale daughters move in lamplight
Their long hair, black or golden, flows
And waterfalls on shoulders, eyes

Contemplate a time and place
That never was nor will be, whose
Trees bear bells and dreams of veils.

But when our daughters move in daylight,
Their locks dammed up in scarves, they see
No trees or white lace in their street

But prams and dustbins, stubbled chins,
And hear cold choristers with lungs
Of steel singing of piston-rings.

Night Music

Darkness and the unceasing sigh and hush
Of the sea, sleepless below the bedroom window,
The slow and gentle molestation of the waves
Fretting the sand and pebbles, soothe the ear
Dismissing grit and sniggers of the day's
Vexations and perplexities, drowning
Those last invaders of the heart's repose.
   And then,
From the room beneath, the punctual music wakes:
Loved and loving hands walk thoughtful on the keys
As mother plays. Now sky and sea are wild
With bells and stars as bright arpeggios rise;
Silver scales – crunched moonlight – move in shoals
Beyond blind nets that reach into the dark.
The child swims through the window into sleep.

The Cowboy of the Western World

He rode into town one summer evening
As the bloodshot clouds presided over
The end of day, the leisurely pacing
Of decent citizens, most of them sober,
Though many intent on altering that.

He left his mount outside the saloon
And swaggered inside and called for liquor;
He felt that every eye in the room
Was fixed on his dangerous challenging figure;
He tilted the insolent brim of his hat.

His pants were tight and his heels were high,
Though his shirt was a temperate but sexy black.
He lit a cigarette, took another slug of rye,
Glanced round the joint then casually
Checked on his weapon with a nonchalant pat.

He stayed for an hour, but met no challenge.
Outside, the sky wore badges and spurs
Enough for a posse; a luminous orange
Spilt light on the sidewalk. When the shooting occurred
He was snug and dreaming in his bachelor flat.

Right Dress

Slither of silk like temperate water over
The humps of hips, delicious as a drink;
Lace froths on flesh as lightly as a shadow
And nylon shines, a sly translucent pink.

Next, the sheer stockings smoothing over knees,
Stretched taut at calves and plumping full of thighs.
The curtains at the bedroom windows press
Back, like constables, the straining eyes.

The sweet and private ritual of dressing,
This beautifying of the self, creates
A painless sense of being loved and loving,
A perfect equilibrium of states.

The frock floats like a fall of mist and roses
Over soft secrets, desiring and desired;
Before the wardrobe mirror gravely poses
Archibald Fullblood, Brigadier, retired.

The Poet's Tongue

With industry and patience he must bring
Together his great arsenal which stores
Blunt cudgels with the very latest thing,
Romantic swords employed in ancient wars
And complicated engines needing great
Skill and practice to manipulate.

And he must travel far in time and space,
Find loot in labs and factories, soil and sand,
Arrange his plunder in well-ordered ways
So what he needs will always be at hand.
And yet, possessing such elaborate means,
He'll constantly invite a puzzled stare
By using – not his intricate machines –
But bits of flint that hit the target square.

One That Got Away

I was alone, desultory line
Drifting in slow-pacing water
When suddenly I felt the tug,
Saw silver twitch in darkness shine
For no longer than a quarter
Of a second. Again, small jerk and drag

And momentary glitter: I knew I could
With skill and vigilance hook this one.
But then I was distracted by
Commotion on the bank where stood
Friendly idlers in the sun
Who, laughing, waved to catch my eye.

Politeness, or a slippier wish
To be esteemed, persuaded me
To greet them, swap some casual chat,
And then they left; but now my leash
Of line was slack; my prey slipped free.
I knew I could not win it back.

I wonder if another man
More serious, luckier than I,
Is richer for my careless loss,
As here in *The Angler's Rest* I stand,
Arms and tongue too short to try
To show how vast and marvellous it was.

UNCOLLECTED POEMS
1975–80

Two Variations on an Old Theme

I

Winter returns, white with patient rage;
Its peckish minutes nibble at my skin.
I am not old enough to cope with age.

Most men mature, grow stoical and sage,
Don't flinch when, as the knives of ice go in,
Winter returns, white with patient rage.

But somehow I have never reached the stage
Where I can take time's punches on the chin;
I am not old enough to cope with age.

No games divert, no medicines assuage
The pain and fear; my overcoat is thin.
Winter returns, white with patient rage.

Mordacious winds come howling from their cage.
There's no escape, I'm pinioned by their din.
I am not old enough to cope with age.

The little space left on the final page
Attends words like 'deceased' and 'next of kin'.
Winter returns, white with patient rage;
I am not old enough to cope with age.

II

It has to come, I know, but I need time;
I'm not prepared; I've got so much to learn.

I couldn't face it with a face like mine.

The soldier is conditioned by his trade:
He treats the whole thing as a family joke.
The airman tells me it's a piece of cake.

The gaunt religious welcomes it with joy,
Flings wizened arms ecstatically wide
And swallow-dives into the awful void.

Gangsters, cops and nurses every day
Observe its policies without a qualm;
For them the end's the last move in a game.

But wait a minute! What about the kids,
Twelve-year-olds, scared aunties, timorous clerks?
All have faced it; surely they've no tricks

I'm unaware of that could make it seem
Less terrible? No, no, yet most have made
Astonishingly little fuss indeed.

If they can take it, there's no reason why
I shouldn't too. I'll be okay, I know –
Oh Christ, I'll always be too young to die!

Old Man in Winter

The cold time again. The seasons dwindle.
The years contract, and yet each day
Is just as long as past days were,
But not the years. Spring flirts and flaunts,
Impatient for the consummation
Of the Summer. It comes,
Is passionate, then languorous,
Heavy with scent and sleep before
The Fall's inexorable tristesse.
But now the winter moils.
My fire is almost out;
The soft white ash still holds

A little warmth though I perceive
No visible sign of heat,
No sanguine glow. The hour is late.
I hear the brawling wind outside
Shaking the branches of the dying elm,
And I am shaken, too,
But subtly, not as the tree is thrashed
By the gale's insensible rage;
A dudgeon more malevolent
And sly perturbs my brittle boughs,
And I, unlike the elm,
Know that my branches shake, and why.
The room grows cold. Now I must climb
To where sleep, wife-like waits.
Another day dies like the fire.
Succeeding seasons shrink.
The years contract, and yet each day
Is just as long as past days were.
Tomorrow may wear snow. I hope
It will, though no more than a tree
Could I say why I wish this to be so.

Reformed Drunkard

He wakes in a new world and wears new eyes;
His tongue is sweet, as if all night
Summer rain has been his drink
And has rinsed his gaze. His razor moves
With confidence around a temperate smile.
He puts on laundered clothing, knows that vigour
Is stored like legal tender in his purse;
His motion is exemplary, moreover
His wife now wears a different face.
That stare of apprehension and reproach
Has disappeared; she looks on him with pride,
Especially when at dinner he declines
Without perceptible distress or effort
His host's warm invitation to take wine.
She smiles, approving, with the smallest nod;
He is her favourite child. The vicar, too,

Approves, has even stated publicly
That he admires the man, regards
His abstinence as evidence of courage.
The vicar is wrong. Courage or its absence
Is irrelevant.
                    Sometimes, not only in his sleep,
He dreams about that other world, returns
To shiver in a grey chemise of sweat.
What he feels is mainly fear, but something more –
Mixed in that pathogenic stew
Are flavourings of desire, relief, regret.
Something warns him not to analyse
The potency and quantity of each.
He walks a straight line very carefully,
Step by step, day by day. It will lead,
He believes, where all lines lead,
But that is not
For him to think about, far less to say.

A Partial View

It floods the world, it surges like the sea,
Unnecessary suffering that men
Inflict on other men, and equally
Ubiquitous the pleasure felt by them,
Those specialists in pain who busily
Immerse themselves in grave research to find
New strains and modes to benefit their kind.
Steve Biko's agony was someone's joy
Who found delight in witnessing a mind
And body, both superior to his own,
Broken and wasted wantonly. Each slug
That smashes through the knee-cap of a boy
In Ulster is a sweet addictive drug
To him who grasps the gun; the scream or moan
Is transcendental music to the thug.
Neat bureaucrats of systematic death,
To outward view impassive and stone-eyed,
Were tremulous and sticky underneath
Smart tunics when they practised genocide.
When hanging by the neck was used to cure

The anti-social habits of the poor
And solve the problems of the men who kill
From passion, lunacy or greed, forever,
A mob of eager aspirants would fill
The market-place petitioning for the prize,
The office of Chief Executioner.
We live in violent times and always did.
The history of the globe is soaked in blood
And excrement, and we do not improve.
My local paper recently described
An incident in a Wessex seaside town:
A little boy, five years of age, was found
Howling in a public lavatory.
His prick had been cut off, this surgery
Performed by one young man assisted by
Two comrades who held fast their helpless patient.
The operation done, they speedily
Departed on their rasping motorbikes.
This scene poisons the sick imagination:
Their laughter darkening the afternoon
Like burning tyres. Black stench. Say what you like,
There's not a day that breaks that is not strewn
With pain and wreckage, smeared with blood and pus,
Reeling with rage and blind brutality.
Of course I know this is a partial view
That fails to take account of those, like us,
Who represent the great majority,
The decent who deplore such cruelty.
For every act of violence we could find
A score of altruistic deeds performed;
Most people, fundamentally, are kind
And hate to see the humblest creature harmed.
If true it is quite understandable,
This pity for the poor, solicitude
For those who are deprived and are unable
To help themselves; in offering them aid
We re-affirm the human; our response
Is rational and we are sane, although
Precariously so. How can we know
That our apparently well-balanced stance
Is set upon foundations firmly laid?
Who knows what levelling stroke is, even now,
Being planned by human evil or the weather?

Indignation may have steamed the glass,
Our vision lost the power of seeing how
Atrocities need not dress up in leather;
Not every yobbo mutters broken type
Nor swings a fist with knuckles made of brass.
The public outrage cannot be concealed;
There is a kind of candour, though not willed,
In blatant executions in broad daylight
That might deflect attention from the plight
Of tortured victims in quiet drawing-rooms,
From libraries where prisoners are grilled
By soft-voiced experts, ruthless and polite,
And from those murders in the afternoons
To chink of teacup and the chime of spoons.
It drowns the children's weeping in the night.
God help us, who are we to act the judge
When fantasies of vengeance warm the blood
And we are gripped by passions we condemn?
We live in violent times and always did.
Tenants of this universal slum
We clamour for a more salubrious home
Yet know that what we are is where we live
And vice-versa. Mankind has not become
Much wiser in its umpteenth million year,
Or gentler, or more generous or just;
More sly perhaps and hypocritical.
Napalm and laser-beam replace the spear,
The ignorant plague gives way to clever dust,
Our language laced by words like 'overkill'.
No nation yet has ever won a war
Yet wars are fought despite the monstrous cost;
Some murders it would seem are ethical.
What is there then to do or say about it?
We could of course anticipate the end
Which mocks all striving yet without which life
Would be unthinkable and all its treasures
Dross, the oldest enemy and friend,
Meet him by way of bullet, gas or knife
Or kinder overdose; but these are measures
Providing answers only to the blind,
Completing the mad circle of destruction.
The rich can build elaborate defences,
Surround themselves with various distractions,

Enlist a corps of connoisseurs and ponces
To cater for their still discerning senses
Or, less sophisticated, they can choose
The blurred and stumbling cul-de-sac of booze
To join at last the swelling exodus
Of immigrants who daily put to sea
Bound for the Happy Isles and lives of bliss,
Utopias of total lunacy.
Our graveyards and insane asylums bear
Plain witness to the popularity
Of stratagems like these. And as for prayer,
The chance of supernatural intercession
Must be at least unlikely, and indeed
Why should God – whose notions of compassion
Have often seemed ironic – intercede?
So what is left? The little consolations
Of human love? Take her to the seaside,
Stand by the window in the sweet night air
And promise to be true to one another.
Yes, why not? But there is something more.
While you stand there swapping vows and kisses,
Hearing the ocean's long withdrawing roar,
Remember that you could be listening to
More varied music than that salty cadence.
When sick and hot from too much of the world
Immerse yourself in pure consoling art,
Press forehead to the coolness of a fugue,
Invite the wordless message to unfold
Its insubstantial scrolls of filigree.
There's always music. But should you wish to hear
The less transcendent language of the tongue
Then choose the harmonies of poetry
Which builds small barricades against confusion;
Or better, be a dancer at their wedding,
Discover there a nostrum for despair,
An unexpected joy that drowns foreboding,
And find yourself, with almost no surprise,
Accepting everything, rejoicing even
That all is as it is, not otherwise;
Though when the music fades and meanings blur,
The hordes remass, you turn again to her
To whom you might conceivably be true
As she, against the odds, might be to you.

WINTERLUDE
1982

Mastering the Craft

To make the big time you must learn
The basic moves: left jab and hook,
The fast one-two, right-cross; the block
And counter-punch; the way to turn
Opponents on the ropes; the feint
To head or body; uppercut;
To move inside the swing and set
Your man up for the kill. But don't
Think that this is all; a mere
Beginning only. It is through
Fighting often you will grow
Accomplished in manoeuvres more
Subtle than the textbooks know:
How to change your style to meet
The unexpected move that might
Leave you open to the blow
That puts the lights out for the night.

The same with poets: they must train,
Practise metre's footwork, learn
The old iambic left and right,
To change the pace and how to hold
The big punch till the proper time,
Jab away with accurate rhyme;
Adapt the style or be knocked cold.
But first the groundwork must be done.
Those poets who have never learnt
The first moves of the game, they can't
Hope to win.
                    Yet here comes one,
No style at all, untrained and fat,
Who still contrives to knock you flat.

The Bombing of the Café de Paris, 1941

Snakehips, the bandleader, wore a gallant grin,
A clip of white cartridges; he and the boys
Tapped natty polished toes to keep the time
Of tango, quickstep, foxtrot, blues and swing;
The basement of the place was deep and safe,
No other-ranks or bombs would be let in.

A boy in Air Force blue danced with his mother;
A sub-lieutenant stroked his girl's silk knee;
Caressing lights lay soft on hair and flesh,
Bright on badges, deep in polished leather.
A major of the Black Watch called for Scotch
And winked at his admiring younger brother.

Oh Johnny, Oh Johnny, how you can love,
That was the song they liked. They could forget
That loving wasn't all that he must do:
Oh Johnny, Oh Johnny, heavens above –
And in the hidden heavens the siren's wailing
Mourned over London and the shattered dove.

But no one there could hear. The music gushed
And wine corks popped like children's wooden guns.
No warning when the bomb came bursting in,
Huge knuckle-dustered fist that struck and crushed
Furniture of wood and flesh; the bang's
Enormous shadow paled; the place was hushed.

Some light remained, and from the ceiling came
Floating down a fine cosmetic dust
That settled softly on the hair and skin
Of the sailor's girl, who, wholly without shame,
Sprawled in ripped clothes, one precious stocking gone
And with it half her leg. No one would blame

Her carelessness for once, and if they did
She would not care. The sailor lay beneath
Dark flood of fallen curtain, quiet and still,

As if he rested on the ocean bed.
The airman's mother sat upon the floor,
Crooned comfort to her child's deaf cradled head.

Snakehips had put away his grin forever.
Music might return, but he would not.
The kilted major found another drink
Then carried out his brother, like an order,
Joining the stunned survivors in the street,
Sick from their meeting with the dark marauder.

While, down below, a woman lay and saw
A man approaching through the powdery gloom;
She could not move trapped limbs. 'Rescue!' she thought
As by her side he knelt upon the floor,
Reached out to finger at her neck and take
Her string of pearls in one triumphant paw.

Outside, the sirens once again composed
A mocking dirge above the crouching town;
Along the blackened streets on nervous wheels
The blinkered ambulances gently nosed,
Ferrying cool instruments of mercy.
An incident of war was almost closed.

War Movie Veteran

You can't tell me a thing that I don't know
About combat, son. I reckon I've seen them all
On the big screen or TV, the late-night show
Or Sunday matinee. I'm what you'd call
An old campaigner; some of them I've seen
Four-five times maybe. I've got so's I
Can tell for sure which ones among that green
Platoon of rookies are the guys to die.
You know the sensitive and quiet kid
Who can't stand rough stuff, says his prayers at night
And never cusses? He's got to wind up dead
But not before we've seen that he can fight
And he's got guts. He ain't afraid to kill
Once the chips are down. The one to see

Turn really yellow is the loud-mouthed mother
That talks like he ain't scared of nothing; he
Will go, expendable. So will the other,
The black guy who's as good as you or me,
And the Jew that's seeking vengeance for his brother.
The comedian – the hero's buddy – could
Come through the battle in one piece or not:
He's only there for laughs, that's understood
By veterans like me. The hero's got
To be alive and kicking at the end.
The one I really like – you know the guy –
The tough top-sergeant, nobody's best friend,
His favourite meal is bullets, blood and rye;
The Krauts he's killed is anybody's guess.
He's made of steel and leather, but you'll find
That he can be the soul of gentleness
With scared old ladies, babies and the blind
Pooch whose master's been knocked off. But never
Think the guy's gone soft: back under fire
He's just as cold and murderous as ever,
He's everything a General could desire.
He'll come through safe okay.
                              I tell you, son,
I could write out the list of casualties
Long before the battle has begun.
I've seen it all. I know the way it is
And got to be. Well, that's what you could call
The human side, psychology I guess.
The other stuff – a cinch to learn it all
In half-a-dozen battles, maybe less.
It takes no time to get the different ranks:
Enlisted men and noncoms, officers,
The names of hardware, ammunition, tanks
And how the thing is planned. You'll think at first
That war is chaos, howl of bullet, shell
And bomb; flashes and thunder as they burst,
Flying shit, hot jig-saw bits of hell.
Not so. It's all worked out before the start.
It's choreographed, like in a dance, okay?
You get to know the pattern. War's an art,
It's one I understand. There ain't no way
That you'll find anyone to tell you more
Than me about realities of war.

Popular Mythologies

Not all these legends, I suppose.
Are total lies:
Thousands of Welshmen at a rugby match
Sometimes surprise
By singing more or less in tune;
Quite a lot
Of bullies may be cowards, though too many
Are not.
It would make sense to revise most saws
About the tall:
For instance I've found that the bigger they are
The harder *I* fall.
Everyone knows about the Scots
And their miserliness,
The way they repeatedly cry 'Hoots mon!'
Though I must confess
I have often been embarrassed by their largesse
And not one
In my hearing has ever said 'Hoots mon'.
Of course the Jews
Are very easy to pin down:
They amuse
With comic names like Izzy, Solly,
Benny, Moses,
And like the Scots they're very mean
And have big noses.
The trouble is you can't be sure
That people with small
Noses and names like Patrick, Sean,
Peter or Paul
Are always to be trusted in fiscal matters.
Not at all.
And what of the famous cockney wit?
You'd hear greater
Intelligence, humour and verbal flair
From an alligator
Than the average East End Londoner.
And suicides?
Those who talk about it never do it?
What of the brides

Of darkness, Sexton, Woolf and Plath?
And those others
Chatterton, Beddoes, Hemingway, Crane?
This band of brothers
All descanted on the mortal theme.
But why go on thus?
Easy, but waste of effort to fill
An omnibus.
Surprising though how people still
Swallow all this.
Prejudiced stuff – not us, of course,
Oh no, not us.

Protest Poem

It was a good word once, a little sparkler,
Simple, innocent even, like a hedgerow flower,
And irreplaceable. None of its family
Can properly take over: *merry* and *jolly*
Both carry too much weight; *jocund* and *blithe*
Were pensioned off when grandpa was alive.
Vivacious is a flirt; she's lived too long
With journalists and advertising men.
Spritely and *spry*, both have a nervous tic.
There is no satisfactory substitute.
It's down the drain and we are going to miss it.
No good advising me to go ahead
And use the word as ever. If I did
We know that someone's bound to smirk or snigger.
Of all the epithets why pick on this one?
Some deep self-mocking irony
Or blindfold stab into the lexicon?
All right. Then let's call heterosexuals *sad*,
Dainty for rapists, *shy* for busy flashers,
Numinous for necrophiles, *quaint* for stranglers;
The words and world are mad! I must protest
Although I know my cause is lost.
A good word once, and I'm disconsolate

And angered by this simple syllable's fate:
A small innocence gone, a little Fall.
I grieve the loss. I am not gay at all.

A Look Inside

A castle of stink,
A vast cold oven,
The meat inside
Is going bad slowly;
Stench and clangs
Rule days and nights;
All it contains,
They are all unholy,
They are untouchables.
Their flesh appals
Even themselves;
They cringe inside it
And dream of freedom
Beyond the walls
Where they may sluice
The grime away,
Put on fresh skin
Of their own size.

On the jubilant day
When the gates smile wide
They do not see
The Chief Screw's grin
And his knowledgeable eyes.
'Take care,' he says,
'And wrap up well.
You'll find it cold outside.'

Over the Wall

It was not a dream,
yet something dreamlike came between
the man inside his quivering bag of skin
and all the scraped and naked world,
percussive colours, swirling trees,
that he now floundered in.
He ran
over the gorse, the humped and bristling tufts
that more than once rose up and kicked
his feet wild, skittering in the air.
The bone ground banged into his ribs,
thumped borrowed breath from snarling lungs;
he rose again
and ran and ran and ran,
eyes crackling with hot salt,
heart slamming protestant,
chest pumping past the point where it must burst.
Irons of cramp screwed tighter on his calves
and thighs dragged heaving chains,
but far away, though thickening by the minute,
he heard, behind his own harsh sobs
and rusty whimperings,
the bloodshot cries of hounds.
He ran
until his body fell
broken, hugger-mugger, on the ground.
He could not move.
He might have been
a rock or mound, a fallen trunk,
dead lump of animal.
He lay
until the outraged engines of his breathing eased,
but still he could not move.
Derisive birds clawed silence, and the trusty sun,
in solitary as ever,
beamed behind gold bars.
His eyes bled darkness on their blinds.
And then he heard them moving near,
the shouts and whistles, growling engines,
the open throttles of the hounds,

and nearer yet
until at last they jostled round.
They carried him on shoulders, like a coffin.
His breathing now was sweet and effortless;
eyes stayed shut. No one saw his smile
as he was borne away to freedom
from the cruel exigencies of choice.

Weaker Sex

However courteous and tender, man
Is in the act of love his love's aggressor;
No matter with what softness he began
He'll finish as her merciless oppressor;
And though the woman often seems to be
Happily unwilling to escape him,
And may display more appetite than he,
The simple fact remains: she cannot rape him.
You think he should rejoice that this is true?
Maybe, but there are worse things she can do.

Last Attack

And how are things with you, old-timer,
Still looking down with your paralysed wink?
We've been around for quite a while now;
We are inseparable, I think –
Barring the chance of some appalling
Accident, that is.
                    I know
More than once I've introduced you
In some peculiar circles, though
You've not complained, seemed generally
Quite happy not to let me down.
We're friends, we make good sense together,
You the verb and I the noun.
I understand. You're getting older.

Well, so am I. But let me make
One more demand then never another –
A last campaign for old time's sake.
Stick up for me tonight old buddy,
Just one more big attack; I'll never
Send you in to fight again.
I know I've promised that quite often;
This time it's absolutely true.
Okay? Good lad. Let's get back in there.
I know I can rely on you.

Winterlude

The lamp is out. Part the curtains, see
Starlight, the gleam of flutes, hear silver ghosts
Call over polar meadows to the glee
Of moon, with taut and luminous skin, who boasts
Percussively, while poplars, like huge ferns,
Spill shadows on the eatable crust of snow,
Blue smoky plumes that intermelt below.
In the far wood the electric owl burns.
The garden privet wears an ermine stole;
Unlathered side of the pine is black as coal.

Leave the curtains open. Turn and see
How, in your room, the furnishings now seem
To rhyme, with altered iconography:
Fluted candlestick and mirror-gleam,
The watchful clock, with folded wings, which stares
At phantom branches latticing the walls,
Nursing like eggs its unreleased wild calls,
The uncracked shells of silence. Your pillow wears
Fresh snow. Your dreams, that the woods of sleep conceal,
Are frail before the mystery of the real.

Of Love and Poetry

When you are in love you want to write –
If anything at all – in verse, not prose.
The same when in a very dangerous plight
Like war or plague, or when enormous doors
Close on captivity or sunless grief.

Not because you want to orchestrate
Your fear and longing in applauded art;
Real love feels no compulsion to inflate
Its properties in rhetoric or smart
Conceits. It seeks a different relief.

Extravagant hyperbole is fine
For those who wish to demonstrate their skill
In verbal cunning and concinnity,
But honest love adopts another line:
Its voice is never hectoring or shrill.

It would eliminate those furnishings
That are not strictly functional, expel
All that is merely decorative until
The poem owns a cell's simplicity
Or rifle's classic beauty that can kill.

On Leave: May 1916

And now, at last, after the swollen journey,
Black stubbled hilarity, tobacco reek,
Each sweating hour tumescent with anticipation,
Arrival happens: creak of garden gate,
Fluting and flutters of welcome, kisses and tears,
Sweet and delicate as pomegranate seeds.
Then out of the heat into the shadowed hall;
Dump kit-bag, rifle, webbing; promissory kiss;
Alone, strip off the khaki itch, stiff wool,
The hunks of boot; loll in fragrant mist
Of steam, relax in healing water poured

By those white hands which have, for anxious months,
When idle, clung for comfort each to each.

Listen. Hear the distant tinkling talk
Of cups and saucers, spoons, as feminine
As silver thimbles; those remembered things,
Fragile domesticities, so frail
These symbols; their trivial chatter a language
Of brittle leaves and petals, a simple grammar,
Which voice of barrack-square or trench would shatter.

Now cleansed and dressed in seven-day light disguise
He hides away harsh garments of his calling,
Brown bandages, the leather, steel and brass,
And, looming in the summer parlour, tries
To hide big battering hands, temper his voice
To speakings like breeze-questioned foliage.
He waits.

He has grown used to long and watchful waitings.
When sunlight is withdrawn and dark moves in,
Pickets of stars are posted in the skies;
The scattered natural musics of the day
Are drawn together, patterned as she plays;
The piano smiles beneath her thoughtful hands,
Those clever, sad and crushable bones.

Lamplight spills pools of gold on polished oak,
Bestows a glimmer on her lowered head;
The music falls, lingering, drop by drop,
Into a brimming silence. Her head stays bowed,
And, though he cannot see her eyes, he knows
Their little glitter contradicts the sly
And pensive disavowal of her lips.

All lamps are out; the clock tacks down the dark.
They climb to where the unsurprisable bed
Attends, composed and tolerant witness of
Pale preparations for the tremulous night.
He sees, with awe and pain and gratitude,
In veiling starlight, her quick nakedness
Flash, slender, incandescent, vulnerable,
Before they lie together, move and cling.

In deeper dark he lies in one man's land,
Hears his own voice cry, wounded; far away
The barrage of big guns begins; the flares
Illuminate the sky and show, below,
The crazy scribblings of barbed wire, the fat
Bulges of stacked sand-bags, shattered trees,
The livid stripped forked branches, tangled hair;
Crushed underfoot, the crimson flowers are pulped.
Then rain begins to fall, the dark saps flood;
Salt stings on her bruised mouth; her tears, and his,
Are slow, small rain on dust that turns to mud.

Lover's Moon

'Love is always either waxing or waning'

> From the code of laws common to all the Courts of
> Love in the English, the French, and the Provençal
> dominions of the twelfth century.

Now, at the full, the luminous white face,
A public clock at midnight wiped clean of hands
And numbers, mesmerizes; that mad and beautiful face.
It is sovereign; we kneel before it, feeling awe,
Feeling dread and joy; each grateful breath worships it,
And when we rise we dance, as the waves dance.

It does not stay like that. It is always changing.
Time will bite with a pig's crunched tearing bite
A scagging chunk from it. Later, filed down
To a paring, the thin sliver gives almost no light,
It slices the eyeball clean, is acid on the tongue,
And in the cold silence its speech is of darkness.

Sleep Talker

In the early hours of the puny day
Whose eyes still swam with dark
She slowly and quietly spoke,
But not to me.
The man she spoke to was handsome –
She told him so –
I felt bound on principle to disagree
But, in fact, I could not know,
Since she was deep in sleep,
So, whomever she was speaking to,
I was unable to see.
It was in the cold hours before the sky
Had paled at all, the time
When the old and tired and unwanted
So often and so quietly die.

Juan in Limbo

He still has stomach for the enterprise;
It swells and sags. Her bare necessities
Compel, but joylessly. Though he denies
The game's a bore his eyes confess it is;
So does the drowsy slug between his thighs.

He knows exactly how the farce will end.
No longer can there be the least surprise.
He doesn't need another female friend.
He's sick of mouthing sugary half-lies
And playing futile games of let's-pretend.

Never again! Rip up that diet-sheet,
And throw those salves and unguents in the bin,
Wear baggy trousers, slippers for the feet,
Shave once a week and breakfast on straight gin;
Don't give a damn how much or what you eat.

The prospect is magnificent, yet plain,

Simple in the way large visions are;
It glows, a little furnace in the brain
As, sprawling on the back seat of the car,
He feels her hungry mouth come down again.

Nightsong

Tonight the dark is wild:
It thumps on silence with blind fists;
In its head the fog-horns moan.
Out there at sea,
Its rage infects the waves.
They could be strangling deck-hands,
Lambasting bosuns, gulping stewards;
Yet here we are, secure and warm,
Though not entirely dry.

Oh my love, that moistness,
Small sargasso,
The swell and heave and hunger
Will devour, devour.
Dear carnivore, my child, my world,
The night is wild.

Nightflight

It is late. The music has been put to sleep.
Our pillows are unwelcoming as stones,
Small boulders wearing coverlets of snow;
Night's silences have nowhere else to go.
Then, out in the blind, enormous emptiness,
Dark wick of sound is lit, it blackly burns.
Soft drilling starts to probe the nervous ear;
A distant hum, it grows until we hear
Distinct annunciation from a cloud,
But even at full pitch it is not loud,
And very soon declivity begins.

It slides away; dark vacancy once more
Is perfect, brims the universal bowl.
Yet, while no words were uttered from above,
A statement has been made – not one we hoped for,
Nor one to unperplex or to console.

Awakening

Now the drowsy morning sidles
Down the hillside where it idles
In the valley of today.
Each awakes to face the other,
Stares as if upon another,
Neither knowing what to say.

Both survivors of the raging
Tumult of the night's assuaging
Hungers that their feasting fed,
Fixed in stasis of attrition,
Drained of passion and ambition,
Later they will count their dead.

The Witnesses

Phantoms stationed in their places
Watch with white and grieving faces
As the lovers tell their lies;
Soon the need for truth or lying
Passes as the lovers, sighing,
Throw aside their last disguise.

Like two burning candles merging
Bodies melt in one white purging
Till the single flame is dead,
Then the thwarted watchers, weeping,
Slowly turn from that calm sleeping,
Seek a truthful, lonely bed.

An Autumn Love

After a night of love he walks
Along a footpath of the park
Where leaves like flattened starfish spread
Their yellow points upon the dark
And gritty surface underfoot.
The morning is preoccupied;
It hangs frail scarves of mist upon
Branches' knuckles, black as soot.
The sun is stunned. A long wait now
For night and her, but they will come
With frost and stargleam in the sky
Where secret flutes of coldness will
Glitter their elusive tune
And she will spread all seasons on
The bed they tenant, welcoming
With leafmeal scent and taste of stars,
Blue summer heat, white blossoming
Of snow and petal, ice and fruit,
At last his grateful entering.

Simplicities

Now that you have gone
I feel a compulsion to write
not literature but something quite
private, for your eyes only to look upon.

It is good for once,
to ignore the demands of art,
utter simplicities of the heart
and happily become your passionate dunce.

Yet instinct compels
me to accept a formal task;
speech from behind ceremony's mask
might chime with the truth and music of bright bells.

So I have chosen
a syllabic measure this time,
linking these awkward lines with a rhyme-pattern
borrowed from Alfred, Lord Tennyson.

All I wish to do
though is something simple as this:
tell you how I still taste your last kiss,
and say, like any dunce, how much I love you.

Points of View

You called it lovely; it was not to me –
Weak line and gnashing colours – yet I know
You did not falsify what you could see.

A lover took his lute and tried to free
His handcuffed passion; music failed to flow;
You called it lovely; it was not to me.

When I admired the soft fur of the bee
You shrank in fear and prayed that it would go;
You did not falsify what you could see.

You said how musically he murmured, he
Who sounded like a mutilated crow:
You called it lovely; it was not to me.

I praised the green panache of summer's tree,
But you preferred to see it wearing snow;
You did not falsify what you could see.

I knew that we must always disagree.
The night descended, menacing and slow;
You called it lovely; it was not to me.
You did not falsify what you could see.

Some Pictures of the Thirties

The stiff pages turn. Most of the photographs
Are faded now; the air the subjects breathe
Is grey, or amber like weak milkless tea;
A huddle of hunched streets, two cenotaphs,
Burglar's caps and scarves; hard to believe
The child I was lived there in 'thirty-three.

Sepia or grey is what each print allows,
Yet I recall cobbles swimming in gold
As, in blue shimmer, a nodding pony pulled
An ice-cream cart along the hollow street
As chopping paces slowly fell, dead bells
Of hooves that measured Sunday's ritual drowse.

Other Sundays, too: festive processions,
Float of embroidered banners, ribbon-skirl,
Well-scrubbed boys, white ankle-socks of girls;
A kind of holiness in those occasions,
An innocence; the fragrance lingers still,
Drifts through the darkening archives of the skull.

But there were other walks, the long grey marches
In silence, save for a mouth-organ's starved wail,
Towards the specious South of broken promises,
Past black, shut factories and frozen churches –
Hunger and shame with medals, a long, long trail
Into a darkness cold and without torches.

Turn the page quickly, brave faces of the Thirties:
Pale concentrated stares of bantamweights,
Hair centre-parted, greased; their whippet bodies
Lean and white. There were few heavyweights
In British rings and none of them could fight.
Put away the pictures. Turn out the light.

But the flickering ghosts will not at once be quenched.
They stay and, with them, many sounds: laments,
Woodbine-hoarse, for charred disasters – trains,

Dirigibles, bi-planes – and those other musics,
The clang of trams, blunt chime of pony's hooves;
And then these fade. The past lies still, yet moves.

Old Man in Autumn

The browsing wind of Autumn
Riffles through the leaves
With sighs and crepitation
No other sound achieves.

The leaves are dry as parchment,
Construe them for their sense;
They yield an unconsoling
Dark intelligence.

Moors Threnody

No living creature moves, only the skies'
Slow turbulence, the slanting rain that shakes
In sudden gusts and flurries as it rakes
The stubborn grass; no sound except the sighs
Of wind and ceaseless hissing of the rain;
No colour, only varied tones of grey
Against the slate the lowering skies display;
The weather and the landscape speak a pain
That we, not they, must for a while sustain
Until this season break, and see, alone,
Close in the foreground the single hunk of stone,
Bleak cenotaph, and one which bears no name.

In a City Churchyard

It is quite small, no necropolis, this;
A hamlet of mortality, a place
For specialists to visit, library
Of lithic manuscripts displayed on green,
Or what might once have been before the long
Urban plague, grey death, had withered it.
Only three students have come here today:
Old lady, shuffling past in canvas shoes
Attached to unimaginable legs;
Old man who sleeps in methylated peace;
A mongrel dog who studies with his nose
Then lifts an indolent leg to make
Brief annotation on a mossy page.
No one else, unless we should include
The solitary stone angel who attends,
Despite the little insults of the birds
And mottling pox of weathers on its skin,
The promised day when trumpet-calls proclaim
Eternal holiday of white on green,
Take-off for grounded angels who may see,
From glorious perch of sunbeam or star's wrist,
Rejuvenated lady, dancing dog,
The sleeping drinker's dream corporified.

Learning

An August day, the shimmering heat outside
Deepens and cools the shadows in this room;
The sofa purrs, one holy shaft of light
Slants from the window through the velvet gloom
Primed with a million winks in static flight.

The child moves secretly about the house:
It is a place re-made, estranged by absence.
From far away a mournful voice calls out;
A horse's hollow walk drops clops on silence.
Rags are bones the voice appears to shout.

All is mystery. The child climbs the stairs.
He enters his parents' bedroom. Though alone
He feels someone is watching and he hears
The faintest sound of breathing, not his own.
He hesitates, then feels amorphous fears

Recede before a powerful need to know
Or gain at least some inkling of the things
He aches to know. Perhaps the drawer will hold
Some answers to his blindfold questionings:
Open, it smells of something strange and old.

He turns some silk stuff over, a comb, a chain
Of fragile silver; then he sees with shock
Red ugliness that swells and coils like pain.
He shuts the drawer and trembles, feeling sick.
Rags are bones the far voice calls again.

The Unimaginable

Though we rehearse the possible disaster,
Dispose the spectral cast,
With self as master,
To hold the real event at bay,
Dredge from the past
The shape of old catastrophes
To make a stay
Against the murderous furies of today,
Anticipate with vigilance and skill
The worst that accident,
Or evil, will
Devise to cripple limb or mind,
None can invent
Their prophylactic fantasies
To stun or bind
That mortal stalker following close behind.

Advice from Jack Pott

View each production as a blend;
Accept from those prepared to lend,
And know just when to make an end.

Follow my advice: be smart
And don't despise the vulgar mart;
There never was much bread in art.

But I'll admit a touch of sham –
Though I've been careful not to ham –
Has made me what today I am:

Financial health, and mental, stable,
Famed for my cellar and my table;
In more demand than those more able.

I have some enemies, I grant,
Who shout their insults, bluster, rant;
I just keep working like an ant.

You see, I've known right from the start,
The muses – every one's a tart:
They want your money, not your art.

They can be fumbled, pinched and pawed
By anyone not overawed:
They double-cross the ones they wed.

You're bound, at first, sometimes to stumble,
And if you take a proper tumble,
Heep-wise rise – be very 'umble.

Well, I've enjoyed our little chat –
I wonder where I put my hat –
What's that damned waiter grinning at?

Youth, Age and Poetry: A Dialogue

'What right have you to judge my poems, old man!'
He cried, eyes scintillant with youth and rage,
'I write in my heart's blood! I am sincere!
I speak the truth about my pain and passion,
Such torment you've forgotten at your age.'
The old man smiled. 'That's neither here nor there.'

'Poetry,' the boy exclaimed, 'unfolds like leaves.
Keats said it and you must admit he knew.
Its factory is the heart and not the head,
The intellect invariably deceives,
A lyric is as innocent as dew!'
'Keats didn't mean quite that,' the old man said.

'What was his meaning then? I'd like to hear!'
The old man spoke: 'The poem's seed will never
Be explained, but Keats well knew that true
Art is always wrought with skill and care,
That poets must be slippery and clever:
That's what I think he knew, or think I do.'

Blenkinsop's Survival Song

The strongest swimmers have been known to drown;
Ambition often sends them too far out;
Rich food is fine but I can't keep it down.

I stay in careful shade while others brown,
Sip water, never spirits, wine or stout;
The strongest swimmers have been known to drown.

Some men are verbal; I'm a common noun;
I moderate my voice and never shout;
Rich food is fine, but I can't keep it down.

Provoked, I'll answer with a shrug or frown
And never throw my meagre weight about;
The strongest swimmers have been known to drown.

Let others strive for banquets of renown,
I never was a natural Queen's Scout;
Rich food is fine, but I can't keep it down.

I'll never win applause as prince or clown,
But I'll avoid the pox, DTs and gout;
The strongest swimmers have been known to drown;
Rich food is fine, but I can't keep it down.

On this May Morning

Dubieties of mist
have been resolved,
branches glitter.
Delicacies of green
unblur, are crisp and clean;
it is a morning to devour.

I drink cool air,
taste earth and crocuses,
eyes are rinsed with dew.
I breakfast on birdsong.
The morning news is ancient
and astonishing.

I am spring-healed
and move *allegramente*
although I know
that not far down the street
they mutter round the pot
who have not lost one yet.

I know, but knowledge sits
in a room in my head
and does not stir.
I lock the door,
decide on this May morning
to stay alive for ever.

Farewell Performance

I know that I'm squeezed dry, an empty skin,
All juices spent. If I go now
Departure will not leave an absence in
The place where once I grew
Plump with songs that only I could sing.
This will not do.

It's all been said: no point in going on,
Trying once more to whistle out
The animals of menace and of fun,
Beasts that would snarl and bite,
The cuddlies, and the other bristly one
That wore the night.

No harking back to glittering bits of glass,
Red and emerald in the sand,
Splinters of innocence in the summer grass,
First hard-on, hot in hand,
Rigor vitae, symptom of disease
With but one end.

And love like a fresh, expensive cigarette,
First drag delicious, glowing till
It greyed to ash, was dropped and then stamped out;
I learnt, too late, it killed.
Addicted helplessly to smoke and sex
I've made my will.

I promise: no more fights of any kind,
Not gloves and formal, British, fair;
Nor belting brutish, boot, or what's-to-hand;

I don't think I could bear
More blurts of blood, teeth chattering on the ground.
I've had my share.
Of slobbering bugles, too; the pounding dark,
Spoiled blankets stiff at dawn with rime
Of children never to be born: the work
Of killing at that time
Was quite respectable: one heard no talk
Of guilt or crime.

I swear I'll write no more. It's all been said.
I'll down my pen and say goodnight.
I'm glad there's no one waiting in my bed;
I'd better douse the light.
No more parades of syllables – I'm glad –
At least … no more tonight.

FUNERAL GAMES
1987

In Memoriam PAL, 2.12.85

I heard the news at one o'clock,
Formal from the radio;
The room seemed sharply cold as though
The air itself had suffered shock.

I was surprised by how those words,
So calmly voiced, could penetrate
The idling heart and resonate
Like softly falling minor thirds.

We met each other once, that's all,
Nearly twenty years ago.
We were not close and yet I know
His death-day stretched beneath a pall

Of melancholy that would leave
Something of its gloom behind,
A broken cord, half-lowered blind,
Although we may forget we grieve.

Of all that happened on that day
Of snivelling December rain
One thing chiefly chimes again:
I did not weep or curse or pray,

But petulantly cried aloud,
'I do not want him to be dead!'
He would have smiled to hear this said,
If he had heard from some high cloud.

Yet I believe that smile would be,
Although ironic, kindly too,
For who would approbate the true
Voice of feeling more than he?

Funeral Games

The slow, black bell seems still to nod, its shadow
Trembles in the gloom, a musky perfume
Faint in the ear and mingling with the sweet
Blue smoky exequies and far receding chop
Of plodding hooves as she again goes in
Through their familiar door and moves inside
The still shocked house. She visits each dazed room
Leaving till last his favourite one – his books,
So many, everywhere, as if, progenitive,
They multiplied and spilled from shelves and chairs;
The recorded Brandenburgs, the piano-lid
Still raised and on the music-rest the Liszt
Consolation Number Three, the pages cold,
And, underneath the window, on his desk
Pencils and speechless sheets of lined A4
With one apart on which a few words walk,
A poem, perhaps, a letter to *The Times*;
It does not matter now. She hoped to touch
And be consoled by something of him here
But nothing can dissolve or penetrate
The robe of ice her heart elects to wear;
These things, his toys, important trivialities,
The best of him maybe, but only toys,
As he and she might be the artefacts
And toys of hands from which they have been dropped,
Once greatly loved and cared for, but not now,
Left in different rooms to feed on dust.

Candle Reflections

I

A yellow whisper in the still midnight,
A single syllable, inverted heart,
Bright petal glimmering behind dark glass,
Its thick white stem unseen by the watcher
Who stands beneath the elm in the lane,

His eyes eager for the arranged message
Of warning or promise: 'Go. Keep away.
He is here!' or 'Come now, oh my love. Yes. Come!'

II

On a summer morning a periwigged forebear
Would see on his desk in the sun's brightness
Among litter of manuscripts, pens and pipes
His nocturnal helpmeet, now exhausted,
Sunk to its chest in its melted swoon,
Squat in its holder, small glazed ruff,
The night's work done. Now in dark cupboards
And dusty drawers they repose like dead brides.

III

Remembered marriage of honey and wax,
Conjunction of sweetness and light, gold halo-ing
The child's fair head at sleeping time,
White presences on silver occasions,
Star-flowering in bell's breath on snowy pasture,
Celebrations at commemorative festivals,
Their tears silent, warm and lenitive,
Cooling to translucent blebs, like pearls.

IV

Their element has always been religious. They
Proliferate in cathedrals, scenting the gloom;
They pray, in chapels, prayers of extreme
Simplicity; their aspect delights children,
It consoles the old; they invigilate
The explanations of the dead, stand sentinel
About the draped catafalque. When power fails
And all the lights go out, they will be needed.

Apple Poem

Take the apple from the bowl or bough
Or kitchen table where in gloom it glows
And you will sense, mysteriously, how
Its fragrant and substantial presence throws
A shadow shape of this one's red and green,
Whatever it may be – Rose of Bern,
Spice Pippin, Golden Russet, Hawthorn Dean –
Across the mind and then you may discern
Through every sense the quintessential fruit,
Perfected properties all apples own,
In this platonic shadow; absolute
This pleasing thing that you alone have grown.

Beneath the apple's skin, its green or gold,
Yellow, red or streaked with varied tints,
The white flesh tempts, sharp or sweet, quite cold.
Its blood is colourless; scent teases, hints
At othernesses that you can't define;
The taste of innocence, so slow to fade,
Persists like memory. This fruit is wine
And bread; is eucharistic. It has played
Its role in epics, fairy-tales, among
Most races of the earth; made prophecies
Of marriages and kept the Norse Gods young;
Shone like moons on Hesperidian trees.

And here, domestic, familiar as a pet,
Plump as your granny's cheek, prepared to be
Translated into jam or jelly, yet
It still retains a curious mystery.
Forget the holy leaves, the pagan lore,
And that you munch on legends when you eat,
But see, as you crunch closer to the core,
Those little pips, diminutive and neat
Containers aping tiny beetles or
Microscopic purses, little beads,
Each holding in its patient dark a store
Of apples, flowering orchards, countless seeds.

The Last King

When the last King has gone into the dark
There will be mourning, though the mourners may
Not know their grieving's cause, nor even mark
That what they do is grieve. And on that day
The sun will seem unwilling to appear,
Its breathings fan unseasonably chill;
But there will be no sweating mob to cheer
The farewell speech and axeman's glinting skill
Or panic at a sudden muzzle-flash
And crack. The last King will not leave us thus.
His dying, silent, soft as falling ash,
Occurring with no ceremonial fuss,
Will be enacted in a hotel room
After his undramatic abdication,
Hearing the whisper, in the deepening gloom,
Of alien seas; his slow assassination
Performed by his own treasonous appetites.
So he will lie, the table at his side
Bearing no royal relics; the fitful lights
From curtain chink and passing cars outside
Show only his dark spectacles instead
As he, fat bag containing cooling bones,
Lies incognito on the common bed.
And afterwards, no orchestra of moans,
No formal, public panoply of grief,
Gun-carriage, sleek black plume or muffled drum,
Yet his uncommon spectre, this last leaf
Now fallen from the doomed tree will become
A drifting presence, insubstantial, faint,
Ubiquitous, a whiff of something rare,
The scent of gold; heard too – complaint
Of ancient instruments on evening air –
And seen at fading moments in the night,
Gold gleam in black recess, lost coin, a glow
Of tiny lamp, quick spark, a dying light
Whose ultimate extinction we now see –
Pretender, slave, republican or clerk –
Will disinherit all, for all will be
Mysteriously diminished by that dark.

The Long and Lovely Summers

How long and lovely were the summers then,
Each misted morning verdant milk, until
The sun blurred through, at first a pallid wen
Beneath the sky's bland skin and then, still pale,
A swollen, silvery dahlia-head, before
It burned to gold on laundered gentian blue.

At noon the picnic by the waterfall,
The bright behaviour of the butterflies
Interpreting the light; the plover's call
Above the rhyming flowers, the sun-baked pies
Of cow-pats, fossilized, antique; the cool
Shades of chestnuts, little pools of night.

Night: frosted mathematics of the stars;
Homages of fragrances; the moon,
Curved kukri-blade of ice; the green guitars
And soft soprano breeze conspired to croon
Late lullabies that soothed us into dream
And on to dawn which new delights would spice.

Things are different now. The seasons mock
What expectations we may entertain.
No, things are not like that – and, taking stock,
It seems they never were. Did not grey rain
Stop play? Storms follow drought? A child was drowned.
In close-up, river nymphs were coarse and fat.

And yet we still remember them – the long
And lovely summers, never smeared or chilled –
Like poems, by heart; like poems, never wrong;
The idyll is intact, its truth distilled
From maculate fact, preserved as by the sharp
And merciful mendacities of art.

When the Bough Breaks

That the daytime's playful breeze could grow to this
Was something that could chill the heart and rip
The breath out of your chest, as the great gale could;
Something that appalled, something with such weight
To put you on your knees, compelling prayer
And trembling gestures of propitiation.
You might look at your child, that tiny rage,
And ask what incubation could start there.

The night was swollen by its bulk and brawn,
Blind giant, flailing ignorant and mad.
Our windows winced and flinched. Outside, the trees
Lashed back and wrestled at each fresh attack;
Clawed grasses shrieked, the mountains deliquesced;
Their falling waters vaporized, swept down,
Went burling through the vales, black avalanche
Of air: a murderous metamorphosis.

But in the morning's glitter all lay calm.
The mountains had climbed back into themselves.
A sly and disavowing breeze blew cool,
And counted leaves and petals where they fell.
We drove back to the city through the lanes
Where sheepish fields were smeared and blurred with
     cream
Of white and yellow flowers. The sky was cleansed.
Through glass it seemed that summer had returned.

Closer to the city all was changed;
Those orderly spruce avenues transformed:
On pavements twisted branches writhed and sprawled,
Their fluttering rags, weak signals of distress.
The small green armaments of conker-shells,
Whose fruit – snug, glossy jewels – would never now
Grow plump in satin darkness, had been torn
Too soon from bludgeoned chestnuts, crushed on stone.

Sun filtered through, but not with certainty.
Air hunched and shuddered every now and then,
As if remembering. Yet, just three days
Ago, we swam in silken waters, drowsed

In honey sun and listened to the low
Susurrus and soft labials of summer.
That things can change like this is something we
Should not forget, although we always do.

The House

Seen only once but unmistakable
That wink of sentience in stone and glass,
The way it seemed almost to smile. Perhaps
That sounds like anthropomorphic gush and yet
Some houses do seem able to express
Primary emotions, even make
Statements of a very simple kind.

This house that you have long been searching for
Might be discovered almost anywhere,
In some suburban road of similars,
Yet you would recognize it instantly,
As love's investigating eyes pick out
One special face among those little masks
Swirling like leaves toward the playground gate.

If isolated, out of town, the house
Would not be found where frozen mountains gash
The sky's dark temples, troubled torrents brawl
And air is curdled with acerbic cries
Of curlews' maledictions and the wind
Whines and blares its hostile messages
Round chimney-stack and rages at the panes.

It would be set where hills are vigilant,
Green charities with aprons stitched with flowers,
Rivulets make jokes among white stones;
The autumn garden would be dazed in mist,
Long grasses palming russets as they fall;
On outer walls the ivy would hold close
Its dusty secrets in the pungent dark.

The house is not impractically large
But there are rooms and corners to surprise,

Unexpected narrow flights of stairs
And thoughtful attics where, from skylight glass,
Blue chutes of gold-dust lean towards the floor,
And from a downstairs room, just audible,
A piano floats a soft adagio.

In town or out, when winter nights come down,
The curtained windows glow, each luminous square
A box of sensual delights from which
You hear rich skeins of sound complected by
A hidden treasury of instruments.
Images of childhood Christmas there
Glitter in warm frost before they blur.

You will at last come to an open gate
Which beckons you to enter, move towards
The possible fulfilment of a wish
Born long ago, its substance now mislaid.
The path is devious and long. Dusk falls.
The trees are whispering caves. God only knows
What house, if any, waits to welcome you.

White Witch

In the village pub the men converse;
Their talk retains the slow and wondering pace
Of older, fading days. One lifts his glass
And holds it to the lamplight like a nurse
Consulting a thermometer, and then,
Reassured, he drinks, then sighs and, satisfied,
He listens, nodding, to the other men.
They speak of *her*, and keep their voices low
As if she might be listening, although
They know she must be far away inside
Her house or, farther still, locked in her dark
And unimaginable fantasies.
She drinks, they say, *gets drunk and yells and cries*
And cusses like a man or worse. She's stark
Crazy when she gets like that. Not right
It isn't, not in a woman, and a lady, too.
She must have been a beauty years ago.

Some shake their heads; the young ones mutter, grin
But furtively, as if she might look in
And see them, listen to their talk. The sight
Of her at window or on threshold would
Gorgonize each drinker where he stood.
She threatens them in ways they can't define,
So they traduce her, ridicule, although
When meeting her on her infrequent strolls
Along the village street they never fail
To greet her with a shifty deference,
Unctuous and excessively polite,
Acknowledged sometimes, though more often not.
On certain days and sometimes in the night
They hear the noises from the tall white house
Beyond the church, the sound of smashing glass
And then those jagged and forsaken howls,
Until the stealthy ambulance arrives
With bandages of silence and soft dark.
When she has gone they feel her presence still
And see her image, white and terrible,
A haunted ruin; yet wisps of splendour stay,
Frail ghosts of glory, a house once beautiful
Now fallen into moribund decay,
And they, the villagers, are like their own
Neat cottages and bungalows which, seen
From Beacon Hill – a distant view – are small
As children gathered round the summer green,
And safe, because they have not far to fall.

The Long Flight

'... a German Dornier bomber crashed into a ploughed field in North
Wales and lay undetected for 43 years. The plane, with its bomb load
intact, was shot down on its way to Liverpool on October 16, 1940 and
buried itself in the soft ground, killing all the crew.'
                                                    GUARDIAN 28.9.83

From darkening Cherbourg airfield they took off
At twenty hundred hours, young crews but tough
And hardened to their work, a bomber squadron
Of Dornier Seventeens. They headed on

Towards the English Channel, their target Liverpool.
Hard to spot against the smeared autumnal
Skies they looked, from earth, like iron crosses
Or, black against pale lunar breast, like brooches,
Bird-shaped, sliding into folds of dark.
And soon, above the Wessex coast, the crack
And thud of anti-aircraft guns hurled up
Their brilliancies of rage, the probe and dip
Of searchlights swung like white sticks of the blind.
One plane was hit. It lurched and bucked, then climbed
But fiery pennants flew from starboard wing
Until the wind's rush ripped them off and flung
Them down to the floor of night. The plane went on
Though engine-cough said damage had been done
And slowly altitude and speed decreased
Till they had lost all contact with the rest.
And so, alone, the broken aircraft droned
Low over Denbigh Moor then turned for home.
Too late. Its single engine faltered, cut:
The pilot snarled and sweated as he fought
To bring back power. The crew was clenched and white,
Silent as the drowned. The plane's nose dipped
And through the wind's black howl they plummeted
To where ploughed earth was goffered like the sea
And, like the sea, earth hungered for the crew.
The plane went down; it sank in troughs of soil,
Down into darkness, deep in loam and marl,
Silent, dark as ocean's shifting gloom.
Then spectral engines purred again: they flew,
Flew blind with shattered instruments for more
Than forty years in fossil silence, war,
With never hope of armistice. Now gulls
And curlews wheel and cry above, their calls
Bleak requiem for what they see down there –
The shadowed shape, the giant bird entombed,
Wings cruciform as if it rode the air.

In Golden Acre Park, Leeds

The sunlight is fresh poured, liquescent gold,
Transparent, yet its body can be felt.
The roses and the rhododendrons float
In verdancy of leaves and fern and yield
Their innocent convictions to the wide
And cloudless stare of blue. And, over there
Past shimmering skin of pond, past beech and fir,
Keeping to the careful paths, the staid
And well-pressed man of later middle-age,
Clean-shaven, solid, shiny-booted, walks
And does not see or hear dark starry larks
And boisterous blackbirds musically enlarge
Upon this jewelled morning in July.
His step is blind, mechanical; his eyes
Are glacial, fixed ahead as if he sees
A frozen bleak horizon far away
From this rejected luxury of air
And colour. Tucked with care beneath one arm,
Packed neatly, like a family snapshot album,
His prudent waterproof is held secure,
A tidy parcelling of navy-blue
Containing rain-seeds, memories of war,
Dark clouds, a little thunderbolt or two.

Bicycle Races, Roundhay Park, Leeds

From far above the amphitheatre's green,
Shrunken by distance, each rider and machine
Are fused into a single thing, alive,
Insectile. Arched backs and beetle heads contrive,
With spindle limbs, to move on shimmering rings
Of fine-spun webs; the starter's pistol stings
Silence like a Christmas-cracker's snap

As they surge forward for the opening lap.
When we draw closer to the track we can
Dissect each insect into thing and man,
And, nearer yet, proximity reveals
The frantic knees, like twiddling thumbs, the wheels
Sizzling on the labile grass below
The ram's-horn handlebars, the wheels that show
How spokes of ice have melted in hot speed,
A silvery blur. The winner's head, black bead,
Is lifted, as he rides across the line,
And, humanized, he smiles. The circled shine
Of spokes now flickers, ticking down, each wheel
Seen first as fine-sliced lemon, then as steel
And rubber now the spell of speed has fled.
The other riders finish, every head
Stays down, seems bowed in misery or shame.
Every man is numbered, but his name
Will be restored when evening comes and he
Puts on his clothes of full humanity,
Drives home, his bicycle strapped on the roof
Of car or van, upturned, a trophy, proof
Of having hunted with the brave; and so
Its wheels, revolving slowly in the flow
Of darkening breeze, may faintly rhyme with how
Shot prey's dead limbs might stir; these wheels could swing
The pendant heart, like some once living thing.

A Victorian Honeymoon

Her features in the frame are pale and blurred
Imprisoned in the glass. Her hairbrush soars
And swoops and rises like an ivory bird
About her stormy head. The misty gauze
Of chiffon at her breast is startled by
A rose's crimson wound; her gaze implores
Reprieve, or answer to her brimming 'Why?'

And there is no reply. She knows that she
Must grow accustomed to this bitter taste,
The gravy of despair. Outside, the sea

Repeats incessant prophecies of waste
And now its slow, unvaried voice contains
A salt intelligence which must be faced:
There is no hope of rescue from these chains.

The links are insubstantial, and they seemed
Not long ago to gleam, a golden prize,
The goal of which, since girlhood, she had dreamed,
Its aureate sparkle dancing in her eyes;
But now, they are custodial; these chains
Are fetters on the spirit; they chastise
Insulted flesh with unimagined pains.

It was another world when it, and she –
Or, rather, that seraphic girl who died,
Whose days were like a charmed eternity
Of summer picnics – were transmogrified:
Green paradise transformed to tenebrous cave.
Her beauty torn, voice shrilled. The tales had lied:
No hope of princely rescue by the brave.

Her husband soon will come and she must smile;
She cannot tell him that it hurts. All day
They trudged the foreign pavements, mile on mile –
Museums, churches, statues – then the bay
As sunset bled across the sky and sea;
Sad twilight as the pilgrimage of grey
And hooded waves moved shoreward endlessly.

Then back to this. She smells tobacco-smoke.
It sickens her. She thinks she hears his tread
Outside the door. She feels self-pity choke,
A bitter caustic potion: pain and dread
Compose their plaint, but pride aborts the cry;
It freezes in the glass; she lifts her head
And sees reflected eyes, resigned and dry.

Hands

Hands can be eloquent, though sometimes they
Mislead us utterly in what they say.

I have seen slender-fingered, candle-white
Supple and fluent hands that many might
Call 'sensitive', 'a pianist's hands', 'artistic';
But these were owned by someone mean, sadistic,
Hostile to art, a gross materialist.
I know another man, fine pianist,
Whose powerful, sausage-fingered, meaty fists
Should hang from goal-keeper's or butcher's wrists,
Yet on the gleaming keys these hands could wake
Ghosts of drowned nightingales in starry lakes.
I knew a fighter, too, fast welterweight,
Whose punches could crack bone and could create
Sudden shattered galaxies in the head,
Yet from his hands alone you might have said
That he was not unusually strong,
For they were hairless, pale, the fingers long.
So many hands will tell us lies, but I
Have never known old labouring men's deny
Their simple character: these never lie.
For years they have manhandled spade or hook,
Shovel, axe or pick until they look
Like weathered tools, mattock, hammer, vice,
Battered, annealed by wind and sun and ice.
I like to watch them rest on tables, knees,
Lifting a pint of beer or with deft ease
Rolling a fag which later burns between
Dark oaken knuckles which have never been
Surely as soft and sensitive to pain
As this pen-pusher's hand I look at now;
But most of all I like to witness how
They lift small, tired grandchildren and hold
Them curled and safe, how gently they enfold
Their always welcome, always cherished guests,
Become protecting, gnarled and living nests.

A Distant Prospect

Class photograph, 1930

This was Standard Three, the school Church Street
Junior Boys', Beeston, Nottinghamshire.

You can tell that it was summer by the way
The children squint and wrinkle at the gaze
Of prophecy as lens and pupil meet.

Also the way they're dressed is a thermometer:
Shirts or jerseys, though a few have come
In Sunday jackets, unaccustomed ties.
This small élite has, pinned on its lapels,
Badges of office, each boy a monitor.

These frown responsibly. And you can tell
By strictly parted hair, its recent wet
Submission to the comb or brush, that they
Might one day be full corporals, shop-stewards,
Under-managers. They will do quite well.

Though few or none will ever own commissions,
Desks or telephones. The unpromoted,
Their heads close-cropped or rough as coconuts,
Grin or scowl. Here and there you see
A stare of undeceivable suspicion.

Three of the boys are specky-four-eyes. Their
Wearing glasses does not imply a legendary
Love of learning: bad eyesight, that is all.
You look at these small faces and you smell
Their element, the grey imprisoned air.

Is one of them the nine-year-old you were?
It's possible. You only know that now
Those few suspicious sceptics seem to see
A menace in the black-cowled camera,
Cold glitter in the lens's inky glare.

Sixty-first Birthday Poem

This is the age at which the bodies
Of unidentified men are found
In streets near public houses or
On tow-paths or waste-ground,
Foul play never suspected; an inch or less
In the middle pages of the local press.

It is the age at which young women
Do not, in fact, avert their gaze;
If their brilliant eyes should chance upon you
They wipe you out like death-rays.
That you might still claim a little virility
Does not reduce your invisibility.

It is the age when all ambition
Has fossilized, each aspiration
Replaced by muted desperation
Or muffling fog of resignation;
No candles for your cake today;
No cake for candles anyway.

The only card in the morning's post
Is from the Department of Disease
And Total Insecurity.
No birthday gifts; there'll be no knees-
Up later at the Horse and Groom:
Today you've got the key of the tomb.

And yet you grin and tap your toe
To the tune of a silent song today,
And it must be lively by the look of you;
'Senile dementia,' is what they would say,
Those men in white coats. But, no matter what,
Hang on to it, pal: it's all that you've got.

Old Man

What he wished to be and what he was
No longer brawl; the grunts and thuds are dumb.
A former bandit in a fat disguise,
No longer prone to injure anyone,
Holster empty and his tired eyes red,
He nods in ancient rocking chair and sighs,
Remembering that lovely loaded gun,
But then recalls the various salt he shed,
And what a nuisance it so often was.
'Great days, all gone; dear comrades, all stone dead.'

He loves them, for the dead do not condemn
Or mock or boss, or say he's telling lies,
But smile and whisper from the darkening gloom,
'You're tired and cold. Come in. It's time for bed.'

Grandfather's Tears

He cries easily now who once maintained
That weeping was a woman's recreation,
His sedentary grief, lubricious tears,
Induced by simulacra of real pain,
Parodies of pathos on the screen –
The blue-eyed death of child or faithful dog,
Honest cop or genial soda-jerk –
Pacific interludes between the bouts
Of stabbing, shooting, putting in the boot.
There are even times when throat and eyes
Flood with compassion at the sight of ads
For dog-food, baby-powder or shampoo,
But never when the unembellished truth
Of newsreels is presented, images
Of famine, torture, violence in the streets.
Grandpa is bored. He goes out for a pee
Or shuffles up to bed.
                        Old man, old baby,
Off you go. Sleep well. You've had your fill
And more of actuality: two wars,
Insult, hunger, treachery and shame,
The ceaseless accusation from the fields
Of darkness and white stones, the whispering
From buried legions of the faceless dead.
Have your good cry which does not hurt at all;
Enjoy that warm release and go to bed.

Grandma in Winter

In her black shawl she moves over the field of snow
With a slow proud strut, like a burgher

Or a fat crow.
The raw sun has oozed on to the lint of cloud,
A pretty smear of pain. The church gathers its little ones,
The stone children, about its skirts
And tells them an old story.

She will join them, stand perfectly still and quiet there.
No-one will notice her.
And when night unfolds
Its old black umbrella with the little holes
She will pray for the blond stones and the friable bones,
The blue melted jellies; those white
Teeth, the small blanched almonds.

Bona Dea

Who can this someone be, this lady walking
Under the frown of yews and cypresses,
Pouting her great pale belly? You have seen her before.
She is, and will be again, someone's mother:
The beak and plumage look familiar.

Her belly is hard-boiled, a white chamber-pot;
She is Señora Humpty-Dumpty below the breast.
Do not chance another keek down there though
As she moves slowly past on her smooth castors.
Her fingers are pale snakes.

Supper-time. She perches on a stone chair
And scoops spaghetti from a bowl of bone.
The sauce is a mix of incantation and theology,
It smells of sins and psalms.
She is eating for two.

When her meal is finished she folds her napkin;
It is stained with mystery. It has wrapped up
Chewed meat and grass, excreta of phantoms,
False teeth and testimony. When the stars titter
Her long stare freezes them.

Company of Women

Miss Steeples

Miss Steeples sat close;
She touched me.
Her hands were white,
Fingernails pink
Like shells of prawns.
They tapped my desk
And, as she murmured,
Numbers blurred.
She smelled of spring
And cool cash chemists.
One summer evening,
Not by chance,
I met her walking
Near the green
Court she beautified
Dressed in white.
In one hand swung
A netted catch
Of tennis balls.
She smiled and said,
'Hello.'
She smiled.
Love-punctured
I could not answer.
At the end of the summer
She went away.
It was her smell I loved
And her fingernails.

Thelma

Thelma was a Brownie.
I never spoke to her
Although we spent a year together

In Standard Three.
I once followed her home
From the Brownie HQ.
There was honeysuckle in the gardens;
Songs of gramophones, too.
The satchel she brought to school
Was made of expensive leather
And in her hair
She wore a slide of tortoiseshell,
My first fetish.
We never spoke,
Not once in all that time.
It was a long spell
And is not over:
When I smell honeysuckle now
It is Thelma I smell.

III

Doris

Doris was fifteen.
Under her unsuitable blouse
Her breasts bounced when she ran.
I kissed her once
And she fled
Giggling and joggling home.
MacFeeney cheered like a football crowd.
I made his nose bleed.
Doris was more exciting
Than cigarettes,
Sweeter than caramels,
More sparkling than sherbet.
For thirteen weeks I saved
To buy her a gift:
It looked like a sucked pear-drop
On a thin chain.
I like to think of it, snug
Between those plump bubs,
Those joys
That age has never withered.
MacFeeney keeps a pub in Mablethorpe.

IV

Kathleen

Kathleen was tall.
My eyes grew dizzy when they climbed
Her legs;
Sometimes they fell.
Her hair was rich
And golden red,
It glowed like fire
Reflected in
Good marmalade.
We walked at night
Under a nervous sky,
Its darkness probed and drenched
By searchlights, jets
Of phosphorescent milk
Thrilling the black air.
Marauding engines grumbled
As we played
With high explosives
Of primed limbs and lips;
Incendiary kisses fell.
My hands grew dizzy when they climbed
Her legs
But did not fall.
At her long cry
All sirens held their tongues.
Her hair was drenched, it spread
Wild and impenitent,
A red and morning cloud
Above a wasted town
That smouldered but already stirred,
Would rise up new again.

V

Barbara

Barbara was small
But in that little space
A charge of sexual voltage hummed

And, when released, it singed and dazzled mad.
I gave her poetry to read:
She judged it 'very nice',
Would rather far
Been offered chocolate or kisses.
One winter night, the pubs all shut,
She crouched beneath the frosty stars
And pissed.
She looked up, grinning, as the glitter hissed.
And that is what I most remember,
Less passion than delight,
More mischief than dark moans –
Quick sparkle, hiss and rising mist,
The frosty stars
And Barbara twinkling wantonly
And wild.

Autumnal

He walks slowly along Cathedral Road and hears
Funereal music in the misty dark.
Leaves tapestry the pavement, days of rain
Have blurred that veined precision, silencing
The drily whispered commentary again.
Beneath a bilious lamp pulped yellows, browns
And slippery blacks are mushed, all definition
Lost as his slow, browsing shoes move through
The mawkish narrative of mortal summer,
Doomed passion poisoned by the murderous hours
And picked by needle minutes to the bone.
Arriving at a house of blinded words
He pauses, enters, climbs up to the room
Where empty bottles, echoes of the dead
Who fell in ancient, half-forgotten battles
Rehearse the perfect silence of a tomb.
The music freezes in his wounded head.

Neighbours

She:
'Leave, my love, before the morning
Drains the darkness from the pane.
Others who ignored this warning
Did not live to love again.

'Stars, those frozen birdsong fragments,
Soon will melt and disappear;
Footsteps on the frosty pavements
Tap out signals you should fear.'

He:
'How, my dearest, can I hasten
From your clinging limbs and lips
Now warm folds of blind sensation
Cause a rational eclipse?

'What if curtain-peeping neighbours
Recognize the man they see?
Let them wave their stage-prop sabres,
They can't injure you and me.'

She:
'Ah, my love, I fear night's ending
Not because your dawn-lit face
Would feed the need of those intending
Our exposure and disgrace.

What I dread is our own gazing,
In the light that tells no lies,
At each other, neighbours, facing
Features we don't recognize.'

Separate Rooms

She lies and smiles in sleep
Ten Tarquin strides away,
Still tastes his nightcap kiss;

Her goodnight whisper stays,
Cavatina in the dark
Auditorium of the heart.
He settles round his grin –
Love's voluntary gull –
Sucks juice from rind of moon,
Supernal, lustral gin;
Picks golden straws from hair
And stores them with her words
In velvet secrecy,
As if quite unaware
These trinkets, which he hoards,
Are pretty trash, and when
Grey day comes barging in
Their glitter will be dimmed;
And, if her sleeping smile
Was caused by dreams of some
Other man than him,
He will not feel much pain
Till night calls up the moon
And in that room again –
Now miles away from this –
She lies and smiles, awake,
And tastes another's kiss.

Great Western Railway Terminus, 1938

The night is sad with rain and sighed farewells;
In each lamp's nimbus needles spin and flicker.
The shelter eaves are strung with nervous bells
Which fall, unchiming, bursting in quick silver.

Two lovers sit like one two-headed creature,
Locked on the platform seat, keyed with desire,
Hiding their little flame from windy weather
And all that wants to slaughter such frail fire.

The waiting locomotive snorts and huffs;
A hissing cloud of steam, a weightless dumpling,
Conceals the kissing lovers with grey fluff;
A whistle starts its chill and painful probing.

The slam of doors. One lurch, the platform settles.
The steam-cloud fades and drifts away, then shows
Again the seat, where no warm lovers nestle:
But two cold strangers, staring at their toes.

Film Shooting

See how they fall, how many ways there are:
Operatic in their own embrace,
Back-flipping over table-top or bar
With gargling yell, disintegrating face,
Arms conducting great finales, or,
Like joke mendacious anglers, wide apart,
Or clutching belly with both hands before
Making deep obeisance as they start
The slow collapsing journey to the floor.

Their costumes alter with the changing scene:
In desert, prairie, on the dusty track
That snakes through scrub towards the dark ravine
They wear the Western villain's garments – black
And battered stetson, shirt and neckerchief.
They need a shave. On modern battlefield,
In Europe or the East, they come to grief
In khaki, grey or green, the face concealed
By helmet-shade and camouflaging leaf.

The urban victims' dress may vary more,
But snappy suits and tipped fedoras are
The usual gear; they croak in liquor store,
In sidewalk filth or, like a blackened star,
Might power-dive from the sky. They could, instead,
Be drilled in restaurant or while at stool,
In some broad's swell apartment on the bed,
Outside a movie-house or by the pool;
There's plenty of locales for getting dead.

Whenever shooting happens we see red
Expressed from neat-punched wound, a signet set
In flesh, soft sealing-wax that runs. The head
Stays more or less intact. That pirouette
Is fake, rehearsed; take it from one who knows.
I was myself once shot, though thank the Lord
Not fatally, as you might well suppose
Could camera objectively record
My cadaverous appearance in repose.

Drinking up Time

Thin trill of bell, a quick bright jet which sounds
Again, sharp auditory chill in smoke
And heated cachinnation of the bar.
The clock's black sleight of hands again astounds –
Last orders called; supplied. Damp towels cloak
Pump-handles, like caged parrots, for the dark.

On the table-top geometry of rings
Is wiped away. We grip the last half-inch
With shifty grins. The end has now begun.
There's no reprieve. The yawning doorway brings
Rumours of the night; we blink and flinch,
Drinking up time, as we have always done.

Fighting Talk

I overhear the woman in the bar:
'They fought like cat and dog,' she says, her lips
Clamped tight and sour, an operation scar.
Her friend nods glazed agreement as she sips
Another gin and tonic. Both are wrong,
For cats and dogs don't fight. When dogs attack
Most cats will run. The exceptionally strong
In spirit stand, sizzling with curved back.
And then the dog will stop and growl and glare,
Retreat within its skin, then slink away.

Human couples fight – no question there –
But not like cat and dog, nor like I'd say,
Any pair of beasts. When couples rise
To slug it out their rage does not diminish
Though they might smile. You see in those cold eyes
That this fight has no rules, is to the finish.

Skirts and Trousers

It is a fact – or would have been until
About a half a century ago –
That any picture showing Jack and Jill
Would carefully preserve the status quo
And represent the boy as wearing some
Type of trousers with his manly shirt
To clothe his legs and privy parts and bum,
While Jill of course would wear some kind of skirt.

Not quite the same today. Some women wear
Trousers all the time (I mean as fact
As well as metaphor). Most choose a pair
For work or play, some simply to attract –
On certain female shapes they look sublime –
And yet I sometimes feel, I must confess,
Regret for those lost days, that faded time
Of whispering hem, that unambiguous dress.

I've often wondered why it's always been
The woman clad in skirts, the man in breeks –
At least here, on the European scene –
Though come to think of it, the ancient Greeks
(The males I mean) wore skirts, the Romans too,
And both held to the view that those who wore
Trousers were barbaric; it's still true
Some Scots wear skirts, by which they set great store.

But in the main, I think it's true to say
That, in most countries we call civilized,
Skirts are emblematic and convey

Essential woman, always recognized,
And yet I wonder why this should be so:
Why bifurcated garments for the man
While women slide both legs inside one O.
We're led back to the place where we began.

I'd take a bet that women's clothes were all
Designed, as now, by men, to satisfy,
Ever since Mankind's primeval Fall,
The same old pride of life and lust of eye
Still catered for today; but something more
Practical: a help when taken short
In labour or providing access for
The randy hunter out for easy sport?

Perhaps. Yet there is something magical
In women wearing skirts. They may look pert
In jeans, but if you seek the lyrical,
Heart-haunting woman, she will wear a skirt;
That single sleeve, concealing in its dusk
Two limbs that glimmer, brush and cross like beams
Of light, contrives a spell, a spectral musk
Which drifts into the coverts of men's dreams.

Naming of Poets

Surprising once, splendid or absurd
The names with which their mums and dads baptized
Those baby boys. A name is more than word;
It is a kind of garment, loose, outsized,
One which the child will slowly grow to fit.
My God, it must have taken years for those
Poor nippers easily to move and sit
Relaxed in such odd vests their parents chose –
Siegfried, Rudyard, Humbert, Algernon, Bysshe.
Later kids were luckier, I suppose,
Were labelled closer to the way they'd wish.

Yet even then got stuck with names in tales
From women's magazines or nominal-rolls
Of public schools (unless they came from Wales),
Names like Stephen, Christopher, Paul and Charles.
But when the second war to end all wars
Had, figuratively, seen these down the drain
Those lucky fathers, safe on Blighty's shores,
Would nomenclate their young with names as plain
As British Restaurant meals, decent, prosaic –
Brian, Alan, Donald – note again
How disyllabic names are all trochaic.

The next lot, though, chose amputated trochees,
Monikers of one blunt syllable –
More fitting for back-woodsmen from the Rockies
Or for the darts-team chalked up in your local –
Pete and Ted, Ken and Fred – yet we
Became accustomed to them in the lists
Of new contributors, and now we see
Them in the Oxford Books of that and this
Without a flicker of surprise, although
I must confess I do, a little, miss
The way those aureate Julians used to glow.

Well, tough diminutives are out and we
Must now adjust to names which look and sound
Like former surnames – Blake and Craig and Lee –
These poets' full names could be switched around
Like those reversible coats that could provide
A quick disguise for crook or private eye.
But in the end the name is no sure guide
To excellence. The stuff we save to buy
And treasure might not bear a famous name
And, if it does, it's no more reason why
We choose it than a picture for its frame.

Collected Poems Recollected

FOR PETER PORTER

Most of us have smiled to see them there
On market stalls, at jumble sales, in rows
On dainty shelves in twilit bookshops, where
Mild yet vulturine explorers nose
Wheezily through seventeenth-century prose
And cough and chumble in that studious air.

Rarely disturbed, these Poets stand in line,
Quaint wall-flowers few will ever ask to dance
And none invite to share good food and wine;
Though you or I might flick a friendly glance
Most look at them, if look they do, askance,
In ways to chill the bibliological spine.

You, Peter, I am confident, could reel
Their names off, get them smartly on parade –
John Greenleaf Whittier (his three names peal
More plangently than any poem he made);
John Drinkwater (his verse, pale lemonade,
May disintoxicate but scarcely heal).

The Manxman, T E Brown (his shut leaves hide
Stuffed blackbird in a cardboard garden), stout
Noble, Bulwer Lytton, side by side
With fair Felicia Hemans; close about
Stand Gawsworth (next to *Ditties of a Scout*),
Great Noyes and Newbolt, monitors to Pride.

More female poets: Dora Sigerson Shorter,
And Edith Sitwell still failing to impress –
Posterity, as critic, yields no quarter –
Dark waiting spaces, especially under 'S' –
Surely for Spender? ... Silkin? ... Please say 'Yes'!
But none for Martial artist, Peter Porter.

For twenty years I've felt your poems were meant
For private shelves at home and in the mind.
The awkward squad, the not quite excellent
Earn, all the same, some homage of a kind:
Who knows for sure where he will be consigned?
Those foothills prove the peaks magnificent.

Sentences

Soldiers serving sentences in Military Prisons and Detention Barracks
are officially referred to and addressed as S.U.S's – Soldiers Under
Sentence.

Who spiked the water at the wedding
    Held in the Sergeant's Mess?
We all know who the fellow was:
          Jay…
          E…
          S.U.S!

Who blew reveille in the dead man's ear,
    Made him get up and dress?
It wasn't the Company Bugler, but
          Jay…
          E…
          S.U.S!

Who fed the whole battalion
    On one man's rations? Guess!
Of course you know; it could only be
          Jay…
          E…
          S.U.S!

Who marched across the sea, his boots
    Bright and dry? Why, Yes!
The smartest man in the Regiment:
          Jay…
          E…
          S.U.S!

Who made the tempest halt, ground arms
    And stand at ease, no less?
The man who knew the word of command –
        Jay...
        E...
        S.U.S!

Who rode a donkey into town
    And cried in his distress?
We don't know why, but we know who:
        Jay...
        E...
        S.U.S!

Who chased the Pay Corps scroungers from
    The place of holiness;
Bashed spuds on Sunday? Who but he,
        Jay...
        E...
        S.U.S!

Who woke the colonel's daughter from
    Death's sleep to wakefulness?
Not Sawbones but the miracle lad,
        Jay...
        E...
        S.U.S!

Who ripped night's bandage from the eyes
    And healed men's sightlessness?
It wasn't the MO's orderly but
        Jay...
        E...
        S.U.S!

Who never wore a pip or stripe
    Yet still achieved success?
Who held the lowest rank of all?
        Jay...
        E...
        S.U.S!

Who got beat up by Itie cops
    To force him to confess?
Who got put on a Two-five-two*?
                    Jay...
                    E...
                    S.U.S!

Who took the Redcaps' fists and boots,
    His face a bloody mess
And then got taken out to die?
                    Jay...
                    E...
                    S.U.S!

                    But

Who swallowed wine and pissed out water,
Couldn't wake up when reveille was blown,
Who screwed Colonel Jairus's daughter,
Ate ten men's rations, all on his own,
Robbed the blind and beat up cripples,
Flogged his donkey right to the bone?

Johnny Evans, he was the fellow,
Ended up high against the bloodshot sky,
Johnny Evans, the barrack-room cowboy,
Arms stretched out like a PTI.
He, and another old Janker-wallah,
One each side of the man who cried
A loud reproach to his stone-deaf father
And promised Johnny, before he died,
A place that night in the Officer's Mess,
He, Johnny Evans, was a Soldier Under Sentence
                    Jay...
                    E...
                    S.U.S!

* Army Form 252: charge-sheet

270

SOLDIERING ON
1989

Reveille

The vitreous dawn is smashed by noise.
The rooster bugler calls out cock-a-hoop;
Dreams break, the pieces drift away,
Quick glimpses of unmilitary things –
White softnesses and silks and secret hair –
Before the coarse and iron-booted Now
Stamps hard and crushes
All such daintinesses in the dirt
And shouts the brute day in.
Blind fingers fumble for fag-ends and then
The overture of coughs and groans begins.
Sergeant someone slams into the hut,
Hoarse muezzin who cries again
The formal exhortations of his faith:
Wakey-wakey! ... Rise and shine!
Drop your cocks and grab your socks
It's re-vall-ee!

Getting Fell In

Get fell in you dozey men!
The Corporal roars.
The khaki bundles clomp from huts
On dubbined boots and get fell in
Beneath a sky of stone
Unfriendly as the barrack square
They clatter on.
The bundles coalesce, are one.
Scorched porridge sniffs the air.
Squad ... stand-at ... Ease!
Squad ... shun!

Move to the right in threes! Right … turn!
By the left … quick … march!
Lay-rye … lay-rye … lay!
The section moves, brown caterpillar,
Feculent plump worm,
With chink and clink of eating irons,
To break the fast of night,
First fodder of the day.

Bayonet Training

From far away, a mile or so,
The wooden scaffolds could be seen
   On which fat felons swung;
But closer view showed these to be
Sacks, corpulent with straw and tied
   To beams from which they hung.

The sergeant halted his platoon.
'Right lads,' he barked, 'you see them sacks?
   I want you to forget
That sacks is what they are and act
As if they was all Jerries – wait!
   Don't move a muscle yet!

'I'm going to show you how to use
The bayonet as it should be done.
   If any of you feel
Squeamish like, I'll tell you this:
There's one thing Jerry just can't face
   And that thing is cold steel.

'So if we're going to win this war
You've got to understand you must
   Be brutal, ruthless, tough.
I want to hear you scream for blood
As you rip out his guts and see
   The stuff he had for duff.

'Remembering this. You're looking at
A bunch of Jerries over there.
    They'd kill you if they could,
And fuck your sisters, mother too.
You've got to stop the bastards, see?
    I hope that's understood.

'All right? Platoon, in your own time,
Fix your bayonets; stand at ease
    Then watch my moves with care.
First, the High Port, done like this:
You cant the rifle straight across
    Your chest and hold it there.

'Note the angle: left hand firm
Around the barrel, half-way down.
    The right hand grasps the small.
Whatever happens never change
Your grip upon your weapon. No!
    I don't mean that at all!

'You dirty-minded little sods!
The next position – that's On Guard –
    You swing the bayonet out
In front of you like this, chest high,
Take one pace forward with your left
    Knee bent. Let's see you try.

'High Port! On Guard! High Port! On Guard!
All right. You've got the rough idea.
    Stand easy and keep still.
And now – Delivery of the Point –
In other words the moment when
    You go in for the kill.

'So watch me now and listen good.
I'll want to hear you yell like me,
    So take a good deep breath
Before you stick the bayonet in.
If you don't kill him with the blade
    You'll scare the sod to death!'

The young recruits stood there and watched
And listened as their tutor roared
    And stabbed his lifeless foe;
Their faces were expressionless,
Impassive as the winter skies
    Black with threats of snow.

Perimeter Guard

His second two-hour duty: the wind
Is now stropped to such
Fine and steely sharpness that
It might slice off a shrivelled lobe or finger.
The stars are brilliant chippings of frozen flint,
Beautiful, but quite indifferent
To sublunar hurt.

His stunned toes are welded together;
He is club-footed
By the weather. The only
Nostrum for such misery and loneliness
Is found in fantasies of somewhere other,
A feminine place, not erotic
But warm, motherly.

Lavender-scented pillow and sheets;
No gruff blankets there:
Soft wool, a cool counterpane
Of candlewick that soothed an infant fever;
Sweet, unsnoring dark. He shuts his eyes against
The stars' impersonal derision
And the wind's malice.

Then dream and the silence are broken
By a sound beyond
The wire and his eyes are filled
With star-sparks like frozen tears; unsure he calls
'Halt! Who goes there?' No one answers. The glitter
Melts from his eyes; then he hears the wind
Whisper: 'Foe!... Foe!... Foe!...'

Lights Out

The pyramids of canvas shrink,
And palely gleam,
Draw closer to each other
As the night
Slips wedges of the dark between.
A steam of mist
Sways above the grasses
Where, like slanted beams of light,
Guy-ropes hide their ends.
Silence is a black sky; then
A sudden burst of sound
Is hung there goldenly, slides down
And then soars back and spreads.

Here is a sadness to confound,
The throat of brass
Is hoarse with centuries of ache;
And, waking or asleep,
We all recall
Bereavements, near or distant, feel
The tears in things.

Then, later, as the tall
Sergeant of the daylight calls
All sections on parade,
The griefs of night are laid aside,
Though they are not mislaid.

Troopship

I

Setting Sail

Leaving Greenock, on a slaty day
When sea and sky profess the same patched grey

Of jankers denim or of prison walls
And fussy tugboats answer seagulls' calls,
All other-ranks are ranged along the rails
To wave goodbye to Blighty's hills and vales –
'Hill and vales my arse!' as they would say:
Back streets of Glasgow, Leeds and Tiger Bay
Are what they'll dream about when they're at sea,
The loci of their shared mythology
Of sexy, willing women and complete
Freedom and success in civvy street.

The coastline melts in mist. The ship rides on
To where the waiting convoy lolls upon
The queasy seas. Destroyers prowl and wink
Quick signals; lean corvettes appear, then sink
And rise again like whippets in high corn;
The horns of merchantmen and tankers warn
The world of darknesses all sailors know.
The swaddies turn away and go below.

The voyage has begun: that is to say
The physical adventure through the spray
And lurching waves beneath which killers lurk –
The guttural U-Boats glide through wavering mirk
Where mines like huge black conker-cases float –
But other voyages begin, each boat
Small tub of flesh and spirit, each a *Me*
That drifts in waters other than this sea,
Trawling the past, or future fantasy,
For brief reprieve from this reality;
The remora, that piscine limpet-mine,
But one unprimed, its amiable design
To keep the vessel safe in anodyne
And friendly seas, may save a few, but more
Will run aground on that unfriendly shore
Where present terrors from the rocks are aimed,
And must be faced and recognized and named.

II

Letters Home

1

Dear Mum and Dad,
                    We're on the high seas now.
I don't know when you'll get to see this note.
I just asked Sergeant MacNamara how
They got the mail to Blighty from a boat
Like this. He says we stop at Gib – we hope –
And mail is put ashore and then flown back.
I'd like to climb inside this envelope
And whizz straight home inside a postman's sack.
I'm kidding really. Life at sea's all right.
The grub's not bad. You're not to worry, Mum.
We're safe as houses here, so you sleep tight
And bet your boots that we will overcome
Our enemies on land and sea. And Dad,
It won't be very long before we drink
A few more pints than what we've ever had
Before. I hope this finds you in the pink –
That's what they used to say in your old war,
Right, Dad? You came safe back and I will too,
So don't you fret. Remember this is your
Lucky lad, the boy you always knew
Would land the right way up. Good night, God bless,
Remember me to Auntie Flo and Dave.
And thank you both for all the happiness
And love and caring that you always gave –
Sounds soft, I know – But still I'm glad it's said.
Night-night again. Keep smiling.
                              Love from Fred

2

Darling Jane,
            I thought I wouldn't write
Until we're off this floating lavatory
But find I just can't face another night
Unless I scribble something you will see

And knowing this brings you an inch or two
Closer, that is all.
                  The other chaps
Are either being sick or telling 'true'
Tales of conquests, then producing snaps
Of wives or girlfriends contradicting their
Boasts of smashing bints and lovely tarts –
Just ordinary girls with mousy hair
And little, cautious eyes that all the arts
Of camera and make-up can't disguise.
I felt an urge to join them and to show
Your picture, but I knew this was unwise
And kept away of course. 'You'll never know
How much I love you' – that's their favourite song,
Or one of them. They sing it through the nose
With much vibrato. Yes, I know it's wrong
To patronize, but how do you suppose
I manage to keep sane? The only way
That works is packing all perceptions in
The salt of irony. And please don't say
It's all my fault, by now I could have been
An officer and gent. I know it's true,
But do believe me when I say I'm not
Perversely setting out to worry you
Or test your love, nor am I showing what
They call 'inverted snobbery'. It's just
That I can't take the farce of rank that's based
On privilege and class. I no more trust
My leaders than I would myself if faced
By those appalling choices war presents.
But don't you worry, darling. I shall pray
That none of God's sadistic jokes prevents
Our being re-united one fine day –
Though who or what I'll pray to isn't clear.
My love, I miss you and I hope that you
Miss me a little too. The words I hear,
Though scented and banal, are not untrue.
Do you remember Burns's lovely song,
'A Red Red Rose'? 'Till a' the seas gang dry…'
Well let us hope it won't be quite that long
Before we are together
    Always,
                  Guy

3

Dearest Darling Peg,
                            You just can't guess
How much I miss you. All I do is think
About the way you looked in that blue dress
You wore at Mum's. I never sleep a wink
Without I dream that I am cuddling you
And sometimes doing other things. I bet
That you can guess what they might be! I do
Love you sweetheart. Ever since we met
That night at the Astoria when I
Asked you for a dance and you agreed
I fell in love and couldn't make out why
You seemed to feel the same. I'll always need
Your love my sweet and hope that you'll need mine.
Remember my last leave? The time they played
That smashing song of Vera Lynn's? The shine
Your eyes had was so beautiful it made
My heart melt like a snowball in the sun.
Don't look at any man while I'm away.
It won't be long before the war is won
And I'll be back. Every night I pray
It won't be long and that you'll wait for me.
I wish now we'd got married when we could.
There's nothing in the world I'd rather be
Than your life's love and care for you for good.
The only thing that stopped me was the thought
That with me on a draft going overseas
And facing action and all that we ought
To wait in case – your Mum and Dad agrees –
In case – you know – I don't come safe through.
You're not to worry love. Of course I will.
How could I not when I've the thought of you
Waiting there? So I'll be yours until
The end of time. Remembering Vera's song,
Yours till the birds fail to sing? I'll be back
My darling love. Let's pray it won't be long.
A million loving kisses
                            from
                                Your Jack

4

Dear Old Bunty,
                    Just a hurried line
To tell you all goes well. The men are fine.
No problems over discipline. I feel
That all, or most, of them are made of steel,
And British steel at that. *Esprit de corps*
Could not be better. Roger is a bore
But knows his job and keeps out of my way.
The younger officers are keen and they,
I'm sure, won't let me down.
                              Keep well my dear,
We'll give the Hun a thrashing, never fear.
Hope you've got some grazing for the mare;
That fellow Jenkins must have land to spare.
My love to both the girls and cousin Maud,
And most of all to you,
                    Your husband,
                    Claude

5

Dear Gladys,
                    Hope you're well. The kiddies too.
I never was a one for writing letters
As well you know. This ship is like a zoo
And I'm head-keeper. Some should be in fetters,
I mean those lads that think they're on a cruise
And all they're here to do is lark about,
And think they haven't got a thing to lose
Because we're out at sea. But they'll find out.
I'll get them on the boat-deck for a spell
Of pack-drill at the double. Then they'll see
I'm still the boss and I know how to quell
Their bolshie little tricks. They think CB
Can't be awarded on a ship. They're right.
We're all confined to barracks in a way.
But I can think up punishments a sight
Worse than what CB is any day.
I'm their Sergeant-Major and they must
Recognize that what I say is law.

That's the way you build the kind of trust
You've got to have in action. Major Shaw
Is like most officers, not hard enough.
But he's not bad. The subalterns are all
Wet behind the ears. When things get rough
I'll have to hold their hands. They're what I call
More gentleman than officer. I mean
They've got posh voices and all that but no
Leadership. One's only just nineteen
And thinks he's still at school. He'll have to grow
To manhood quick when we go up the blue.
The other day he called me 'Sir' then tried
To act as if he hadn't, but he knew
I'd heard him and he blushed up like a bride.
Well, Glad, I reckon this is just about
The longest letter that I ever wrote.
If Billy's naughty give him one good clout
And tell him that his Dad will make a note
Of all his bad behaviour and he'll pay
When I get back. A hug and kiss for Lil
And lots saved up for you until the day
That I come home.

Your loving husband,
Bill

6

Dear Mother,
                        Just a little note to say
That all is well and that you need not fuss.
The food is good, my quarters are OK.
Though Sergeant-Major Sharp's an awkward cuss
And sometimes makes me feel a frightful ass.
He's one of the survivors of Dunkirk
And served in India on the Khyber Pass
Or some such place. I just don't like his smirk
Whenever I inspect my chaps or when
I give a little pep-talk on morale.
He doesn't even hide it from the men.
It's so embarrassing. I think I shall
Quite firmly tick him off. Well anyway
I mustn't bore you talking army shop.
Everything's been peaceful till today.

Just half an hour ago we had to drop
Some depth-charges which means a hostile sub
Is prowling pretty close. I don't suppose
The Navy boys will let him sink our tub.
Let's hope they're wide awake and on their toes.
Regards to all chums at the tennis club,
My love to Jill and send me one of those
Curly briar pipes, you know the kind
That Sherlock Holmes was always seen to smoke
Though his, I think, was meerschaum. Never mind
If they are scarce or you are feeling broke;
I've no doubt I'll survive without.
                                    Well, mums,
I'd better finish this. I've lots to do.
Don't think I sit here twiddling idle thumbs –
First, boat-drill, then a lecture to sit through.
They keep us on the trot. Now don't you let
The rationing and air-raids get you down.
I know the war is far from over yet
But we'll come through, and won't we paint the town
Fifty shades of red when I come back!
First, the job in hand! then fun and games.
Keep smiling mother. Remember me to Mac
And Mrs P.
                        With lots of love from
                        James

7

Dear Ron,
            Well, here I am at sea. I bet
You never thought the sods would ever get
Yours truly on a troopship. Nor did I.
The buggers had an escort standing by
To pick me up as soon as I got out –
Full magazines, one ready up the spout:
They'd a shot me through the bollocks if I'd run!
Handcuffs too. What else could I a done
But go along with them? I tried to slip
The cuffs. No dice. They got me on the ship
Before they took them off and even then
I never moved a step without two men
Detailed as my escort till we got

Out of sight of land. I don't know what
They thought I'd do – dive overboard, I guess,
And swim three miles or so in battledress.
Not likely mate! But don't think I'll agree
To join the true-blue warriors and be
A willing dish of cannon-fodder. Me,
I'm going to stay alive and let the rest
Get blown to Kingdom Come. It's maybe best
For me to say no more – you never know
Who gets to read your mail. I've got to go
And see old Holy Joe for what he calls
'A little friendly chat'. A load of balls
Is what I call it. Still, I'll get a smoke
And cup of chah. He's not a bad old bloke,
An old brown-hatter if he had the guts.
You know the type: straight out of *Comic Cuts*,
All Adam's apple, teeth and great big ears
And with that silly smile you get with queers.
It's funny how they fancy us hard men
And wouldn't swap one wicked sod for ten
Well-behaved lance-corporals.
                                        Well, I hope
You'll soon be out the nick. I know you'll cope
With all the bullshit that they dish out there.
We'll meet up, you and me, some time, somewhere,
And have the greatest piss-up ever was.
Don't let the bastards grind you down because
You're worth more than a million of them, Ronnie.
Okay?
          Keep smiling.
                              Your old china,
                                        Johnny

8

Dear Hilda,
              Goodness knows when you'll see this
Or where I'll be when you are reading it.
You simply can't imagine how I miss
Our times together when we used to sit
After evensong with Ovaltine
And chocolate biscuits in those halcyon days
Before this beastly war. I do not mean

I'm sorry I joined up though there are ways,
I now believe, in which I could have served
Both God and country more effectively
At home. The trouble is I'm too reserved,
Too *different* from the men who come to me
For help or comfort. They can't understand
My language or my values, nor I theirs –
They might be natives of a different land.
One of them's just left. He sits and stares
And smokes my cigarettes and might as well
Be a chimpanzee for all the sense
Of contact that I feel. I tried to tell
Him something of God's mercy and immense
Capacity for loving even those
Most sinful and debased. I should explain:
This soldier, Johnny Evans – broken nose
And shifty eyes – was handcuffed on the train
In case he ran away. He's what he calls
A real Detention Wallah, spent more time,
He proudly claims, behind the Glasshouse walls
Than with his regiment. His only crime,
As far as I can see, consists in his
Failure to conform and toe the line.
I tried to tell him how the sinner is
Most dear to God. I quoted Karl Barth's fine
Sermon on what he has called the First
Christian Fellowship – the thieves nailed there
With Christ, enduring agony and thirst
As great as His, sharing His despair,
Not knowing they would finally attain
Life everlasting. Jesus did not choose
To die with those who knew what they would gain;
His partners were the scum of slums and stews,
The most despised – oh, Hilda, please excuse
My preaching on like this! Truth is, I feel
That men like Evans show that I'm no use
At all as Padre. When I said, 'Let's kneel
And say a simple prayer together, pray
For help and guidance in the strife to come',
He said, 'No thanks. I'd best be on my way.
But don't mind me. And say one for my mum.
She swallows all that stuff.' I could have wept.
The strange thing is he makes me feel so weak,

So lacking in experience, inept
And somehow less than masculine; a freak.
Ah well, forgive these feeble bleatings, dear.
Things might improve when we are under fire.
I've been assured there's nothing quite like fear
Of sudden death or maiming to inspire
Religious feelings. Only yesterday
Sergeant-Major Sharp was heard to say
There's nothing like old Jerry's eighty-eights
To make a whole battalion start to pray.
Evans says that he'll put on his skates
Long before he gets in range of guns.
I think that he perhaps exaggerates
His lack of spirit. He said that he who runs
Away lives to run another day.
Such cynicism – but I ramble on.
Please give my kind regards to George and tell
Him that I'm sure that he, if anyone,
Will care for my parishioners as well
Or better than I did.
                              Must choose a hymn
For church parade.
                              Goodnight, God bless,
                                        from Tim

III

Port of Arrival

It is like coming back to somewhere known,
Or dreamed about for years, its features grown
Familiar yet imprecise, now blurred
By frequent fingering, observed and heard
But in another life. The place we see
Is just as we imagined it would be
Except its furnishings are somehow less
Spectacular, more drab, and we confess
To disappointment, something like a sense
Of loss, of being cheated. The difference
Between the cherished image and the real
Is that of tone. Unlike our bright ideal
The buildings we see now are not pure white

But ochre with a hint of pink; the light
Is not that pale and deliquescent gold,
But harsh, acescent, and it does not hold
Expected spicy perfumes but the scent
Of urine, sweat, and various excrement.
And yet the sky's fresh, smoothly-ironed blue
Is as we knew it would be, and the few
Dusty palm trees near the jabbering quay
Are those dark frozen fountains they should be.
The women, in their long black robes, conceal
Behind their yashmaks all they think and feel
And, like the fellahin, appear to be
Models for the scriptural pictures we
Remember on the walls of Sunday School.
Incongruous beside them, stands the cool
And polished Captain with his little squad
Of other-ranks, less elegantly shod
And clad, who stand at ease in front of rows
Of stationary trucks. Two camels doze
Like dusty hillocks mounted on thin props.
Hoarse shouts and rattlings, then the gangway drops.
The order comes for us to disembark
And, like the crowd emerging from a dark
Cinema, we blink as we see sores
And milky, sightless eyes, wounds, not from wars,
But death and ignorance. The beggars' cry
Despairingly demands baksheesh. The sky
Remains serene, its smooth indifference spreads
A seamless canopy above our heads,
Nor does that bland composure seem to feel
The presence of the great dark birds that wheel
And drift on lazy, outstretched wings which throw
Their black prophetic shadows here below;
And, while no smear of threatening cloud appears,
Faint thunder whispers in our wondering ears.

Swearing In

What a fucking awful mob,
The Gordon fucking Highlanders.
That fucking bastard sergeant, I'll
Smack him in the fucking gob –
   He's put me on a fucking fizzer
For sweet fuck-all the rotten fucker.
I'll kill the fucker, so I will.
I'm on a fucking charge tomorrow –
   it's fucking pay parade an' all –
   and I'll be on a C fucking B,
Seven fucking days at least – what for?
Just for being fucking me.
An idle boot-lace, that's what he
Pegged me for the rotten fucker,
Idle boot-lace? Was it fuck!
He hates my guts so fuck my luck,
I'll kill the fucker so I will.
Fucking arseholes here he comes,
Garbage from the fucking slums.
He'd kiss my arse in Civvy Street
And call me 'sir', the little shite –
Look out China! On your feet,
He's coming over … 'Yes Sarge! Right!
Right away Sarge! Very well!
At the double … I'll do my best
Yes Sarge … Right Sarge – ' Fucky nell
I hope to fuck he was impressed.
You never know, the fucker might
Tear that 252 to bits
And I'll get pissed tomorrow night
Instead of doing fucking jankers –
But no! All NCOs are shits
And fuck-pigs, ponces, poufs and wankers.
He'll never let me off that charge –
'Right! I'm coming jildi Sarge!'

Varieties of Bastard

Not a bad old bastard, Captain Treve.
He only give me seven days CB
For being two days absent without leave.
That bastard what was previous OC
Would sling you in the bastard nick for less.
He give me fourteen bastard days last time
Because they said my bed-space was a mess!
What would he give you for a proper crime?
It's a bastard when your Company OC
Detests your bastard guts. When he got sent
To BHQ I shed no tears, not me.
Life's been all right since then. Old Treve's a gent
Compared with him. The CSM's not bad:
The bastard's strict but fair. And Sergeant Green's
A decent bastard underneath. I'm glad
It's his platoon I'm in and not McQueen's.
By Christ, McQueen's a proper bastard, mate.
You'd have to go to Hell to find one worse,
And there he'd be contender at his weight:
Corporal Watson's gentle as a nurse,
As nice a bastard as you'd wish to meet,
And all the lads is just about the best
Bunch of bastards you could find, a treat
To soldier with.
             All right, get dressed.
Stop wasting bastard time. We'll get to town
Just as the pubs is opening, if you shift
Yourself a bit. Then first of all we'll down
A dozen pints of bitter pretty swift
And then we'll get some crumpet at the dance.
Can't dance? I know you can't. No more can't I.
But that don't mean we got no bastard chance
Of picking up some bints, and that's no lie.
And if the bastards brush us off we'll wait
Outside the bastard hall, and if they've got
Their boyfriends with them all the better, mate.
We'll get both effs – a fuck and fight, that's what!
Come on then, you old bastard, let's be quick.
I tell you, mate, of all the bastards in
The whole battalion you're the one I'd pick
To be my right-hand man through thick and thin.

FFI

'Get fell in for FFI!'
'What's FFI mean Sarge?'
'You'd better call me Sergeant or
You'll find you're on a charge.'

'Sorry Sergeant'
     'All right son,
FFI means free
From horrible infections like
Scabies and VD.

'Now listen. If you've copped a dose
Of syphilis or clap
Don't claim you caught it from the seat
Last time you had a crap.

'The MO might be stupid like
Most officers and gents,
But don't believe that even them
Is total innocents.

'The quack, he knows about these things,
So just take it from him:
The only way to get poxed up
Is from an arse or quim.

'There's only two men in this mob –
And this you ought to know –
Who *can* catch pox from toilet seats:
The Chaplain and MO.'

Rifle Inspection

My God, your rifle's manky!
You're on a fizzer lad!
I don't know what you think you're at!
You'll drive me bleedin' mad!

Both sights is fucking filthy!
There's spiders up the spout!
Last time you used it on the range
You never boiled it out.

You what? You lost your pull-through?
Right then, you must expect
Another charge as well as this –
Losing by neglect.

You're for the high-jump, sonny;
I almost pity you.
Meanwhile you'd better beg or steal
Pull-through and four-by-two.

What's the thing they learn you
At your mother's knee?
The best friend of a soldier's his
Lee Enfield 303!

Your best friend is your rifle:
So don't you let me see
You treating yours as if it was
Your bitter enemy.

Yes, treat it like your sweetheart,
Your baby or your wife.
Look after it! Maybe one day
The thing will save your life.

But now you're on a fizzer,
And when your pals is free
Tomorrow night to go to town
You'll find you're on CB.

And you'll be doing jankers
When they're out on the piss.
All right platoon: be warned by this!
Attention and dismiss!

Sanitation Wallah

I joined up in the 'thirties, like
  Lots of other blokes
Who couldn't get a bleedin' job.
  I never told my folks
But signed my soul away to get
  A pint and twenty smokes.

The King's Shilling's what they give you then,
  Once you signed your name
And sold yourself like merchandise –
  I'd only myself to blame,
And if I'd a known what was to come
  I'd a joined up just the same.

It's not that nature meant me for
  A soldier's life, that I
Was made of the stuff of military men
  What say they'd sooner die
Than let the name of the regiment down,
  That's not the reason why.

I suppose I can't imagine life
  In civvy street at all;
I don't know how you ever get up
  Without revalley call;
Truth is, a soldier never grows up
  Though he might be six feet tall.

The army, it looks after you,
  Just like a bleedin' nurse,
Though a bit more heavy-handed like
  And more inclined to curse.
It feeds and clothes and tucks you up:
  Things might be a damn sight worse.

Although I'm London born and bred
  I joined a Scottish crowd.
My ancestors, you see, was Scotch –
  My name is Jim Macleod –
And when I first put on the kilt
  By Jesus, I was proud!

The other blokes all laughed at me
  And called me Sassenach
And other things much less polite:
  I don't blame them, looking back.
I wasn't one for making pals,
  Just hadn't got the knack.

Stirling Castle was the place:
  We learned to move in threes,
Did weapon-training, drills and guards
  And got down on our knees
To scrub a hundred barrack floors
  Before going overseas.

Egypt suited me all right;
  I've always liked the heat;
And, when the Padre chose me for
  His batman, life was sweet:
All I had to do was keep
  His kit all clean and neat.

The cushiest job you'd ever get;
  Trust me to ruin it!
He used to leave his cash around;
  I only took a bit,
A few bob now and then, but he
  Split on me, the shit!

I lost the job of course, but worse
  I had a two-month spell
Of pack-drill at the double in
  That place next door to hell
They call Detention, where I slept
  On stone in a reeking cell.

I done my time and then went back
  To what life was before
The cushy batman's job, except
  I now was even more
Unpopular with everyone.
  Then came the bloody war!

I didn't think, when I joined up,
    I'd ever have to fight.
One taste of it was quite enough;
    I never dreamt that fright
Could chew you up and spit you out
    The way it did that night.

Our mob was ordered to attack;
    Sidi Barrani, the place.
The night was cold, a vicious wind
    Flung sand in every face
And choked and blinded us as we
    Advanced at walking pace.

Machine-gun bursts and eighty-eights
    Chattered, roared and flashed;
I heard the wounded wailing loud:
    Those bodies had been smashed
As mine at any moment might
    Be broken, gored and gashed.

Well, I survived that night somehow
    But on the following day
I took my old Lee Enfield, then
    I blew two toes away:
I'd swear it was an accident
    Whatever they might say.

It did the trick. I never saw
    No action after that.
When I came out of hospital
    They called me filthy rat
And things much worse but, at the base,
    I prospered and grew fat.

They made me sanitation wallah,
    And that's what I shall be
Until my time's expired for good,
    And it will do for me.
We all end up as we deserve:
    We *are* our destiny.

A sanitation wallah is
    The lowest of the low;
He cleans the men's ablutions and
    Each morning has to go
And empty all the chocolate-pots –
    Not soldier's work, I know.

But I think it is much better than
    Slogging up the blue
And digging in, scared shitless, when
    They've got a line on you,
Or lying in a shallow grave,
    Or I think I think I do.

Detention Wallah

'What did you do in the war Daddee?'
    'Lots of jankers, son:
Coal fatigues and scrubbing floors,
    Bashed spuds till I looked like one.

'Guards and pickets, rifle range,
    Chucking Mills grenades;
Kit-inspections, FFI's,
    Lectures and parades.

'Weapon-training – mortar, Bren –
    Forced marches at the double;
Bayonet-practice and PT,
    And never out of trouble.

'Always getting pegged for crimes
    Like dirty brasses or
An idle bootlace, petty things
    Is what they did me for.

'The officers and NCOs,
    They had it in for me;
When other lads was out on pass
    I was on CB.'

'But what about the war Daddee
   When the fighting started?'
'I took a powder, sonny-boy.
   I hastily departed.

'I wasn't going to get myself
   Blown to smithereens.
They'd never get me on that boat
   By any kind of means.

'I shoved my towel and shaving gear
   In my small pack and ran.
I got a lift to London in
   A big removal van.

'The red-caps, they soon picked me up;
   I got three months detention;
The glass-house, son, is hell on earth –
   There's things I just can't mention.

'Everything you do is done
   Always at the double;
That means you never walk, but run,
   Or else you're in real trouble.

'Each day I scrubbed the barrack-square
   Before PT began,
Down on all fours – if not a dog,
   Then something less than man.

'PT, son? What is that, you say?
   It's supposed to make you fit.
Pure Torture's what we knew it as,
   Whatever *they* called it.

'The whole idea, you see, was this:
   To make you suffer so
That even if Hell lay outside
   You'd volunteer to go.

'Not me though, son. I thought, "OK
   You treat me like a brute –
Those hours of packdrill, insults, blows
   And putting in the boot – "

'Lots of that there was, my lad.
    They'd beat you till you bled
And stick you into solitary
    With water and dry bread –

' "You treat me like an animal
    And that's just what I'll be,
Cunning, tough and obstinate:
    You'll never master me!"

'They never did, though I done more
    Glasshouse time than most;
So long I spent in solitary
    I came out like a ghost.

'But son, my spirit, underneath,
    Survived it all intact;
They thought they'd crushed me like a bug
    But I had won in fact.'

'But Daddee, what if everyone
    Had done the same as you?
We would have lost the war, Daddee,
    And lost our country, too!'

'If everyone had been like me
    No war could have occurred;
That's logic, son, can't be denied
    So take your old Dad's word.'

Old Sweat
or The Gift of
Tongues

Get some service in;
Your knees aren't brown yet, lad.
I might not be as old but I'm
Smarter than your dad.

So don't you try and come
The wide-o, clever dick.
Don't use them long posh words with me:
Your voice gets on my wick.

You haven't got no pips,
So talk the way we do.
That lah-di-dah will make the blokes
Piss all over you.

So drop them fancy airs,
You know they make me mad.
When you was in your Daddy's bag
I was in Baghdad.

Because I've got no rank
Don't mean I've got no sense.
When I complain you're like a kid
I don't mean no offence.

I just mean you don't know
The how and where and why
Of proper soldiering at all:
Your number isn't dry.

I've served in foreign parts –
You wouldn't know the names –
I speak the lingos and I know
The wog's little games.

Experience is what
Learns you more than schools
And colleges that turns out squads
Of educated fools.

How many of them speak
Six languages, like me?
French, German, Arabic as well
As Itie and Parsee.

You what? That's only five?
I'm well aware of that.
The sixth one's what I'm talking now
You dozey little prat.

You might know Greek and Latin,
But let me tell you, pal,
Them's useless in Bombay or here
Beside the Sweet Canal.

Compree mon Kamerad?
Jig-jig, parley-voo,
Shufti zubrick, quois-kateer
San fairy ann, napoo.

Achtung, maleesh, sai-eeda,
Mafeesh faloose, buckshee;
Juldi, wahled, mangarea,
Promenade sheree.

Ears and eyes wide open
That's the way it's done;
Shut your trap, put in some time,
You'll be a man, my son.

Twelve-Hour Pass

I'm beezing up my toe-caps and I'm shining all the brass;
Buttons, cap-badge, gleam like gold; I'm on a twelve-hour
    pass.
Last night I pressed my strides between my bed and
    palliasse.
It's true I'm just a lance-jack but I've got a bit of class.
I've used white chalk on my one stripe and shaved and
    trimmed my tash;
I'm off to town. This time I swear I'll get myself a bash.
My hair is slick with brilliantine; I mean to cut a dash.
Tonight at the Astoria I bet I make a splash.
Bints like a man in uniform, or so folk always say;
I'm all set up, I look a treat, I've got a full week's pay.
If I pick up a bint tonight and she don't want to play
I swear I'll put one on her chin and shag her anyway.
That might sound hard, but so is life, and everybody
    knows
A bint says No when she means Yes, and that's the way it
    goes.

They get what they deserve and what they really want from
    you;
They've only got themselves to blame; we all know this is
    true.
There's nothing they like better than getting took by
    storm,
Pertickly if the man is one that wears a uniform.
Well, cheerio and wish me luck; tonight's the night, lads,
    so
With swagger-stick and blancoed prick I'm off to meet the
    foe,
'Cos we all know the enemy is not the Kraut or Jap;
It's that pretty little honey-pot with furry booby-trap.

Drinking Song

Tonight's the night so, by the right,
Right wheel! Then sink your liquor.
We're on the town; I've half-a-crown,
But Jim's got half a nicker.

We'll spend the lot no matter what
We feel like at revallee;
Them that think it's wrong to drink
Is sissy or dulallee.

Another bar, another jar,
No time for idle chatter;
We've had our fill of guards and drill
And now we're on the batter.

So drink up, son, we'll have some fun,
And when they've shut the boozers,
A bloke or dame, it's all the same,
Us buggers can't be choosers.

But, while they serve what we deserve
And much prefer to crumpet,
We'll kill our thirst with rapid bursts
As long as they will pump it.

So one last toast: the Holy Ghost,
Pure spirit, so they tell us;
The Padre he can get it free,
But I'm not really jealous.

Fill up your glass; this is our Mass –
See how the bottles glitter –
We are content, our sacrament
Potato-crisps and bitter.

THREE LOVE SONGS

I

The Sentry's Song

Fist clamps frozen on the rifle;
Frost and north-east malice stifle
All desire;
When the duty-stint is ended,
Flesh and soul will be attended
By kind fire.

Warmth and rest, and then soft dreaming;
Images of love's sweet scheming
Re-awake
Those intensities of yearning
Which set mind and body burning
For her sake.

Guardroom, uniform, and webbing
Fade and drift away; their ebbing
Leaves a bright
Shore where man and woman wearing
Mufti of silk skin are pairing
In delight.

II

The Corporal's Song

O, Dolly dear, you're more to me
Than my third stripe. I long to be
Close to you and once more see
Your eyes, their starry beauty;
Those other things I ache to do
I hardly dare confess to you:
I'll love you always – that is true –
Beyond the call of duty.

The lads in my platoon would grin
If they could see what happens in
My head but they could not begin
To understand love's power.
They think I am a man of steel
And could not guess at what I feel,
That X-Rays of my heart reveal
A single, fragile flower.

So roll on next weekend, my sweet;
I'll get a pass and we will meet
As always on Victoria Street,
And I shall hold you tightly.
O love, it seems too long to wait;
At times I feel I almost hate
This life that keeps us separate,
Prevents our loving nightly.

And yet, when all is said and done,
There's nothing like the roar of gun
And rifle's spite when war's begun
To make a soldier frisky.
The man who flirts with death and life
Is one who can excite his wife,
Like gleam and danger of a knife,
Make loving sweet, but risky.

III

The Defaulter's Song

Although I miss you, dearest heart
I would not have you with me here
To see me play this clownish part
Clad in penitential gear.
More than pain or loss I fear
Humiliation's sickly taste:
The sky seems one enormous sneer
As I crouch here, ashamed, abased.

I'm peeling spuds, enough to serve
A hundred hungry men. I feel
That this is worse than I deserve,
This scullion's role. I did not steal,
And tried my hardest to conceal
My lack of keenness to become
The sergeant-major's sworn ideal –
Unquestioning and blind and dumb.

Of course you never thought of me
As hero or as fighting-man.
There was a time I tried to be
Dead regimental but that plan
Was blown to bits when I began
To fall in love with you, my sweet.
Now nothing could be dearer than
A nest for us in civvy street.

I'll peel away like wedding-bells,
And do my jankers with a grin.
I think of you and my heart swells –
And something else – my senses spin
To dream of when we can begin
Our life together when we're wed
And you and I will snuggle in,
Like little spuds, our marriage bed.

Pipes and Drums

Slow, bandaged hammer-beat of drum is tolled,
Three booming spondees; pause, and then three more;
Then rattling side-drums chatter out their din,
Machine-gun rapid, as the pipes begin.

Pipe-major Mackie leads his men in march
And counter-march; kilts sway and swing; the wild
Barbaric voice of triumphs, griefs and fears
Floats dreams of banners, plumes and glittering spears.

Scotland the Brave, Hey, Johnny Cope, before
A change of tempo for the grave slow march:
The Flowers of the Forest are withered away, and then
The tunes of glory swagger out again.

The flagrant splendour still contrives to seize
The yielding heart; the mind almost believes
The tales this pageant tells, almost ignores
The excremental horror of all wars.

The pipers' boasts and lamentations fade;
Night and silence drape the barrack square.
A bugle sounds Lights Out; the last note dies,
Its sadness certain truth where all else lies.

Route March Rest

They marched in staggered columns through the lanes
Drowsy with dust and summer, rifles slung.
All other-ranks wore helmets and the sun
Drummed on bobbing metal pates and purred
Inside their skulls; the thumping tramp of boots
On gravel crunched. B Company had become
A long machine that clanked and throbbed. The reek
Of leather, sweat and rifle-oil was thick
And khaki on the body of the day.

All dainty fragrances were shouldered out
Though thrush and blackbird song could not be stilled
And teased some favoured regions of the air.

They reached a village and the order came
To halt and fall out for a rest. The men
Unslung their rifles, lit up cigarettes,
And sprawled or squatted on the village green.
Opposite the green, next to the church,
The school, whose open windows with wild flowers
In glass jars on the sills framed pools of dark,
Was silent, cool; but from the playground sprayed
The calls of children, bright as buttercups,
Until a handbell called them in from play
And then B Company was ordered back
To fall in on the road in their platoons
And start the march again.
                                        Beyond the church
They passed a marble plinth and saw the roll
Of names, too many surely for this small
Community, and as the files trudged on,
Faintly from the school, like breath of flowers
But half-remembered, children's voices rose:
'All things bright and beautiful,' they sang,
Frail sound, already fading, soon to die.

Church Parade

Faint breath of flowers but, overwhelming this,
A heavier scent of dust and holiness
As sunlight, strained through gold and purple glass,
Slants down to gild the altar and the cross.
An organ, sounding less than healthy, groans,
And slowly the battalion, in platoons,
Files on heathen boots into the House
Of God. They settle, sheepish, in their pews.
Above the pulpit, on the wall, a board
Bears numbers like an oculist's testing-card.
Memories stir and tease; this heavy, sweet
Mysterious air and sound can propagate

Sensations from the treasurable past,
A nervous awe and momentary thirst
For goodness; boredom settling like the dust;
A sense of something frail and pure, now lost.

PTIs

In the echoing gymnasium they shout,
Though 'shout' is too robust a word for those
Falsetto, yelped commands to stretch and bend;
There's something else androgynous about
The way they bounce and pirouette and pose:
Effects that few, if any, could intend.

Oddly insectile, too: their legs look thin
In hugging navy blue; their sweaters striped
In horizontal red and black, though each,
Whether dark or fair, possesses skin
That superfluity of health has wiped
Clean and lent the texture of a peach.

Despite big biceps and aggressive jaws,
That look of chorus-girl or model stays.
Their shiny stares are innocent of wit
Or curiosity; all human flaws
For them are physical, and their blank gaze
Is colder than the glass that mirrors it.

Casualty – Mental Ward

Something has gone wrong inside my head.
The sappers have left mines and wire behind;
I hold long conversations with the dead.

I do not always know what has been said;
The rhythms, not the words, stay in my mind;
Something has gone wrong inside my head.

Not just the sky but grass and trees are red,
The flares and tracers – or I'm colour-blind;
I hold long conversations with the dead.

Their presence comforts and sustains like bread;
When they don't come it's hard to be resigned;
Something has gone wrong inside my head.

They know about the snipers that I dread
And how the world is booby-trapped and mined;
I hold long conversations with the dead;

As all eyes close, they gather round my bed
And whisper consolation. When I find
Something has gone wrong inside my head
I hold long conversations with the dead.

War Graves at El Alamein

When they were little children they explored
Forests dense with dangers, were pursued
By beast, or giant wielding knife or sword
And terrified they found their feet were glued
Firmly to the ground; they could not scream
Or run, yet they were never stabbed or gored
But always woke to find it just a dream.

Years and nightmares later they became
Old enough to put on uniform,
And in parched throats they gagged upon the same
Taste of childhood terror in a storm
Of killing thunder they must battle through.
Now, unimportant pieces in the game,
They sleep and know that last bad dream was true.

Naming the Names

Carved on slabs of silence
　　The litany of names
Outlives glass and palimpsest
　　And time's lithophagous flames.

They cannot be buried in darkness
　　With the white, staring dead
And their obsolete dreams and weapons;
　　They cannot be unsaid.

Nor can we be deaf to the bitter
　　Psalming of those nouns,
The names of the rivers and valleys,
　　The broken, beautiful towns.

The Somme, like guns' far thunder,
　　Ominous, yet with a sigh,
Passchendaele, Mons and Wipers,
　　Graveyards where multitudes lie.

Arras, Bapaume, Vimy Ridge,
　　The Marne, Loos and Cambrai,
Dark stains on the pitiful ribbons
　　That will never fade away.

They are written in blood; and I wonder
　　If those later slaughter-grounds
Dunkirk, Alamein, Arnhem,
　　Will ever join these sounds.

Will my children's children tremble
　　And sigh to hear them said,
And taste that bitter-sweet liquor
　　Flavoured with pity and dread?

Or will the words be merely
　　Names glanced at on a map?
Arromanches and Pegasus Bridge,
　　Caen, the Falaise Gap.

A TIME FOR FIRES
1992

Escapologist

The year was nineteen-thirty,
The place, Eccles.
In the market square, on cobbled stones,
Dark and slimed from recent rain,
Two men had drawn
A few spectators in a ring
Around the space where one
Would now perform.
His skin was pale,
A bluish white, the pallor of boiled cod.
The arms were thin and muscles unheroic.
Those who looked on
Swapped shifty glances,
Wore the same uneasy grin.
An old cloth cap, for pennies, yawned in mud.
The man's assistant manacled his wrists;
Both feet were chained
And he was lowered to the ground
And wrapped from neck to feet
Inside a canvas shroud, then firmly strapped.

The long thin bundle lay
Trussed tight, the head
The only part of him in sight.
And then his struggle to escape began.
Those swivelling eyes were not theatrical;
This thing was real. I read
The language of imprisonment and fear
As that stained, capitate, long parcel
Jerked and bucked and squirmed
In dirt, on obdurate stone.

A few spectators left
And, as they walked away,
The small explosions of their grins,
Becoming laughter, flared, then sputtered out.

And still he wrestled, writhed and fought;
His face contorted, broke beneath the strain:
Those eyes could burst;
Spittle laced the jagged mouth.
This was the face of someone who could die,
A parody of death and birth.

And now, though half a century has passed,
Something of my fear can still defy
Reason and the years,
And I remember how, when he at last
Threw the canvas cloak and chains aside
And sucked in liberal air,
The witnesses did not applaud,
Though some of them threw pennies in the cap,
That few, if any, could afford.

Frying Tonight

Outside, the dark breathes vinegar and salt;
The lemon window seems to salivate,
Draws peckish kids, black moths to candlelight.

Inside you may sit down to eat, or take
Your parcelled supper out into the night.
On each white halo of a china plate

Dismembered golden dactyls form a nest
About the scab of batter which, when split,
Confesses flesh as white as coconut.

Beneath investigation of bright fork
The naked body breaks and separates,
Unfolds its steaming leaves, in smooth soft flakes.

Sleek, plump bottles, bodies almost black
Hold vinegar on all the table tops
Like little holy sisters in white caps.

And on the counter in a gallon can,
Floating blindly in translucent brine,
Small green dirigibles loll still, becalmed.

Those silver vats behind, they all contain
Hot lakes of oil: when fresh peeled chips are drowned
They spit and sizzle like a thousand cats.

In front a patient congregation stands;
These serious communicants who long
To feel warm parcels solid in their hands.

Later, at home, replete, they may spread out
Stained paper cerements, read about old scores,
Dead scandals, weddings, unimportant wars.

Bobbie

'We used to drink Green Goddesses,' she said.
'I don't suppose you even know the name.
At least you've heard of Pimm's. He had a red
MG, my boyfriend did. We'd go to Thame
And stay at Fothergill's pub, the famous one,
Or else nip down to somewhere by the sea
And spend the day just idling in the sun.
And when the long and lovely night began
We'd leave the bar and go outside where we,
And maybe one or two new chums, would dance
There on the esplanade to music from
A gipsy barrel-organ. Such romance
You can't believe, and all along the prom
Coloured lanterns glowed like fairyland.
We'd dance and dance, my dear, and all the time
You'd smell the seaside smell of sea and sand
Behind the lilac, honeysuckle, lime
And *Passing Clouds*, and there, below the sound
Of tango, waltz and foxtrot, you could hear
The hush and sigh of breakers on the strand
And suck and gurgle underneath the pier.
Things were different then, sheer poetry dear;
Such gorgeous lingerie we used to wear.
My boy friends, every one a gentleman;
You'd never hear one raise his voice or swear,
Not like today. Oh, things were different then.
My escort never came without some flowers
And chocolate liqueurs, nice things like that.

They were the days of sunshine and sweet showers.
The dancing days of silver saxophones
And roses.

                    Well, thank you for our chat
And for the drinkie too. It's time to go.'
The lipstick marking where her mouth had been
Curved slightly upward at each end although
Her eyes remained unchanged, glass splinters, green,
Like Christmas-cracker jewellery, the gleam
Not quite derisive, watchful, undeceived,
Not asking to be wanted, but believed.

The Party's Over

A Kind of Elegy

Some years ago – forty or so, I'd guess –
Among the literati of the day
It was fashionable to praise the pure *simplesse*
Of the artist's eye, and you would hear them say
In The Fitzroy or Wheatsheaf, or write in some review,
How the painter or poet with his innocent eye
Perceived a world rinsed by primeval dew,
And marvelled like a child. Maybe. But I
Was never quite convinced although I knew
Of poets, painters and composers who,
Outside the practice of their art, would be
Judged as, if not 'childlike', 'immature'.
One, a poet, died quite recently,
Whose bloodshot vision no one would call 'pure',
And yet he wrote with passion and some wit
And made his own bleak music from despair,
Snarling at life, as if he hated it,
Those obloquies a kind of putrid prayer.
His last appearance, just before he died,
Was at a party given by a friend
Whom he had known for years, and there he tried
To squeeze more from the night than it contained,
Growing more excited with each drink,
Frantic for affection and applause.

The less indulgent guests would purse and shrink,
And even his kind host was seen to pause
Before responding to appeals for more
Booze, and love, and flattery.
                    At length
The first departing guests moved to the door;
Soon others followed, sensing that the strength
Which welded this occasion's symmetry
Had suddenly begun to leak away.
'The party's over,' someone said; but he,
The ageing poet, was resolved to stay:
'The party isn't over! Mustn't be!'
Indignation and entreaty brimmed his eyes;
His look was like a child's of two or three,
Grey hair and ravaged face, a slipped disguise.
'It isn't over yet!' he cried again.
'Oh yes it is,' they said, and made him go
Out into the night of grown-up men
Who laugh, and wave, and slam car-doors and know
The safe road home.
                    Last seen, the poet stood
Blanched and isolated in the chill
Blaze of headlamps, as if carved in wood,
Almost like a winter tree, until
The silver glitter of his piss began,
Rose arching from his centre to descend
On unaffronted hollyhocks and on
A world where all the parties had to end.

The Larkin Room

'A Larkin Room is to be established at the University Library'
                                                        TLS

The walls subfusc with age and nicotine,
Their floral pattern only just
Discernible behind the solid haze;
Two wooden chairs, a table in between,
And in grey air the scent of dust,
As music from a hidden speaker plays.

Bechet, or King Oliver perhaps,
Jazz certainly. The littered books
Are all in English: fiction, mainly light;
Sly female wit and rough stuff from the chaps
Who write of race-courses and crooks;
Nothing even mildly recondite.

Of twentieth century poetry you'll find
Owen, Betjeman, Auden, all
Well-fingered, loved, and, by the narrow bed,
The poems of Thomas Hardy which divined
A wilderness that should appal,
Yet play a marvellous music in the head.

The table holds a saucer-souvenir,
A pair of cycle-clips and sprawl
Of scrawled-on paper, pens, elastic-bands,
And from the ceiling's centre, like a tear,
A single light-bulb hangs; one wall
Displays a photograph of Frinton Sands.

The curtains, faded like a slattern's skirts,
Conspire to keep the daylight out;
They almost meet, not quite, for one is short,
Permits thin gleam of sunlight in to flirt
With dancing dust-motes' prickly rout,
But makes no promises of any sort.

Matches

I saw him often, so often that I ceased,
Almost, to notice him. So now I visualize
A photograph or something like a still
From an old movie, shot in black-and-white.
The mood is one of darkness, but not night.
Rain grizzles. It is probably November.
He is standing near the entrance to the Underground
Outside Victoria Station with his tray
Of matches no one buys, though once or twice,
A hurrying traveller drops a coin or two
On the tray. He wears a burglar's cap
And overcoat discarded by a man

Of greater size. Suspended from his neck
A grimy cardboard sign rests on his chest
That few have stopped to read, and written there,
In faded capitals, is this: KID FRANCIS,
LIGHTWEIGHT CHAMPION OF THE WORLD. NOW BLIND.
The picture does not show the scenes behind
The stony pupils of his eyes, nor can
We know what those clubbed ears may listen to
From peopled darkness in the stadium
Beyond the white-drenched altar of the ring.
Perhaps a kind of mercy operates,
Prevents his seeing what this world is like,
In which a king is brought to beggary,
And almost everyone is blind to him.

Access to the Children

The polar bears are sculpted lumps of snow.
If they feel sympathy it doesn't show.
The monkeys are absorbed in their own business;
Their nimble, unrestrained indecencies
May or may not express contempt for those
Who watch uneasily or move away
With furtive eyes to where the zebras stay
Quite still, great dusty humbugs on four stilts,
No more concerned than that giraffe who tilts
And sways in useless camouflage and shakes
His high disdainful head above the groups
Or pairs, the Sunday fathers and their young,
The sullen sons and daughters, little troops
Of conscripts, heirs to marital mistakes.
Their pouting faces blubbered, rouged and stung
By cold and petulance. Each father's grin
Has frozen to a desperate grimace.
He wonders if he'll be invited in
When they get back to what was once his place,
Deciding to refuse with some excuse
In case he finds that he will have to face
His smug usurper's patronizing gaze.

At last the withered daylight starts to fade
And darkens like a leaf. It's time to go.

The children, sick from sweets and lemonade,
Trail towards the gates to start the slow
Journey to the Underground and home.
Early lamps throw bars of yellow light
Across the path, and spectres of the reek
Of stale captivity steal through the night,
Lingering like smoke in hair and clothes,
And will not disappear next day, or week.

Elaine's Story

This happened when I was eight years old.
I was wearing my silver bracelet
That Grannie gave me for my birthday.
Mummy was not there. I did not know
Where she had gone. It was a dark day
And it smelled of Monday. In the hall
The telephone started to ring. And ring.
Daddy was at home. I don't know why.
He was a policeman then. Not now.
He stays at home and looks after us.
I saw him pick up the telephone.
Yes, he said, Yes. He said it again.
Then he said, I see. I don't think
He could see though. His eyes were like glass
Or more like ice. They began to melt
And I saw his face starting to break.
The pieces did not fall on the floor
But they did not seem to fit together
Like they ought to do. I felt frightened.
His face is better now, looks mended
But not the same. His eyes don't either.
Mummy did not come back home. I kept
Asking where she was but now I've stopped.
I've stopped asking anything. Grannie
Said she is with Jesus and happy.
I pretended that I believed her.

Snowfall at Night

The slow and spectral dance is on:
Seven million tiny veils, each one
Frail as a martyred leaf, begin
Their blind work of hypnosis;
And all is so mysterious,
And most mysterious of all,
The more than silence of the fall.

Now, at the window your warm brow
Is sluiced by coolness of the glass,
And sarabands of flakes endow
The heart and eyes with ease; alas,
An ease that, like the fall, will pass.

So these slow gestures of the snow
Bestow a present from the past,
Enchantment close to innocence
Which, like the whiteness, cannot last.

Watering the Flowers

Week upon week of heat,
A summer that the young
Are spellbound by and grateful for,
And we, the old,
Remember from a long-ago Arcadia;
No rain for many days:
The garden soil is cindery with the need
For fresh, celestial waters, healing draughts.
And so I come,
Watering-can in hand,
To ease distress of hyacinth,
Peony, heart's-ease, dahlia and rose,
And they lift grateful faces to the spray,
Silvery and cool,
From my beneficent hand.
They think that I am God.
I care for them in their bright parishes;
I send their roots rain.

Later, lapped in lamplight,
Implicated in
A cello's lovely lucubrations
In the key of C,
I think about the flowers,
Their possible theology,
And wonder what satanic image might
Perturb their peace:
A biped, like their God? Like me?
Though one not bringing sustenance
But bending over them
To cloak the sun and cast a gloom
In whose grim shadow gleam
Steel blades to cut their slender throats?

Or could it be
A quadruped that squats and squirts
Envenomed rain and buries bones
In their dark place of genesis?

Lacrimae Rerum

Whatever is remembered and preserved
In photographic images or words,
In music or those spectral, yet unblurred,
Pictures that may flower inside the head,
However bright, faint shades of loss intrude,
Presences of tears, unshed or shed.

One summer night I walked across the Heath,
Alone and lonely, even then past youth;
The moon gleamed white and curved, a tiger's tooth.
And then, surprising as a starburst, came
Those voices calling to me from the gloom,
Inviting me to step into a dream:

A midnight feast; young men and girls had spread
White linen on the grass, on this displayed
Wine, fruit, various meats and bread.
They were servants from a neighbouring hotel,
Italians, Spaniards, Cypriots, as well
As waitresses from Leeds and Liverpool.

They welcomed me to share their food and wine;
Their friendliness was absolute, it shone
More brightly than the moon's apprentice shine;
We shared, not only nourishment, but bliss,
Yet even in that glade of blessedness
A brackish hint of dawn soon chilled the grass.

Another scene: inside a hotel room;
Jalousies are shut against the sun,
A noon of sensual delights, perfume
And cream of skin, such pungencies!
Gold powder swirls in dusk as voices rise
In contrapuntal music of wild cries.

But, even while love's lexicon
Is rapturously incarnated in
That shadowy room, outside small sounds begin:
Thin whimper of a baby and the sigh
Of rising wind that will, before the day
Is done, bring rain from misanthropic skies.

Now, warm in lamplight on this winter's night
I listen to a Mozart work for flute
And orchestra in D: again I note
How that pure statement just a little aches
With threads of sadness, even in its jokes,
And sigh with pleasure at the noise it makes.

The Better Word

Bonfire: (orig. bone-fire) a great fire in which bones were burnt in the open air.
SHORTER OXFORD ENGLISH DICTIONARY

Summer's petals shrivel in the cold
And dim atelier of memory;
Their scent is difficult to resurrect.
Sensitive potatoes have grown old;
First sweetness lost, they're stout and coarse, like me;
Their toughened skin is maculate and flecked
With warts and wens. This is a time for fires
In gardens and in grates. Outside, the trees
And shrubs are vague and sorrowful in mist;

Stems of clematis, like tangled wires,
Torment the trellis. Under apple trees
Rotting Bramleys deliquesce when pressed
Beneath my heavy tread. In spite of all
The sodden earth and vaporous air I stack
Branches, twigs, stale news, a magazine,
Some broken toys, aborted poems' stained scrawl,
All things that fire is eager to attack,
Or will be when I splash the paraffin
On wood and paper, add the match's flare,
Like so... Soon leaves of flame fandango, flaunt
And wrangle in the smoke; an ancient scent,
Both sweet and acrid, spices swirling air;
Faint images and far-off speakings haunt
The weather in the skull, all redolent
Of unspecific loss; but then, as plain
As if the child were by my side, I hear
The voice from almost thirty years ago
Of my son, Toby, calling me again
To make a 'grandfire', and the word is clear:
Let's make a grandfire dad! And still I know
As I knew then, that through mishearing or
The infant tongue's recalcitrance he'd found
A better word than 'bonfire' for this blaze
Whose flames are now gone widdershin and roar
And crackle, spitting pips of sparks around,
In truly grand and not ossiverous ways.

On the Chevin

November and the rowan berries burn
In brilliant clusters in their dark green caves.
Disgruntled clouds sag low with unshed rain.
The path that runs through now dishevelled woods
Of oak and birch and conifer is mulched
With decadence of fallen leaves on moss
As soft as felt beneath the feet. No dogs
And tumbling summer children to be seen.

A man and woman walk, their pace so slow
It seems to tease the notion of arrival.
The colour of their clothes rhymes with the weather.

This couple is quite unremarkable,
Unless joined hands could waken interest.
Her head tilts slightly to her right and rests
An inch beneath his shoulder, his inclines
Towards her own. They do not seem to speak.

At last the footpath's terminal is reached,
An area where patient cars are parked,
And here they disengage their hands and pause,
Face to face, quite close, though silent still.
The long embrace and kiss don't quite occur.
They turn away to different cars. Doors slam.
Both engines snarl. His car moves off, then hers,
In opposite directions, gathering speed.

The Spell

She will not come.
He works with brush and mop and pail, and sees
Suds glitter, deliquescent diamonds, where
The citrous fragrances ascend to please
Grateful nostrils of the morning air;
And yet he says: *She will not come.*

She will not come.
He places flowers in vases to dispose
About the house to sweeten space and light –
Lily, jasmine, emblematic rose –
He trims the lamps in readiness for night,
Yet still he says: *She will not come.*

She will not come.
But he puts on his coat, goes out to buy
Honey and brown eggs and wine and bread,
Apples, grapes and cheese and medley pie,
Returns to spread fresh linen on the bed,
But says again: *She will not come.*

She will not come.
Collusive twilight veils the brooding skies;
A chill breeze whispers like a distant sea;
He waits in deepening darkness with closed eyes.
As spell against its own fulfilment he
Repeats the words: *She will not come.*

She Speaks the Words

At last she speaks the words he longed to hear:
Lying in his grateful arms she sighs,
'I love you,' and he looks into her eyes
And sees, in each, the glitter of a tear;
And, when again she breathes the words, he feels
In his euphoria a glint of fear.
The music of her voice is sad, reveals
No trace or echo of his own elation,
And underneath the melancholy steals
A contrapuntal note of accusation.

Anniversary Interview

Since you've been partners for so long may I
Face you with a question that you might
Find very difficult indeed to answer.
Are you happily in love with her?
Well, I don't know; the question's made of words.
What happens if I shuffle them like cards?
They turn up meaning something more or less
Significant, though still ambiguous.
In love with her, and *happily*, you said.
That *in* has always seemed a little odd –
In debt, in jail, in terror, in despair –
The preposition seems to chime far more
Matily with bleaker nouns than that
Liquid syllable you'd never shout.
Try *with her happily in love*. It makes
A certain sense, except that *in* still irks;
Or *happily with her in love*. This could
Mean happy me because she loves. I'll spread
The words out one more time and that's the last.
Oh yes, the sequence now makes sense; the best,
The only honest, statement I can make
After all these years; it may sound weak,
But here's the answer your five words now give –
Rip up semantics, syntax and such stuff,
For I am in her, happily, with love.

Stunt Diver

A jangle of coloured lights, though darkness hissed
Beneath those motionless or spinning glitterings,
The fairground called to us with pounding blare
Of noise and we ran eagerly towards it,
Children of a dying day, our fists
Bunched tight about the pennies we would lose.
1936, the year, though we
Knew nothing of Cordoba, Saragossa
Or Berlin. The fairground was our El Dorado
And there, among the whirling brilliancies,
We saw the tower of scaffolding
With the little platform on the top
Just visible against the glowing sky.
And at the foot a water-tank was set,
Cubiform, not more than twelve feet square,
And, propped against this vat, a blackboard leaned
On which the words were chalked: '*Tonight at 9
Stan Linbergh England's greatest diving ace
Performs his death-defying dive through flames.*'

By nine o'clock a crowd had gathered round
And we had waited patiently to keep
As close as was permitted to the tank.
A small man in a tilted opera hat
Striped with the colours of the Union Jack
Shouted through his conic megaphone,
Exhorting everyone to keep well back
Because the water in the tank would blaze
With dangerous flames when Captain Linbergh dived.
More waiting: then at last the hero came.
'Make way!' the patriot shouted and the crowd
Heaved and rustled as a path was made
For Linbergh to walk through. His head was bowed;
He wore a greatcoat with the collar pulled
About his ears. He looked like one condemned.
He reached the tower, removed his overcoat
And briefly shuddered. We could see the flesh
Of arms and shoulders, legs; and we were shocked
To see how soft and white they looked, not carved
From dark, heroic metal or tough teak
But hurtable, almost a girl's pale limbs.

Then he began to climb.
                    We watched his slow
Insectile progress up the trembling tower
And saw, as he drew closer to the small
Platform at the top, his movements seem
To grow more tentative and slow. But he
At last stood there, transformed by distance to
A manikin, Tom Thumb, a something more
Or less than ordinary man. The crowd
Now held its breath as if it stood up there
And was about to dive, while, on the ground,
His partner swung an arm and shouted out,
'Now keep right back!' and in a second flames
Leapt, blazing from the water in the tank,
And Linbergh dived.
                    It was no Tarzan dive,
Slow-motion, breasting air with swallow grace
And swooping downwards like a feathered dart;
No: Linbergh dropped, a heavy stone, so fast
We still stared upwards after he had plunged
Through fire into the tank and dowsed the flames
With that explosive crunch. And then he rose
Shaking water-shrapnel from his head,
And heaved his glistening body from the tank
And climbed down to safe earth. He raised one hand
Acknowledging the patter of applause,
And then put on his coat. His partner moved
Among the crowd, his upturned hat become
A begging-bowl.
                    We did not move away,
Held there by an unreasonable sense
Of being cheated: there must be more to come.
Stan Linbergh and his partner had both gone;
The dark mass of the crowd began to break
And crumble, trickling off towards the lights
And noises of the roundabouts and stalls.
At last we, too, turned slowly from that place
And with a single backward glance we left,
Not speaking, sulky with the sense of loss,
Robbed of something none of us dared name.

Afternoon Men

'... drunkards, afternoon-men, and such as more than ordinarily delight in drink...'

BURTON: THE ANATOMY OF MELANCHOLY

What has happened to the afternoon-men
Now that the afternoon clubs have closed?
They shawled themselves in twilight when
The sun was bright and the old folk dozed
On benches in the public park;
Each sought his own dim, pungent den
And drank in that expensive dark.

While serious people worked away
In office, factory, shop or field,
The afternoon-men went in to play;
They slouched or shuffled, lurched or reeled
Through doors that knew their shadows well –
The *Mandrake, Caves, ML* – to stay
And drink till they, or darkness, fell.

The *Marie Lloyd*, known as plain *ML*
By the afternoon-men, was a paradigm
Of all such clubs: pervasive smell
Of stale tobacco, patina of grime
On the walls and floor; and, on the bar,
Filled ashtrays and fake asphodel:
A babble of noise like a small bazaar.

Failed scholars, ponces, purblind seers;
Poets, sepia with nicotine:
Rayner, Ruthven and their peers,
Louis and Terence, would all convene
Daily with their thespian mates,
Felix and Pat, whose furtive fears
Would soon be realized in their separate fates.

They have all gone into the world of dark,
The wise, the witty, the dumb and the trite;
Charon has welcomed them on to his barque –
It was all a rehearsal for the last night.
The doors of the Clubs are locked and the rust
Forms in the wards and the message is stark:
The afternoon-men have been joined with the dust.

Watching the Cricket

Sun simmers in a gentian sky,
White blossoms of small clouds hang still
Above the elms, in whose spread stain
        Of shadow go
Plump and strutting pigeons. High
Above the trees two skylarks spill
Their sparkling notes like silver grain
        On us below.

White flash and smack of ball on bat;
A shout, and like a frightened thing,
Scurrying on hidden paws
        Across the green,
The ball is chased; a soft white hat
Spins down, a dove with broken wing;
We hear small flutter of applause:
        You have the scene.

Now note that bench where three old men
Sit and watch and rarely say
More than a muttered word except
        To show dismay
And some contempt, recalling when
They were young enough to play,
How keen they'd been and more adept
        In every way.

Then, after tea, as shadows grow
Longer on the grass, the old
Men speak even less and their
        Eyes half close;
How much they see is hard to know,
Or if the little hint of cold,
Glinting in the evening air,
        Disturbs their doze.

It's almost close of play, and they
Surely hear the umpire cry
The final 'Over!' If they do
        They only yawn

And stretch and, when they turn away,
Seem not to see, as day must die,
Their separate nights are beckoning too,
        As stumps are drawn.

Second Sight

Poor eyesight has its compensations,
allows access to a world whose furniture
surprises. I remove my glasses
as I walk with my whippet
in the summer park and, instantly, she melts
into the green earth and disappears.
Irked by her continued absence I begin
to whistle and to call her by name,
and I am again startled
at her small yelp as I stumble over her.

I am gulled by the scattered white stones
which suddenly ascend and punish the air
with slapping wings. The beautiful girl,
as in Greek myth, is changed
by my proximity into a laurel.
A fallen paper bag starts to bark.
In the distance I see trees as men talking.
I resume my spectacles,
expecting the commonplace.
It is revealed, rinsed with recent theurgy.

Shadow on the Snow

The old man wore a gown of morning light.
Through silvery translucence and against
Smooth ermine hiding wintry grass from sight
He felt his scarecrow body, gaunt and flensed.

He looked up at the sky, as cleansed and blue
As on the morning of its making; no
Smudge of cloud or wink of wing; a new
World fashioned by the legerdemain of snow.

But he was old; the same warped gallows frame;
Yet, on the white before him, strode the tall
Figure, soldierly, erect, not lame,
Impervious to pain, not aged at all.

Advent

From the back doorstep, seen through steam
Of mist powdered with faint fall
Of drifting rain,
Square lozenges of yellow gleam
Against the blackened schoolhouse wall.
Though it is morning, lamplight floods each pane.

Beyond the windows children sit
At little desks. I hear and see
And even smell
The scene as I imagine it,
Or conjure it from memory,
Self-enthralled by this deliberate spell.

It is the last month of the year
Bedecked in coloured paper-chains
With tinselled hair,
Dispensing artificial snow. I hear,
Or almost hear, the treble strains
Of carols sweetening the studious air.

I see the faces, which are one,
Girl or boy, multiplied:
Each wears the same
Rapt smile and gleaming hair, fine-spun
And weightless cap of gold; the wide
And wondering gaze in light of candle flame.

I turn away, go back inside
To kitchen warmth and shut the door:
An old man's room,

Populous with shades; a hide
For revenants whose nightly spoor
Trail slender silver ribbons through the gloom.

The children's eyes and voices press
Inside the borders of recall
Insisting on
An innocence, no more or less
Authentic than my ghosts' thin scrawl
Whose meaning I decline to brood upon.

Fading Away

As frail as wedding veils lace curtains float
Inside the bedroom window, swirl and swell
Bellying, exhale and then retreat,
Pause tremulous above the ledge until
Another boastful flourish is impelled
By floral breath of summer, cool and sweet.

This girlish dancing of the curtains mocks
The masculinity which governs here:
The polished shoes and boots arranged on racks,
The monkish dressing-gown hung on the door,
Framed photograph of his old brigadier,
Piled copies of the *Tatler* in neat stacks.

The Colonel's daughter, Joan, and Mrs Beese,
Take turns to sit with him. For them these days
Are long but not, Joan thinks, for him who lies
In drugged and sunless limbo – yet who knows
What images might terrify or tease
Behind the sculpted lids of those closed eyes?

That night, her daily tour of duty done,
Joan lies between stiff sheets and cannot sleep:
The little bedside lamp that she keeps on
Paints figures on the walls; there's no escape
From what awaits to sidle close then leap
With cudgel, blade, or blunt and loaded gun.

She is afraid. Her bedroom is not safe:
It's strange, those childish pictures on the wall,

Books and trinkets from another life;
She's often heard it said that people feel
The same at forty as they did when small.
Not her. The future's glinting like a knife.

She switches off the bedside light and hears
Dark silence seeping through from father's room,
Exhausted ocean that no longer roars;
She longs to drown in that warm flood and dream
Reversals of the images of doom
And carnage from his lost, unholy wars.

And sleep, at last, she does till morning calls
With avian scratchings on the window pane;
She stirs and wakes, and instantly she feels
Convinced that he has gone. She is alone
And will, her mirror tells her, so remain,
Attentive to the crunch of carriage wheels.

On the Melton Mowbray Train

His book is open; he seems to read
But his deceitful eyes are in fact
Fixed on the grey woman opposite.
He watches her with a kind of greed,
Not for what she is now in the act
Of denuding – a banana – but
Something less innocent. She wears steel-
rimmed spectacles; behind the lenses
Her eyes almost squint as she inclines
Her head towards her tall, pallid meal.
His own lips open as it enters
Her mouth. He lowers his eyes, resigns
Himself to the calmer diversion
Of literature and, as he does so,
He reflects, with only mild surprise,
That, in senescence's bleak season,
He appears, if anything, to grow
More prone to impure thoughts, not wiser
But nastier.   His destination

Reached, he leaves the train, sets out to go
Into the town, pleased with his disguise,
Bufferish, genteel, and all it hides,
Where they breed horses and make pork pies.

Old Shaver

I am surprised by how young I look
In the mirror, now it is misted by steam.
It is true I have removed my spectacles
And the mirror is of such circumference
That my defoliated skull is not revealed.
This simulacrum of youth does not greatly perturb;
Its mild mockery is not malicious.
The unambiguous script of wrinkles, and the furrows
Carved deep, like cicatrix, are smoothed away;
Even the whites of the eyes have lost
Their rubineous glaze.
                                        I do not stay
And stare for long, but address myself
To what I am here to do. I beard my jowls
With snowy foam, then coax, with keen steel,
Protestant bristles from my jaws and chin.
This operation done I rinse and dry,
Replace my spectacles to face the day,
And what is there, and always had to be.

The Other Word

Confluence of contradictions are contained
In the weft of the word: soft scrolls of mist,
Infusion of swan's feathers, white hush
Hovering over unfathomable dusk,
Slow griefs of watchers gowned in wax,
The sleeping head sunk in snow,
Filled by the pillow; the hidden hand
Swinging the bell to bring the children in;
Light drained from the looking-glass;
Silence when all breathings cease;

Padlocked iron gates, the green pagodas
Unstirred by erotetic breeze, by breath,
That single and defiant rhyme;
Here is something to be knelt before,
Acknowledged tutelage of love,
Sable regency and, over all,
That mercy, inexorable and pure.

Aide-Mémoire

Must not forget: write to Martha Frame.
But no. I'll telephone. It costs about the same.

Write that review for the TLS.
I've read most of the book – well, more or less.

Prepare my lecture for the 23rd.
Rough notes will do. They won't listen to a word.

And write, I really must, to Terence Snow.
Oh Jesus Christ, I can't! He died four months ago!

It's terrible how quickly we forget,
How cruelly ephemeral the pain and the regret.

Last week I thought of Iris, quite by accident –
The name on a seed-packet – and I recalled her scent

And the way she smiled as she peeped through her hair,
As if from behind a curtain, both shy and debonair.

And only last night I thought of Ivan and Fred,
Shot down over Hamburg. For five decades they've been
    dead,

But I hadn't thought of either for many years,
And, when at last I did, it was with more fear than tears.

Some faces and names are forgotten, I must confess,
All sucked away into that black hole of nothingness

Where all must go, including me, I'm afraid,
To linger briefly in a living mind or two, then fade.

So now I think of those words from a poem still dear to
    me:
'*Memory fades, must the remembered perishing be?*'

Telegram

Logic, grammar, each grey vocable
Broke into pieces when the telegram
Fell from her faint fingers, dainty bomb
Exploding on the carpet like a bubble.

No punctuation, though beyond the glass
Of veiled french-windows could be seen a few
Dark circumflexes printed on the sky
And yellow commas scattered on the grass.

Mummy was distraught and Daddy proud,
Each isolated in parentheses.
Silent exclamations marked her cheeks,
But he stood staring at a distant cloud,

Private, pleasurable to contemplate.
He almost smiled. Never had she felt
Such hatred for the man, or so much guilt
Remembering her son and her delight

And pride reflecting his exuberant joy
In those twin asterisks that gleamed upon
Each epaulette: her own sweet subaltern,
Unchangeably her gentle, aureate boy.

At least she cannot see him now he lies,
A black full-stop punched neat between white eyes.

Owl Faces

An early autumn night; the leaves are still;
No whispered bedtime legends to be told;
In huddled clusters apples gleam, pale gold;

The moon-washed air is motionless until,
As if the moon itself must now confess
A sadness it has struggled to withhold,
It publishes aloud its loneliness.

As that cool ululation soars and dives,
Small sonic meteor, across the skies,
The echo lingers and, before it dies,
A yet more plaintive twin of it contrives
To follow down the track the first has scored:
Its plangency and echo emphasize
How almost perfect silence is restored.

And in the darkness underneath the trees
Recent windfalls nestle in the grass;
The skin of each is smooth and cold as glass;
And you may lift up any one of these
And carry it indoors and take a bright
Knife and halve, then quarter it, to face
Four faces staring from their unlocked night.

Night Out

And when Night
Darkens the Streets, then wander forth the Sons
Of Belial, flown with insolence and wine.
PARADISE LOST, BOOK ONE

Saturday and early evening;
In little houses, where savoury phantoms
Lurk on the stairs, the lads are busy
At kitchen sink or bathroom basin;
They scrape and rinse and titivate, anoint
Their skins with famous unguents and choose
Carefully the clobber for the coming night.

Obedient muscles swell, blue serpents writhe.
They decorate their limbs with bracelets and frail
    chains.
Mums are kissed or carelessly *tarrahed*;
Then out to where the town lies welcoming,
Perhaps a little scared but open wide,

They wander forth, rehearse their shouts.
The bars wear necklaces of lights, like girls.

Blue scarves of smoke unfurl and swirl;
The juke-box thrashes silence till it howls;
Torn mouths shout mad hosannas. Soon
The lights will die. Last Orders has been called.
The doors are open and the pavement feels
The crack and splash of noisy yellow streak
Across its dark and sweating face of stone.

Back to the streets: glass trembles to be smashed.
Buttocks, white as Wensleydale, are bared
To mock the moon; moonstruck they roar
And swill from can and slurp from polystyrene,
Swallowing their venomous viatica.
Blue flashes whirl their whining whips
And compound fractures whimper in the dirt.

Sunday, and a grey, exhausted quiet
Lies on the morning streets; the asphalt
Advertises jaundiced asterisks of puke
And crumpled cans and jagged bottle shards.
Church-bells begin to toll, lugubrious,
And those few worshippers who venture out
Move on slow, mournful feet, as to a funeral.

Bush Vet

That's what they call me. Know what it means?
A veteran of Nam, that's vee-et-nam,
You might have heard of it. It's history now.
The bush, that's where I live,
Up there. You see the trees against the sky,
The forest on the hillside like a pelt?
That's home for me,
Miles away from any living soul.
I come down here
Maybe once a month, or less than that,
To get supplies, oil for the lamp,
Coffee, cans of beans and stuff,
Whisky and tobacco, chiefly them.
A couple, maybe three times, in a year

I get to come in here and hang one on,
Not for company you understand.
I don't get lonely in the bush.
It's other folk, like those guys over there,
That make you feel the loneliness come down.
No sir, I got no need of company,
I like it fine up there.
When I first picked the place
So long ago,
I can't recall exactly when,
I fixed a kind of bivouac.
I slept in that while building me a shack.
It took a while but I'd got time enough.
It don't look great, but keeps the weather out,
And other things. There's memories of Nam
I just can't talk about. Bad things.
I think a lot and sometimes I read books,
That's when I'm feeling tidy in my head,
When I can concentrate. Mostly though
I dream about what was and might have been.
But here's a crazy thing I'll tell you now:
After I got back from Nam
And got my discharge, tried to settle down,
I couldn't make it. Mostly couldn't sleep
And if I did, oh man, the dreams I had.
But here's the crazy part. I missed it all.
I wanted to get back – well, part of me –
I dreamed about the palm groves and the paddies,
The water buffalo, the bamboo hills,
The wooden ploughs the oxen used to pull,
The peasants working in the fields,
The elephant grass that sliced you like a knife,
The leeches, mud and shit, the fear.
Even that.
I got depressed, got mad. I couldn't help it.
Couple a drinks and I could kill,
Kill anyone you understand.
I had to get away.
I'm safe up there.
There's water near my shack, a stream.
I don't need halizone for that.
Truth is I'm just not fit for anything,
I mean for living in a city,
Or anywhere with ordinary folk.

I seen too many killed, too many kids
And women, little children, cooked alive.
I seen too much. I need to clean my eyes,
My hands as well. I never will.
In the bush up there I'm safe, I'm tame.
If any human being does get shot
That person will be me. By friendly fire.
That's what they called it when a guy
Got wasted by a buddy's careless stray.
They called it friendly fire.
It happened all the time. And what the hell
Difference does it make, a VC slug
Or M14, you end up dead the same.
I sometimes wish I had.
There's some things I don't want to ask myself,
And yet the questions sneak up in the night
And grab you by the throat. Or should I say
The question there's no hiding from.
What was it for?
The killing and the fear, the suffering, the shit?
What was it for? And if the question's bad
The answer's worse. Nothing. That's the word.
You know what nothing is?
Nothing is a hole with nothing in it,
A round black emptiness with nothing round it,
A hole punched in a human skull,
When all the flesh has rotted, gone.
Nothing is the muzzle of a gun,
Dark centre of a whirlpool made of steel,
The dark beyond the dark.
Emptiness beyond all emptiness,
Silence under silence,
Nothing is the answer to it all.

In Memoriam CMH

There are many days when I never think about him.
I do not apologize, nor would he wish me to,
And I write this to gratify a quite selfish whim:
Having no picture of him I shall have to make do
With this rough sketch when his memory grows dim:

One of a dying species from the human zoo.

He was lean and fierce and could stun you with a surprise
Weapon of geniality. His rages would make
Walls tremble like virgins; tusks menaced, and from his
    eyes
Flashed sizzling tracers, but after each violent quake
The peace it left was like the calm when a great storm dies
And his smile came sweet and white as a wedding-cake.

He believed in capital punishment, but not in God.
He loved his wife, gave her expensive presents and hell.
Each evening at exactly half-past-six he would plod
Upstairs to take his bath. At seven a tactful smell
Of soap ushered him into his study where he stood
Sinking a double whisky before the dinner knell.

I use 'knell' not merely for the rhyme. He made each meal
A grave occasion and like a mad pathologist
He dissected his food, probing with mistrustful zeal
For evidence of crime. Gloom and silence like a mist
Shrouded the feast. Then he swallowed his ritual pill
And belched, swore and muttered like a drunk
    ventriloquist.

Each morning he rose at precisely seven o'clock
To perform calisthenics for which he was too old.
His bones were like dead branches over which a loose
    smock
Of dried flesh was hung. Not for decades had muscles
    rolled
Under that wizened skin. Yet we felt no wish to mock
His strenuous folly, nor dared we attempt to scold.

He had fought at Mons and Wipers. In seventy-four,
One evening of reminiscing, his musings strayed
Back to his army days; then he asked about my war,
Had I enjoyed it? I said I would sooner have stayed
At home. Those times, for me, were frightening or a bore.
He said, 'I don't know what it feels like to be afraid.'

And I believed him. He was vain, bigoted and brave,
Tyrannical, a great snob. He often made me wild.
I should have hated him, but I did not. He gave
Prodigally of love, hate and cash. Often reviled
He stood firm by his views. And now he is in the grave
Grief multiplies for one, part father and friend, part child.

Four Roys

It is a curious, if fairly obvious, fact
That people, celebrated or quite unknown,
Seem to grow into their Christian names, expand or
    contract
According to whether they should be seven or seventeen
    stone.
But it's not as simple as that. A Christian name
Generally regarded as dull, or even absurd,
May be alchemized by a great possessor's fame
Into something noble and ennobling; this has occurred
For instance with Poets Laureate – though by no means
    all –
With Alfred (Tennyson, not Austin) a name
Was rescued from the dandruffy drab and became,
Briefly, royal again. William, a name that few would call
Especially resonant before its conjunction with
    Wordsworth (not Whitehead)
Grew soberly strong; those like Naham, Cecil, and Colley
Are condemned, like their owners, to the ranks of the
    benighted
Or recalled, if at all, as embodiments of vanity and folly.
God alone knows what posterity will make of Ted.

Now, all of these generalizations about Christian names
Are a windy prelude to a fragmentary recollection
Of four acquaintances, two of them now dead,
All of them bearing the first name of Roy,
Three of them practitioners of the art of versification
And one I have not seen since I was a boy
And will not see again who, if he felt the temptation
To make poems, resisted it. What he *did* make
Was model aeroplanes. I envied him this skill.
His ambition, which neither mockery nor mother could
    shake,
Was to be a bomber pilot. He would never fulfil
His other longing – to be one of Greyfriars' Famous Five,
Preferably Harry Wharton, though I think he would have
    settled
Even for Billy Bunter – which could never come alive,
Except in imagination, of course, though once, when
    nettled

He actually shouted, 'I say, you beastly cad!' and this
Was in the playground of Queen's Park Council School
Where everyone was too astonished to take the piss.

Most of us regarded him as a kind of holy fool.
His other dream, though, was briefly fleshed. He died in
    flames
In flak-ripped skies over Berlin. The other dead one
Was killed in 1957 in a car-crash in Spain.
He and I were not close friends, each fed on
Quite different ideological and literary grub
Though we did share one experience: together we were
    thrown
Out of the Windsor Castle, not the royal seat but a pub
In Notting Hill Gate. He had a reputation
For being a fighting man based chiefly, it seemed to me,
On reports of a small altercation
He had with a fellow poet not known for his ferocity.
I found him soft and mild though of substantial size.
He wrote some blustering satire and sweet lyrics but
    translation
Was his true strength: he made fine versions of one of
    God's great spies,
St John of the Cross, of Lorca and of Baudelaire.

About the two living Roys I have little to say,
Knowing neither very well. Enough that they both care
Seriously for their craft and each in his own way
Has written poems that delight and go on delighting.
The prospect of sharing a compartment with either or both
On a long railway journey would be distinctly inviting.
Well – where was I? – oh yes, names. To tell the truth
I'd forgotten what I was supposed to be on about –
Christian names: four men, three poets and one not,
All named Roy. Not a strong name. It is without
Power, despite its echo of 'King'. It would suit a swot,
Someone neat and correct, or a senior boy-scout.
It is not, as the young might say, much of a turn-on,
Though, come to think of it, I can't imagine what,
They would have to say about the Christian name Vernon –
Who could wear comfortably such a name? What kind of
    man?
I can't think what they'd say. Or perhaps I can.

Dylan Thomas Country

A bowl of seasons at the hills' feet,
     A helmet of weathers;
At night the white owl, fat and shining,
Blinks among scattered crumbs and trinkets
     And the sleepless sea
Over and over sighs and surrenders.

This day decides on rising to sport summer;
     It comes out dancing;
The green dress shimmers with relucent beads;
Little houses and enormous horses
     Whinny their waking;
Trout practise their scales in the waterfall pool.

In this country, and in all but one season,
     A plump boy
With apple cheeks where no worm burrows
Whistles and wonders with blue amazement
     At the mystery and joy,
The promise of this day and all its fellows.

And should the next day wake up as winter
     Its snow will be sweet
On the tongue, friendly to toes and fingers,
Chilblains glow only in the evening sky,
     Complected with darkness
To parcel the mistletoe, the evergreen and manger.

The circus of Spring then dazzles the hamlet
     With trumpets and flags;
The laughter of daffodils waves to the master,
A chorus of crocuses seasons the singing,
     The big cats roar
But will never molest the boy of Easter.

The fall does not happen at all in this country
     Where uncles are huge
And tremendously gentle and aunts are funny;
No insults, no harpies or hangovers rage,
     No gaol here or factory,
No college of pain, gigantic infirmary.

This country welcomes the rarely enchanted,
    The meagre and sour;
Here they rip off their collars of caution,
Ethical serge, their boots and galoshes,
    They dance and munch flowers
Though the worm eats the face of the boy of Autumn.

Flying Blind

Soft, blundering fog has neutralized
The morning sky, and from that foul
And padded air is recognized
The aircraft's stretched catarrhal growl.

A plane about to land, we hope
In safety though, on looking through
Imagination's telescope,
We see that they are hoping too.

And some within that metal case
Dictate a message straight to God;
They stare through glass but only face
The day's enormous smothering wad.

It bandages the windows tight
However much they crane and peer;
Their voices flutter on a bright
Chilly thread of perfect fear.

Everyone becomes a blind
Longing for the feel of earth
Beneath his feet, amazed to find
How much one stepping-stone is worth.

And they are right to be afraid,
Though wrong about the aircraft's fate,
For they should fear the ambuscade
Crouching there beyond the gate.

Poetry Now

How is it done?
Shift your glass into your left hand;
Drink southpaw for a while;
Lead with the right,
Jab and jab, persistent;
With luck you'll see
The trickle soon become a flow.

Don't get excited and impatient now.
Be resolute
But wary, cool,
And don't be tempted to show off.
Erato is in your corner
Who never tells you why you do it,
But sometimes tells you how.

English Summer

It's August in England and time for vacation;
A full hour of sunshine would cause a sensation.
The weather's called 'fine' if the rain isn't falling
And few of us curse at the wind's catawauling.
It's usual in Blackpool or Morecambe or Brighton
To crouch in a shelter and watch gulls alight on
The crests of the curling and shit-bearing breakers,
Or bleakly stare out over grey salty acres;
And later, at nightfall, more *forte* than *piano*,
Hear choirs of brass monkeys all singing soprano.

Getting Over It

They said, 'Don't worry: you'll get over it.'
And they were always right; you always did.
The wounds healed up and didn't hurt a bit.

After a time of course. Meanwhile you hid
The fact that you were hurting, or you tried;
Not always easy for a pampered kid:

Disappointments over which you cried –
The model aeroplane that wouldn't fly,
The whispered promises that always lied,

Then stumbling into love, the biggest lie
As things turned out; you thought your heart would break,
But you recovered from it by and by.

And so it rolled – betrayal, belly-ache,
Rejection, blows, a dozen kinds of shit:
There wasn't any kind you didn't take.

When flesh and eyes were sore with dust and grit
You seemed a static target none could miss,
They said, again, that you'd get over it.

And they were right. Though no one told you this –
That on the other side lay the abyss.

Talking Head

Take the unfleshed head, the strict skull;
Hold it in the palm of your left hand
While, with pincers of right forefinger and thumb,
You carefully select a plump, green grape.
Delicately place the grape in the socket
To the left of where the nose once jutted.
If it does not fit perfectly discard it.
Choose another, and another, until you find
One that plugs in snug. Over the twin cavity
Place a black, piratical eye-patch,
Secured by a wide elastic band.
The choice of hat is yours, a beret perhaps,
A tricorne, sou'wester or a large tea-cosy;
Something sporty like a cricket cap or boater;
Nothing, I suggest, explicitly sacerdotal.
Next, into that empty smile, or snarl,
Insert a partly smoked cheroot or half corona.
Then decide on a topic of conversation,

Not too contentious but not tedious either.
Avoid mentioning rivers, bells, masonry and flowers.
Listen carefully and you may be instructed
Though not, I fear, amused or comforted.

Home Movies

We, the guests, sit in pink twilight.
The cosy box we occupy
Is pretty and warm;
We might be dolls,
But we are men and women,
Have eaten well,
Dressed in appropriate uniform.

Flavours, savoury and sweet, still linger
Pleasantly, but what we ate
Is not quite free;
Now is the time
When payment is exacted,
Not cash of course,
But another quite painful fee.

'Painful', perhaps, is over strident
To designate that grey malaise,
Boredom's sick
And stifling ache;
Our ordeal is beginning:
On the screen
The pictures flicker, blur, then click

Sharply into focus, recognized
With gleeful cries: '*Oh look! There's Paul,
A Proper Mister
Universe!
And that one on the donkey's
Peter's friend
Who fancied George's younger sister.*

*Wait for this though! This will slay you!
Judy's fancy swallow-dive!
She swallowed half*

The swimming-pool!
That's the place we stayed at –
Rather pricey.
Now this will really make you laugh!'

It did. The laughter sounded rather
Less than joyful, but it came,
Enough for Paul,
Our kindly host.
One cure alone for us though:
To see our own
Dear lineaments dancing on that wall.

Interview with the Author

'Your oeuvre is not complete. May I suppose
You have a clear conception of its close?'

'I can't foresee the end, and if I knew
I think I'd hide the dénouement from you.'

'Well, what about the origins? How long
Did you reflect, make notes, upon the throng
Of characters and scenes before the act
Itself of starting on the artefact?'

'Longer than you or anyone will know.'

'What you have so far published seems to show
A passion for crude violence and lust
That could be called obsessive. Now, I trust
You will not think me puritanical
In finding much of this mechanical,
And scarcely edifying. Why do you
Make humans beasts or engines, as you do?'

'You are mistaken there. I have no skill
In metamorphosis. My creatures will
Their own behaviour, shape identities.
I made them, yet the paradox is this:
I cannot change their world from what it is.'

'I see. Your characters assume their own
And independent natures. They alone
Determine what events will come to pass?'

'Well, yes. But only certain ones, alas,
Attain autonomy and power, and they –
The wicked – rule and have the final say.'

Apostate

He climbs the steps that look like slabs of cheese,
And when the glass doors glide apart he feels
No surprise at all. He enters, sees
How like a statesman's coffin the long desk gleams
And how, behind it, the woman shines and smiles
With eyes and teeth as bright and cold as nails.
The scratched air bleeds an odour, sour and sharp,
The scent of staples; then the drumbeats start
And, with the drumming, a thin high whining noise.
He knows that he was wrong to come. The caves
Were better far than this.
                                                    The sliding doors
Are now shut fast and, when he turns, he sees
Reflected in the sheet of glass his face
Fragmented by panic and despair.
The woman's smile has gone and left no scar.
The hungry cold outside is sweet as choice.